Aspen Handbook for Legal Writers

ASPEN PUBLISHERS

Aspen Handbook for Legal Writers

A Practical Reference

Second Edition

Deborah E. Bouchoux, Esq.

Georgetown University
Member, District of Columbia and California (inactive) Bars

Wolters Kluwer
Law & Business

AUSTIN   BOSTON   CHICAGO   NEW YORK   THE NETHERLANDS

Aspen Publishers
Attn: Permissions Department
76 Ninth Avenue, 7th Floor
New York, NY 10011-5201

To contact Customer Care, e-mail customer.care@aspenpublishers.com,
call 1-800-234-1660, fax 1-800-901-9075, or mail correspondence to:

Aspen Publishers
Attn: Order Department
PO Box 990
Frederick, MD 21705

Printed in the United States of America.

4 5 6 7 8 9 0

ISBN 978-0-7355-6856-3

Library of Congress Cataloging-in-Publication Data

Bouchoux, Deborah E., 1950–
    Aspen handbook for legal writers: a practical reference / Deborah E.
    Bouchoux. — [2nd ed.].
        p.   cm.
    Includes index.
    ISBN 978-0-7355-6856-3
    1. Legal composition. I. Title. II. Title: Handbook for legal writers.

KF250.B68 2009
808'.06634—dc22   2009003048

About Wolters Kluwer Law & Business

Wolters Kluwer Law & Business is a leading provider of research information and workflow solutions in key specialty areas. The strengths of the individual brands of Aspen Publishers, CCH, Kluwer Law International and Loislaw are aligned within Wolters Kluwer Law & Business to provide comprehensive, in-depth solutions and expert-authored content for the legal, professional and education markets.

CCH was founded in 1913 and has served more than four generations of business professionals and their clients. The CCH products in the Wolters Kluwer Law & Business group are highly regarded electronic and print resources for legal, securities, antitrust and trade regulation, government contracting, banking, pension, payroll, employment and labor, and healthcare reimbursement and compliance professionals.

Aspen Publishers is a leading information provider for attorneys, business professionals and law students. Written by preeminent authorities, Aspen products offer analytical and practical information in a range of specialty practice areas from securities law and intellectual property to mergers and acquisitions and pension/ benefits. Aspen's trusted legal education resources provide professors and students with high-quality, up-to-date and effective resources for successful instruction and study in all areas of the law.

Kluwer Law International supplies the global business community with comprehensive English-language international legal information. Legal practitioners, corporate counsel and business executives around the world rely on the Kluwer Law International journals, loose-leafs, books and electronic products for authoritative information in many areas of international legal practice.

Loislaw is a premier provider of digitized legal content to small law firm practitioners of various specializations. Loislaw provides attorneys with the ability to quickly and efficiently find the necessary legal information they need, when and where they need it, by facilitating access to primary law as well as state-specific law, records, forms and treatises.

Wolters Kluwer Law & Business, a unit of Wolters Kluwer, is headquartered in New York and Riverwoods, Illinois. Wolters Kluwer is a leading multinational publisher and information services company.

In memory of Josephine LaPointe Bouchoux
much loved by her many students and her family

A teacher affects eternity; he can never tell where his influence stops.
—Henry Adams

summary of contents

Contents   xi
Foreword   xxi
Help for Writers   xxv
Acknowledgments   xxvii

Section One ■ **The Mechanics of Writing: Grammar, Punctuation, and Spelling   1**

Chapter 1   Grammar   3
Chapter 2   Punctuation   29
Chapter 3   Spelling   53

Section Two ■ **Features of Effective Legal Writing and Organization   71**

Chapter 4   Features of Effective Legal Writing   73
Chapter 5   Organization and the Writing Process   115

Section Three ■ **Legal Documents, Legal Conventions, and Common Legal Writing Blunders   127**

Chapter 6   Legal Correspondence   129
Chapter 7   Legal Memoranda   153
Chapter 8   Legal Briefs   169
Chapter 9   Pleadings and Transactional Documents   187
Chapter 10   Legal Conventions and Legal Writing Blunders   205

Section Four ■ **Postwriting Steps and Document Design   215**

Chapter 11   Postwriting Steps   217
Chapter 12   Document Design   227

Appendix A   Citation Form   235
Appendix B   English as a Second Language   249
Appendix C   Sample Appellate Court Brief   259
Appendix D   Answer Keys to Challenges   279
Appendix E   Glossary of Terms   297
Appendix F   Glossary of Usage   303
Appendix G   Sample Case Brief   317

Index   319

contents

Foreword   xxi
Help for Writers   xxv
Acknowledgments   xxvii

Section One ■ The Mechanics of Writing: Grammar, Punctuation, and Spelling   1

Chapter 1. Grammar   3

A. Introduction   4
B. Sentence Fragments   4
C. Run-On Sentences   4
D. Subject-Verb Agreement   6
   1. Multiple-Word Subjects   6
   2. Indefinite Pronouns   7
   3. Collective Nouns and Company Names   8
   4. Intervening Words   9
   5. Inverted Sentence Order   9

E. Modifiers   10
   1. Misplaced Modifier Phrases   11
   2. Misplaced Prepositional Phrases   11
   3. Limiting Modifiers   12
   4. Dangling Modifiers   12
   5. Squinting Modifiers   13

F. Split Infinitives   14
G. Pronouns   15
   1. Personal Pronouns   15
   2. Pronoun Agreement   17
     a. Indefinite Pronouns   17
     b. Collective Nouns   18
     c. Generic Nouns   18

3. Pronoun Reference   18
  a. Ambiguous References   18
  b. Implied References   19
  c. Vague References   19
  d. Indefinite Use of *It* and *They*   19
4. Use of *Who* and *Whom*   19
5. Use of *That* and *Which*   20
6. Reflexive Pronouns   22
7. Gender-Linked Pronouns   23
  a. Six Techniques for Gender-Neutral Language   23
  b. Constructions to Avoid   24
  c. Letters   24
  d. Closing Thoughts on Gender-Neutral Language   25
8. Special Pronoun Situations   25
  a. Use of *We* and *Us*   25
  b. Comparisons with *Than* or *As*   25
  c. Gerunds   26
9. Shifts in Pronouns   26

H. Conjunctions   27
1. Coordinating Conjunctions: *And, But, For, Nor, Or, So, Yet*   27
2. Correlative Conjunctions: *Both-And, Either-Or, Neither-Nor, Not Only-But Also, Whether-Or*   27
3. Subordinating Conjunctions   28

Chapter 2. Punctuation   29

A. Introduction   30
B. End Punctuation   30
1. Using Periods   31
2. Using Question Marks   31
3. Using Exclamation Points   32

C. Commas   32
1. Rules for Comma Use   32
2. Comma Misuse   37

D. Apostrophes   39
1. Possessives   40
  a. General Rules   40
  b. Proper Names   40
  c. Special Situations Involving Apostrophes   41
2. Contractions   43
3. Numbers and Letters   43

E. Colons   44
F. Semicolons   45

G. Quotation Marks   46
H. Parentheses   47
I. Other Punctuation Marks: Dashes, Hyphens,
    and Slashes   49
    1. Using Dashes   49
    2. Using Hyphens   50
    3. Using Slashes   51

Chapter 3. Spelling   53

A. Introduction   54
B. Strategies to Improve Spelling   54
    1. Use a Dictionary   54
    2. Develop a "Hit List" of Commonly Misspelled Words   54
    3. Pronounce Your Words Carefully   55
    4. Use Misspelled Words as Passwords   55
    5. Use Mnemonic Devices   55
    6. Don't Rely Only on Your Spell-Checker   55
    7. Proofread Carefully   55
    8. Learn Some Spelling Rules   55

C. Compound Words   58
D. Capitalization   60
    1. General Capitalization Rules   61
    2. Capitalization in Legal Documents   63

E. Abbreviations   65
    1. General Principles   65
    2. Legal Abbreviations   68

Section Two ■ Features of Effective Legal Writing and Organization   71

Chapter 4. Features of Effective Legal Writing   73

A. Introduction   74
B. The Plain English Movement   74
C. Accuracy   75
    1. Introduction   75
    2. Word Choice   76
    3. Vague Words   78
    4. Intentional Vagueness   79
    5. Word Connotation   79

6. Special Word Problems: Made-Up Words, Slang and Colloquial
   Expressions, and Offensive Language   80
   a. Made-Up Words and Phrases   80
   b. Slang and Colloquial Expressions   81
   c. Offensive Language   82

D. Clarity   84
   1. Elegant Variation or the Slender Yellow Fruit Syndrome   86
   2. Negatives   87
   3. Word Order   89

E. Readability   90
   1. Prefer the Active Voice   91
   2. Use Lists   92
   3. Use Parallel Structure   94
      a. Introduction   94
      b. Coordinating Conjunctions   95
      c. Correlative Conjunctions   95
      d. Comparisons   95
      e. Lists and Headings   96
   4. Avoid Nominalizations   97
   5. Avoid Legalese   98
      a. Introduction   98
      b. Indirect Writing   100
      c. Pretentious Writing   100
   6. Keep Subjects and Verbs Close Together   102
   7. Use Forceful Words   103
   8. Repeat Strong Words and Phrases   104
   9. Vary the Length of Sentences   104
   10. Use Effective Transitions   105
   11. Avoid Shifts in Tense   106

F. Conciseness   109
   1. Introduction   109
   2. Omit Needless Words   110
   3. Avoid "Throat-Clearing" Introductions   111
   4. Avoid Redundancy   112
   5. Avoid Repetition   114

Chapter 5. Organization and the Writing Process   115

A. Introduction   116
B. Order and Internal Organization   116
   1. Outlines   116
      a. Brainstorming and Freewriting   116
      b. Clustering and Tree Diagrams   117

c. Story Telling 117
d. Percolating 117
e. Reverse Outlining 118
2. The Paper Chase: Using the Legal Authorities 119
3. An Overview of Most Writing Projects 119
a. Introductory Section 119
b. Middle Sections and Paragraphs 120
c. Conclusions 121
4. Using Position and Voice for Emphasis 121
a. Start and End Strong 122
b. Bury Negative Information 122
c. Use Passive Voice 122
d. Avoid Forceful Language 122
5. Avoid Micro-Editing During the Drafting Stage 123

C. Methods of Writing 123
1. Writing by Hand 123
2. Dictating 124
3. Using a Word Processor 124

Section Three ■ Legal Documents, Legal Conventions, and Common Legal Writing Blunders 127

Chapter 6. Legal Correspondence 129

A. The Elements of a Letter 130
1. Introduction 130
a. Letterhead 130
b. Date 130
c. Special Notations 130
d. Inside Address 130
e. Reference or Subject Notation 131
f. Salutation 131
g. Body 132
h. Closing and Signature Block 132
i. Reference Initials, Enclosures, and Copies 133
2. Format Considerations 134
a. Size of Paper and Spacing 134
b. Arrangement and Indenting 135
c. Margins and Justification 135
d. Widows and Orphans 135
e. Font and Typeface 135

B. The Audience and Tone for Legal Correspondence   136
  1. Who Will Be Reading This Letter?   136
  2. What Is the Purpose of This Letter?   137
C. Types of Letters   137
  1. General Correspondence   137
  2. Demand Letters   138
    a. Elements of Demand Letters   139
    b. Some Common Pitfalls in Demand Letters   139
  3. Opinion Letters and Their Elements   142
    a. Date   143
    b. Introductory Language   143
    c. Review of Facts   143
    d. Opinion   144
    e. Explanation of Opinion   145
    f. Recommendations   145
    g. Instructions   145
    h. Protection Clauses   145
  4. Electronic Communications   149
    a. Communicating by Email   149
    b. Communicating by Facsimile   150
    c. Communicating by Telephone and Voice Mail   151
    d. Communicating by Text Messaging   152

Chapter 7. Legal Memoranda   153

A. Introduction   154
  1. Be Objective   154
  2. Be Specific   154
  3. Be Thorough   154
B. Format of Memoranda   154
  1. Heading   155
  2. Question(s) Presented   155
  3. Brief Answer(s)   156
  4. Statement of Facts   156
  5. Analysis or Discussion   156
  6. Conclusion   160

Chapter 8. Legal Briefs   169

A. Introduction   170
B. Tips for Writing Briefs   170
  1. Be Persuasive   170
  2. Be Honest   171
  3. Know the Rules   171

C. Trial Court Briefs   172
1. Introduction   172
2. Elements of a Trial Court Brief   172
   a. Caption   172
   b. Introductory Statement   172
   c. Statement of Facts   173
   d. Argument   173
   e. Conclusion   174
   f. Signature and Date   174
   g. Certificates of Service and Compliance   174
   h. Exhibits   174
   i. Order   174

D. Appellate Briefs   174
1. Introduction   174
2. Elements of Appellate Briefs   175
   a. Cover Sheet   175
   b. Identification of Parties   175
   c. Table of Contents   175
   d. Table of Authorities   175
   e. Jurisdictional Statement   176
   f. Constitutional and Statutory Provisions   176
   g. Question(s) Presented   176
   h. Statement of the Case   176
   i. Summary of the Argument   177
   j. Argument   177
   k. Conclusion   177
   l. Signature   177
   m. Certificates of Service and Compliance   177
   n. Appendix   177

Chapter 9. Pleadings and Transactional Documents   187

A. Pleadings   188
1. Introduction   188
2. Format of Pleadings   188
3. Using Form Books   189
4. Legalese   192

B. Transactional Documents   193
1. Introduction   193
2. Drafting Considerations   193
3. Elements of Transactional Documents   194
   a. Introductory Matter   194
   b. Recitals   194

c. Consideration   195
d. Operative Terms   195
e. Standard Provisions   195
f. Signatures   195
4. Using Form Books   195

Chapter 10. Legal Conventions and Legal Writing Blunders   205

A. Legal Conventions   206
1. Defined Terms   206
2. Repetitive Terms   206
3. Labels   206
4. *Including But Not Limited to* Phrases   207
5. Money Amounts   207
6. Numbers   207
7. Initial Phrases   207
8. The *Whether* Clause   207
9. d/b/a References   207
10. Law Firm Names   208
11. Ordinals   208
12. Pagination   208

B. Common Legal Writing Blunders   208
1. Labels and Numbering   208
2. Defined Terms   208
3. Supporting Authorities   209
4. Conclusory Language   210
5. Including Facts   210
6. Other Legal Authorities   210
7. Tone in Court Documents   210
8. Title Headings in Statutes   210
9. Complete Discussion   210
10. Concurring and Dissenting Opinions   211
11. The Complete Package   211
12. Use of Headnotes   211
13. Addressing Readers   211
14. Authors of Court Opinions   212
15. New Topics   212
16. Citations   212
17. Over-Quoting   212
18. Mini-Conclusions   212
19. Headings   213
20. Use of First Person   213

21. Use of Party Names   213
22. Tense   213
23. Writing *This Case*   214
24. Abbreviations   214
25. Collective Nouns   214
26. Cross-References   214
27. The Biggest Blunder—Violating Court Rules   214

Section Four ▪ Postwriting Steps and Document Design   215

Chapter 11. Postwriting Steps   217

A. Introduction   218
B. Proofreading Stage One: Reviewing for Content and Meaning   219
C. Proofreading Stage Two: Reviewing for Technical Errors   220
   1. The Effect of Technical Errors   220
   2. Using a Style Sheet   220
   3. The Limitations of Spell-Checkers   220
   4. Techniques to Slow Down   220
   5. Asking for Help   222
   6. Using Templates and Forms   222
   7. Using Technology to Help with Proofreading   222

D. Proofreading for Others   223
E. Proofreaders' Marks   223
F. The Final Run-Through   225

Chapter 12. Document Design   227

A. Principles of Document Design   228
   1. Introduction   228
   2. Paper   228
   3. Typeface   228
     a. Typeface or Font Style   228
     b. Mixing Typefaces   229
     c. Roman Typeface   229
     d. Proportional or Monospace Typeface   229
     e. Size of Typeface   229

B. Formatting and Layout   230
   1. White Space and Margins   230
   2. Justification   230
   3. Spacing   231

4. Document Length 231
5. Headings 232
   a. Placement 233
   b. Phrasing 233
   c. Emphasis 233
   d. Lists 233
6. Visuals 234

Appendix A. Citation Form 235
Appendix B. English as a Second Language 249
Appendix C. Sample Appellate Court Brief 259
Appendix D. Answer Keys to Challenges 279
Appendix E. Glossary of Terms 297
Appendix F. Glossary of Usage 303
Appendix G. Sample Case Brief 317

Index *319*

> Reading maketh a full
> man; conference a
> ready man; and writing
> an exact man.
>
> Sir Francis Bacon

foreword

In many professions it is sufficient to perform a task, such as the athlete who plays a game or the artist who paints a portrait. The legal profession, however, rests on communication and requires its professionals not only to know the law but also to write about it. Legal writing takes many forms. Some documents, such as internal office memoranda, are intended to explain the law to the reader. Other documents, such as court briefs, are intended to persuade the reader. No matter what the form of the document, however, it must be accurate, clearly presented, readable, and concise.

The good news is that good legal writing is simply good writing. It should not differ greatly from other forms of writing. On the other hand, there are some quirks to legal writing that deserve special attention. Legal writing is more formal than other forms of writing. For example, the use of contractions is rare, and the use of the personal pronouns *I, we,* and *our* is uncommon (because the focus of a document should be on the client's position, not on the writer's opinions).

This Handbook is designed to be a thorough guide that legal writers can use to answer not only the "big" writing questions (such as determining the elements of a court brief) but the many "small" questions that continually occur during the writing process (such as when a comma precedes the words *and* and *but,* when the word *court* should be capitalized, and when the writer should indent quotations).

The Handbook begins with the mechanics of writing: grammar, punctuation, and spelling. Errors in these technical areas will distract the reader and detract from your message. Once a writer has mastered or reviewed these basics, the writer will be ready to address the characteristics of effective legal writing, namely, the tools used to ensure writings are accurate, clear, readable, and concise. The next section of the Handbook is devoted to legal documents. The most commonly prepared documents in law practice are described: letters, memoranda, court briefs, pleadings, and transactional documents. Sample letters, a sample memorandum, and trial and appellate briefs are included. Sections on standard legal conventions and common legal blunders are included in Section Three. Finally, the Handbook concludes with a thorough treatment of proofreading and editing your work and designing it to be visually appealing. The inside front cover shows you the brief table of contents and the inside back cover reminds you of the elements of a well-written project. Mark up your Handbook, put comments in the margins, and use sticky notes to flag frequently used sections.

Throughout the Handbook, references to helpful writing websites are given and exercises are provided to challenge your understanding and mastery of topics. Additional exercises are provided on a CD-ROM available from your instructor. To reduce clutter, examples are generally shown in italics rather than enclosed by quotation marks.

The Appendixes provide an overview of citation form, a guide for English as a Second Language learners, a sample appellate brief, answer keys for the Challenges in the Handbook, a Glossary of Terms used in this Handbook, a Glossary of Usage, describing and defining some frequently confused words in the legal profession, such as *affect* and *effect*, and a sample case brief.

As to citation form, Appendix A shows examples of frequently used citation forms. There are two primary guides on citation form: *The Bluebook: A Uniform System of Citation* (Columbia Law Review Ass'n et al. eds., 18th ed. 2005) (*The Bluebook*), which is the oldest and perhaps still most widely used manual on citation form, and ALWD & Darby Dickerson, *ALWD Citation Manual* (3d ed., Aspen Publishers 2006) (*ALWD*, called "all wood"), created by the Association of Legal Writing Directors to provide an easy and efficient alternative to the user-unfriendly *Bluebook*. In many instances, the *ALWD* format for citations is identical to *Bluebook* format. Appendix A gives examples of some citations for both *ALWD* and *The Bluebook*, but this Handbook is not meant to be a citation guide. Additionally, although every effort has been made to refer to useful websites, those sites can change both their content and addresses without notice. References to websites are not endorsements of those sites.

This second edition of this Handbook includes several new features, including the following:

- New exercises and challenges to test mastery of topics discussed;
- Information on readability tests;
- Updated websites;
- New information on using reverse outlining to organize writing projects;
- Expanded information on preparing tables of authorities for court briefs;
- A project proofreading and editing checklist; and
- New sample documents, including a sample opinion letter in Chapter 6, a new sample legal memorandum in Chapter 7, a new sample trial court brief in Chapter 8, and a new sample case brief as Appendix G.

This Handbook is designed to be used as a supplement to the texts you use in your writing classes and not as a replacement for those texts. Use the Handbook to provide additional information on the writing process and to enhance your understanding of the preparation of various legal documents. Use the Challenges and supplementary exercises to test your mastery of the subject matter. A reference tool such as this Handbook introduces you to concepts you will study in more depth in your legal writing courses and serves as a refresher of some writing basics you learned before you began your legal education. Thus, the Handbook serves as another tool in your writing arsenal and a complement to your assigned writing texts, which provide comprehensive information on legal analysis.

Finally, writing is a skill that you can master by repeated practice. If you are inexperienced at writing, keep practicing. Enjoy writing and understand that your writing not only says something about the topic you discuss but also something about you. Make sure your finished project is understood by the reader and reflects well on you.

Deborah E. Bouchoux
Spring 2009

help for writers

No matter what their level of experience, there are two tools that all writers need: a dictionary and a style guide. Dictionaries help you determine the spelling and usage of words, and style guides provide basic rules of grammar and punctuation as well as information on usage in general. A good dictionary can be found in any bookstore. Consider using a well-known dictionary, such as *Merriam-Webster's Collegiate Dictionary*, now in its eleventh edition. As to style guides, which are also available in most bookstores and online, consider the following:

- *The Chicago Manual of Style* (15th ed. 2003). *The Chicago Manual of Style* is considered the classic guide for writers and editors; however, it includes a great deal of information about publishing, which is not particularly pertinent for legal writers.

- *The Gregg Reference Manual* (10th ed. 2005) by William A. Sabin. This excellent reference manual, published by McGraw-Hill Irwin, contains not only comprehensive information about writing basics (with numerous examples) but also information on preparing letters and tables and on editing and proofreading. Its coverage is very thorough, and it answers nearly every question imaginable about punctuation, grammar, usage, and document formatting and presentation.

- *The United States Government Printing Office Style Manual* (29th ed. 2000) (*Style Manual*) is the definitive source on writing for the federal government. The *Style Manual* is available for downloading and printing at www.gpoaccess.gov/stylemanual.browse.html. The *Style Manual* is arranged in easy-to-read chapters. For example, Chapter 3 presents rules on capitalization and Chapter 8 presents rules on punctuation. The *Style Manual* is an excellent, free resource and its use is approved by *Bluebook* Rule 8 and *ALWD* at 7, which direct readers to the *Style Manual* for issues not addressed by *The Bluebook* or *ALWD*.

Finally, no book on writing would be complete without an endorsement of *The Elements of Style*, by William Strunk, Jr. and E.B. White, now in its fourth edition. This "little book" has long been considered the classic and authoritative source for writers. Portions of *The Elements of Style* are available at www.bartleby.com.

acknowledgments

I would like to express my sincere appreciation to the many individuals who contributed greatly to the development of this text. As always, my first thoughts and gratitude go to Susan M. Sullivan, Director of the Paralegal Program at the University of San Diego, who gave me my first teaching job and opened the door to a thoroughly gratifying career. Sue has been a valued friend as well as a much-admired colleague over the years.

A special thank you to my family: my husband, Donald, and our children Meaghan, twins Elizabeth and Patrick, and Robert, for their patience and understanding while I completed this text. A special thank you goes to Robert for his computer "tech support."

Many thanks also to the various reviewers who evaluated the manuscript on behalf of the publisher. Their comments were insightful and instructive. I have also received continuing evaluation from my students throughout my more than twenty-year career as a legal educator. I am especially indebted to the ESL students in my Advanced Legal Research and Writing class, Summer 2003, who provided their thoughts and comments on legal writing when English is a second language.

Finally, a special thank you to the individuals at Aspen Publishers who generously provided guidance and support throughout the development of this Handbook, including Carol McGeehan, Publisher; Melody Davies, Executive Editorial Director; David Herzig, Executive Legal Editor; Betsy Kenny, Developmental Editor; Kaesmene Harrison Banks, Senior Editor; and Teresa Horton, Copy Editor. A special thank you to Rick Mixter, Director of Digital Development, who was the chief advocate for the Handbook and guided it from inception to publication.

Aspen Handbook
for Legal
Writers

The Mechanics of Writing: Grammar, Punctuation, and Spelling

■ **Section One** of the Handbook reviews some of the common rules of grammar, punctuation, and spelling. Flaws in these technical areas, such as awkward sentence construction, incorrect punctuation, and spelling errors, distract readers from your message, make them doubt your abilities, and reflect on your carelessness. The way you communicate communicates information about you. Make sure you're right not only with regard to the big issues, such as case analysis, but also with regard to the little issues, such as the mechanics of writing.

chapter 1

Grammar

StyleLinks

www.gpoaccess.gov/stylemanual/index.html
The Government Printing Office *Style Manual* is one of the most widely accepted manuals on English usage. The entire *Style Manual* is available at this site.

http://owl.english.purdue.edu/owl
Purdue University's Online Writing Lab offers excellent information on grammar as well as exercises and answer keys.

http://grammar.ccc.commnet.edu/grammar
The site provides an excellent and thorough *Guide to Grammar & Writing* offered by Capital Community College. Numerous interactive quizzes are designed to test knowledge.

www.fas.harvard.edu/~wricntr
Harvard University's Writing Center provides useful information about grammar, punctuation, and writing, as well as links to other writing resources (including ESL resources).

www.kentlaw.edu/academics/lrw/grinker/LWTA.htm
Subtitled *The Law Student's Guide to Good Writing*, this excellent website offered by Professor Mark A. Grinker of Chicago-Kent College of Law provides explanations and examples of rules of grammar, punctuation, and good writing. Exercises and answers are provided.

http://law.case.edu/faculty/friedman/raw
The website "RawData" offers excellent information about legal writing together with numerous links to other excellent writing sites. Select "Writing."

A. Introduction

We use correct grammar to communicate clearly. Don't let the traditional rules of grammar and its incomprehensible terms (such as *pluperfect* or *subjunctive*) intimidate you. You do not need to know the names of the parts of speech to be a good writer, just as you do not need to know all the parts of a microwave oven to be a good cook.

B. Sentence Fragments

The sentence is the cornerstone of all writing. A well-written sentence conveys information to the reader. A poorly written sentence causes confusion and ambiguity. Legal writing is more formal than many other kinds of writing, and an incomplete sentence in a legal document will be noticed immediately. Thus, although you may see sentence fragments in novels and other types of writings, they are not acceptable in legal writing.

Sentence fragments (also called *incomplete sentences*) are usually caused by the failure to include a subject and a verb in a sentence. Fragments also occur when writers assume that a *dependent clause* (one that cannot stand on its own) is a sentence by itself.

To remedy sentence fragments:

- Attach the fragment to an adjacent complete sentence (usually by correcting punctuation); or
- Make the dependent clause or fragment into a complete sentence.

Sentence Fragments	Corrections
The plaintiff pointed to the defendant. The man who was wearing the red tie.	The plaintiff pointed to the defendant, who was the man wearing the red tie.
I proposed two changes. Revising section one and omitting section four.	I proposed two changes: revising section one and omitting section four.
The plaintiff was late for the hearing. Which infuriated the judge.	The plaintiff was late for the hearing, which infuriated the judge. *or* The plaintiff was late for the hearing. This tardiness infuriated the judge.

C. Run-On Sentences

In many ways, a run-on sentence is the opposite of a sentence fragment. A run-on sentence combines two sentences into one. There are two causes of a run-on sentence:

- A comma joins two main clauses (this type of run-on sentence is usually called a *comma splice*); or
- No punctuation joins two main clauses (this type of run-on sentence is sometimes called a *fused sentence*).

Fix these sentences by inserting the correct punctuation (usually a semicolon, if the two clauses are closely related) or by making the clauses into separate sentences. In many cases, a comma splice can be fixed by using a coordinating conjunction (the words *and, but, for, nor, or, so,* and *yet*) after the comma.

Comma Splices

Please have the paralegal edit the complaint, it must be filed today.

Corrections

Please have the paralegal edit the complaint; it must be filed today.
or
Please have the paralegal edit the complaint. It must be filed today.

The defendant was early for the trial, his attorney was not.

The defendant was early for the trial, but his attorney was not.
or
The defendant was early for the trial. His attorney was not.

Fused Sentence

The jurors were deadlocked they could not reach a verdict.

Corrections

The jurors were deadlocked; they could not reach a verdict.
or
The jurors were deadlocked. They could not reach a verdict.

Challenge ? Sentences

Rewrite the following to correct them.

- He was not prepared for trial. If you want my opinion.
- He summarized the transcript. Because his supervisor told him to.
- Blake drafted the brief. Which was longer than the court rules allowed.
- The attorney drafted the complaint, he included both causes of action.
- Ask the clerk to file the answer, it must be filed by Friday.

D. Subject-Verb Agreement

A subject must agree with its verb. Singular subjects correspond with singular verbs (as in *The plaintiff is testifying*) and plural subjects must correspond with plural verbs (as in *The plaintiffs are testifying*).

Most problems in subject-verb agreement occur when:

- A subject has more than one word;
- The subject is an indefinite pronoun (such as *everyone*);
- The subject is a collective noun (such as *committee*); or
- Words or phrases intervene between the subject and the verb.

1. Multiple-Word Subjects

☐ **Rule One: Subjects joined by *and* usually take a plural verb.**

Incorrect	Correct
The judge and the jury was unpersuaded by the witness's testimony.	The judge and jury were unpersuaded by the witness's testimony.

 Try mentally replacing multiple-word subjects with the word *they* to determine the correct verb, as in *They were unpersuaded by the witness's testimony.*

Exception to Rule One: When the parts of the subject describe a singular idea or are thought of as a unit, they are singular and take a singular verb, as in Macaroni and cheese is my favorite lunch.

☐ **Rule Two: Singular subjects joined by *or* or *nor* usually take a singular verb.**

Incorrect	Correct
Neither the defendant nor his counsel were prepared.	Neither the defendant *nor* his counsel *was* prepared.

☐ **Rule Three: Plural subjects joined by *or* or *nor* take a plural verb.**

Incorrect	Correct
Either the records or the receipts is missing.	Either the records *or* the receipts *are* missing.

☐ **Rule Four: When a singular subject and a plural subject are joined by *or* or *nor* (or *neither* and *nor*), the verb should agree with the nearer subject.**

	Correct
	Either the jurors or the *judge has* left.

Note, however, that sentences such as these "sound" better with plural verbs; thus, try to place the plural subject nearer to the verb.

Better

Either the judge or the *jurors have* left.

☐ **Rule Five: When a compound subject is preceded by the words *each* or *every*, the verb is usually singular.**

Correct

Each plaintiff, defendant, and witness *was* present in the courtroom.

2. Indefinite Pronouns

Indefinite pronouns are pronouns that do not refer to a specific person or thing. Many of them end in *-one* or *-body*.

Indefinite pronouns can be singular or plural. Singular indefinite pronouns take singular verbs and plural indefinite pronouns take plural verbs. Following are some common indefinite pronouns:

Singular Indefinite Pronouns	Plural Indefinite Pronouns
anybody	both
anyone	few
each	many
either	several
every	
everybody	
everyone	
neither	
nobody	
no one	
somebody	
someone	
something	

Correct Examples

- *Each* of the complaints *alleges* malpractice.
- *Everyone* in the courtroom *was* seated.
- *No one was* absent from the board meeting.
- *Many* of the documents *were* missing from the file.
- *Both* contracts *contain* errors.
- *Neither* of the plaintiffs *lives* in the county.

Caution: A few indefinite pronouns (all, any, more, most, none, *and* some) *can be singular or plural depending on the word to which they refer.*

Correct Examples

- *All* the board *members were* present for the meeting.
- *All* the *money is* counted.
- *Some documents were* missing.
- *Some* of the *jewelry was* appraised.

3. Collective Nouns and Company Names

Collective nouns are nouns that stand for a group of people or things, such as *committee, corporation, crowd, evidence, jury, staff,* and *team.* These collective nouns are usually singular because they refer to the group as a unit and they thus take singular verbs. The word *court* is also viewed as a collective noun (even when there is only one trial judge), and it is always treated as a singular word. Similarly, organizational names (General Electric Company or Starbucks Corporation) are usually treated as singular.

Incorrect	Correct
The jury have adjourned to deliberate.	The jury has adjourned to deliberate.
The evidence show probable cause.	The evidence shows probable cause.
The court have decided the case.	The court has decided the case.
The board of directors have passed a resolution.	The board of directors has passed a resolution.
Starbucks are holding their annual meeting today.	Starbucks is holding its annual meeting today.

If you wish to discuss the individuals that compose the unit, use the following forms:

Correct
The jurors have adjourned to deliberate.
The members of the court have decided the case.
The members of the board of directors passed a resolution.

Note, however, that in British usage, collective nouns are usually treated as plurals, and thus it would be common to read *The team are playing at home today.*

Tips → On Singular Nouns

- Watch for the word *the* before a noun because it is often a signal that the word that follows is singular, as in *The committee has nominated its officers.*
- Organization and company names are usually treated as singular nouns, as in *Microsoft Corporation has posted its quarterly earnings.*
- Expressions of time and money are usually singular, as in *Three hours is enough time to edit the brief* and *One hundred thousand dollars is the settlement offer.*

---

4. Intervening Words

Subject-verb agreement problems often occur when words or phrases (often prepositional phrases) intervene between a subject and its verb. These intervening expressions often confuse writers, who may be tempted to match the verb with the noun in the intervening phrase rather than with the subject of the sentence. To be correct, identify the subject of the sentence, and ignore intervening words.

Incorrect	Correct
The discrepancy between the books and the accounting records have been resolved.	The *discrepancy* between the books and the accounting records *has* been resolved.
The remainder of the goods to be distributed are in storage.	The *remainder* of the goods to be distributed *is* in storage.
One of the best experts are available.	*One* of the best experts *is* available.

Caution: Phrases or words such as together with, including, *or* in addition to *do not change the number of the verb. If the subject is singular, select a singular verb; if the subject is plural, select a plural verb.*

Correct Examples

- The *attorney*, together with the paralegals, *has* reviewed the contract.
- The *exhibits*, as well as the report, *show* a pattern of traffic congestion.

5. Inverted Sentence Order

In most sentences, the subject is placed before the verb, as in *The witness lied.* When this standard sentence structure is inverted and a verb precedes its subject, make sure they agree.

Correct Examples: Enclosed *are* two *copies* of the contract.

In the written proposals for settlement, there *is* a *suggestion* for compromise.

Caution: Be careful with sentences beginning with there is *and* there are. *These expressions signal that the sentence is inverted. Be sure to use* is *for singular subjects and* are *for plural subjects.*

Correct Examples

- There *is* an *exhibit* in the folder.
- There *are* many *options* to consider.

Challenge ❓ Subject-Verb Agreement

Select the correct word.

- Neither Paul nor Pamela is/are attending the conference.
- The witness, together with the experts, have/has testified.
- The last thing the firm needs is/are attorneys without practical experience.
- The staff have/has prepared their/its report.
- Most of the money is/are available for settlement.
- The expert and the attorneys has/have left.
- Either the jurors or the bailiffs has/have requested a break.
- Either the document or the attachment was/were altered.
- Neither the tenant nor the landlords have/has filed a complaint.
- Management has/have decided to submit the proposal.
- Don't pick a juror just because he or she is/they're available.
- The set of rules that govern/governs federal litigation is the Federal Rules of Civil Procedure.

E. Modifiers

Modifiers are words that modify other words by describing, limiting, or qualifying those other words. An adjective such as *big* is a modifier because it describes another word. Adverbs (such as *slowly*) are also modifiers. Modifiers should be placed as close as possible to the words they modify.

1. Misplaced Modifier Phrases

The term *misplaced modifier* refers to a modifier that has been located in a sentence in such a way as to cause ambiguity (and often humor). To avoid trouble with modifiers, keep phrases and words close to the words they modify.

Consider the following examples of misplaced modifiers:

- *The defendant was described as a tall man with a hat weighing 180 pounds.*
  (This sentence suggests that the hat weighs 180 pounds.)
- *He provided exhibits to the attorneys on CD-ROMs.*
  (This sentence suggests that the attorneys were on CD-ROMs.)
- *He placed a transcript on the table that was blue.*
  (This sentence is confusing because it isn't clear whether the transcript is blue or whether the table is blue.)

To remedy a misplaced modifier, move the modifying phrase close to the words it refers to or modifies.

Correct

- *The defendant was described as a 180-pound, tall man with a hat.*
- *He provided exhibits on CD-ROMs to the attorneys.*
- *He placed a blue transcript on the table* or *He placed a transcript on the blue table.*

Similarly, a 2007 headline in the *Washington Post* announced "Woman, 30, Is Found Shot in Home by Children," suggesting incorrectly that the children had shot her. A correctly worded headline would have read "Slain Woman Found at Home by Her Children."

2. Misplaced Prepositional Phrases

One common type of misplaced modifier is a prepositional phrase that is located in the wrong place in a sentence. Consider the following examples:

- *These guidelines provide tips for protecting your safety from our staff.*
  (This sentence suggests that the staff cannot be trusted with your safety.)
- *The attorney will discuss my proposal to fill the excavation pit with the corporation's officers.*
  (This sentence suggests that the pit will be filled with the corporation's officers.)

To remedy this error, place prepositional phrases after the words they modify.

Correct

- *These guidelines from our staff provide tips for protecting your safety.*
- *The attorney will discuss with the corporation's officers my proposal to fill the excavation pit.*

3. Limiting Modifiers

The following words, all of which are called *limiting words* because they restrict the meaning of other words, are notorious causes of ambiguity and should be placed immediately before the word or group of words you intend to limit or restrict.

almost
even
exact, exactly
hardly
just
mere, merely
nearly
only
scarcely
simply
sole, solely

Review the following sentence: *The witness identified Jack as the burglar.* Now consider the placement of the word *only* in the following versions of the sentence:

- *Only* the witness identified Jack as the burglar.
- The *only* witness identified Jack as the burglar.
- The witness *only* identified Jack as the burglar.
- The witness identified *only* Jack as the burglar.
- The witness identified Jack *only* as the burglar.
- The witness identified Jack as *only* the burglar.
- The witness identified Jack as the *only* burglar.

Note that varying the placement of the word *only* in the sentence can produce seven different meanings. For clarity, place these troublesome words immediately before the word or words they are intended to limit or describe.

4. Dangling Modifiers

A modifier is said to "dangle" when it does not logically modify anything in its sentence. Most dangling modifiers occur in phrases introducing sentences (especially in phrases beginning with an *-ing* word), and although the phrases include a verb form, they do not include a subject. This modifier isn't merely separated from the word it modifies, it is missing a subject to modify.

Dangling

- *Upon entering the conference room, an exhibit came to my attention.*
  (This sentence suggests that the exhibit entered the conference room.)
- *Waiting in the courtroom, his eyes became tired.*
  (This sentence suggests that the eyes were waiting in the courtroom.)
- *When not in use, the city stores the display in a warehouse.*
  (This sentence suggests that the city is not in use rather than that the display is not in use.)

To remedy a dangling modifier, either identify the actor immediately after the introductory modifier, or reword the modifying phrase so that it identifies the actor.

Revised

- *Upon entering the courtroom, I noticed an exhibit.*
  (The actor *I* is identified immediately after the introductory phrase.)
- *As he waited in the courtroom, his eyes became tired.*
  (The modifying phrase is reworded to identify the subject *he*.)
- *When the display is not in use, the city stores it in a warehouse.*
  (The subject *display* is identified in the introductory phrase.)

5. Squinting Modifiers

A squinting modifier is a modifier placed so that it is not clear whether it modifies the word before it or the one after it, as in the following sentence:

- *Lawyers who prepare briefs often can improve their writing skills.*

The placement of the word *often* renders the sentence capable of two interpretations: Lawyers who prepare many briefs improve their writing skills or lawyers who prepare briefs can often improve their writing skills.

Fix a squinting modifier by moving it so that it clearly refers to the intended word.

Revised

- *Lawyers who often prepare briefs can improve their writing skills.*
- *Lawyers who prepare briefs can often improve their writing skills.*

Tips ➡ For Correcting Dangling Modifiers

Most sentences that include dangling modifiers are written in the passive voice. Changing to active voice corrects the dangling modifier because an actor or subject is identified in the phrase that begins the sentence.
  Example:

- When a boy, my father changed careers (passive voice).
- When *I* was a boy, my father changed careers (active voice, actor identified in modifying phrase).

Challenge ❓ Modifiers

Rewrite the following.

- Unclear and too long, the judge has ordered us to rewrite the brief.
- Moving the exhibits, her back was hurt.
- Having arrived late, a reprimand was issued by the judge.
- Reviewing the deposition, the error was obvious.
- The judge agreed to admit the evidence with misgivings.
- Reviewing the exhibit, the errors were apparent.
- I anticipate help in proofing the brief from everyone.
- New attorneys who attend depositions often gain confidence.
- Fix the following newspaper headline: "Detective's Hunch Led Him to Attack Suspect."

F. Split Infinitives

An infinitive is the word *to* together with a verb, as in *to run, to plead,* and *to scream.* An infinitive is said to be "split" when a word (usually an adverb) is inserted between the word *to* and the verb, as in *to quickly run, to convincingly plead,* and *to loudly scream.*

Most writing experts now recognize that there is no formal rule against splitting an infinitive, and split infinitives are commonly seen in nonlegal writing, including newspaper articles; however, legal readers tend to be conservative and may be annoyed or distracted by a split infinitive. Because most split infinitives are so easily corrected (by merely moving the adverb that causes the "split" after the infinitive), correct them when you can and avoid splitting an infinitive unless you want to place emphasis on the adverb or you need to remedy an awkward-sounding phrase, as in *to boldly go where no man has gone before.*

Split Infinitive	**Corrected Infinitive**
The attorney asked me *to thoroughly review* the documents.	The attorney asked me *to review* the documents *thoroughly.*
The judge ordered us *to immediately produce* the documents.	The judge ordered us *to produce* the documents *immediately.*

☐ **Rule: Do not insert *not* or *never* in an infinitive because the result is awkward and incorrect.**

Split Infinitive	**Corrected Infinitive**
She agreed *to not examine* the witness.	She agreed *not to examine* the witness.

Tips → The Old Rules

Because legal writing is more formal than other styles of writing and because legal readers are notorious perfectionists, err on the side of caution so readers will not be jarred by your usage. Thus, whenever possible, comply with the "old" rules of writing in legal documents:

- Avoid splitting an infinitive;
- Avoid starting a sentence with a conjunction such as *and* or *but*; and
- Avoid ending a sentence with a preposition.

In most instances, there is a quick fix for violations of these old rules. For example, to remedy the split infinitive *to promptly investigate*, reword as *to investigate promptly*.

Ending a sentence with a preposition is something up with which I will not put.

Attributed to Sir Winston Churchill

G. Pronouns

Pronouns are words that replace nouns. Thus, consider the sentences *John filed the complaint* and *He filed the complaint.* In the second sentence the word *he* is a pronoun because it replaces the proper noun *John.* There are many different kinds of pronouns, including personal pronouns, indefinite pronouns, and reflexive pronouns, but all pronouns must always agree with their *antecedents* (the word or phrase to which the pronoun refers).

1. Personal Pronouns

Personal pronouns (*I/me, you, he/him, she/her, we/us, they/them*) change forms depending on whether they function as the subject of the sentence or the object of the sentence. Most problems occur when there is more than one subject or object. For example, writers seldom have difficulty with a sentence such as *Give the document to me* (and would never write *Give the document to I*); however, when another party is added to the pronoun, as in *Give the document to John and me,* confusion often results.

☐ **Rule One: When a pronoun functions as or replaces the subject of a sentence, use *I, he, she, we,* or *they.***

Incorrect	Correct
It was me who prepared the contract.	It was I who prepared the contract.
James and her drafted the brief.	James and she drafted the brief.
Either him or me will do the cite-checking.	Either he or I will do the cite-checking.
Us on the jury voted to convict the defendant.	We on the jury voted to convict the defendant.
It was them who informed the police.	It was they who informed the police.

☐ **Rule Two: When a pronoun functions as or replaces the object of a sentence, use *me, him, her, us,* or *them.***

Incorrect	Correct
You must give John and I directions.	You must give John and me directions.
We urge you to release Susan and he from their employment contracts.	We urge you to release Susan and him from their employment contracts.
She has provided the committee and we with the budget analysis.	She has provided the committee and us with the budget analysis.
Between you and I, the defendant is guilty.	Between you and me, the defendant is guilty.

 For Pronoun Use

As an aid to determining which form of pronoun to use, omit or cover up the noun and the word *and* accompanying the pronoun. This will provide a clue as to which pronoun to use.

   Example: You must give Ted and me the police report.

Omit or cover up the words *Ted and* so that the sentence reads,

   You must give _____ the police report.

This reading makes it clear that the correct pronoun is *me.*

It is customary to place the pronouns *I* or *me* after other pronouns or subjects. Thus, write *Deliver the records to Jack and me* rather than *Deliver the records to me and Jack.* Similarly, write *She and I attended the meeting* rather than *I and she attended the meeting.* There is nothing grammatically incorrect with the second presentations, but custom (and perhaps modesty) dictates that we refer to ourselves after we refer to others.

2. Pronoun Agreement

A pronoun must agree in number with its antecedent (the word the pronoun stands for or refers to). Singular antecedents take singular pronouns and plural antecedents take plural pronouns.

In most instances, writers instinctively choose the right pronoun based on what "sounds" right. Thus, writers seldom have difficulty with a sentence such as *The jurors brought their notes into the jury deliberation room.*

There are a few instances, however, that tend to cause problems for most writers: the use of indefinite pronouns or collective nouns or when a prepositional phrase or several words intervene between the subject and the verb.

a. Indefinite Pronouns

☐ **Rule: Use a singular pronoun when the antecedent is a singular indefinite pronoun.**

Some antecedents are indefinite, meaning that they do not refer to any specific person or thing. The most common indefinite pronouns that take a singular form are as follows (note that many end with *-body, -one,* or *-thing*):

anybody, anyone, anything
each
either
every
everybody, everyone, everything
much
neither
nobody, no one, nothing
one
somebody, someone, something

When these indefinite words serve as antecedents of pronouns, select a singular pronoun.

Incorrect	Correct
Somebody forgot to file their papers.	*Somebody* forgot to file *his or her* papers.
Does everyone have their contract?	Does *everyone* have *his or her* contract?
Each fraternity member had their cap.	*Each fraternity member* had *his* cap.

Although these correct examples show proper usage, you may wish to avoid the expression *his or her* if it strikes you as wordy or stuffy. As discussed later in subsection 7, there are several ways to remedy such constructions. For example, the first example could be rewritten as *Somebody forgot to file the papers.*

b. Collective Nouns

As discussed in Section D.3, collective nouns (nouns that stand for a group of people or items) such as *committee, corporation, crowd, court,* and *jury,* are usually singular and take a singular pronoun. Watch for the word *the* before a noun because it is often a signal that the word to follow is singular.

Incorrect	Correct
The corporation is holding their annual meeting next week.	The corporation is holding *its* annual meeting next week.

If you wish to discuss the individuals composing the unit, for clarity use the following form:

	Correct
	The corporation's shareholders are holding *their* annual meeting next week.

c. Generic Nouns

A generic noun is one that could refer to either men or women, such as *athlete, attorney, defendant, juror,* or *plaintiff.* These generic nouns usually take a singular pronoun, as in *An attorney must present his or her argument* or *A juror will be compensated for his or her time on the jury.* As previously discussed, many sentences with the phrase *his or her* can be reworded to eliminate awkwardness, as in *The attorneys must present their arguments* or *Jurors will be compensated for their time on the jury.*

3. Pronoun Reference

A pronoun must relate clearly and specifically to its antecedent (the noun to which the pronoun refers).

a. Ambiguous References

A pronoun is ambiguous when it could refer to two possible antecedents. Thus, make sure that any pronoun used in a sentence refers clearly to one antecedent. This ambiguity often occurs when writers substitute pronouns for names. For example, consider the following sentence: *The document Ellen drafted for Teresa was given to her for review.* It is unclear whether *her* refers to Ellen or Teresa.

There are two ways to remedy such an ambiguity:

1. Replace the pronoun with the appropriate noun, as in *The document Ellen drafted for Teresa was given to Ellen for her review.*
2. Revise the sentence if you do not wish to repeat a noun, as in *Ellen, who drafted the document for Teresa, was later given the document for review.*

Ambiguous	Revised
Dan told Bill that he needed to draft the contract.	Dan told Bill that *Dan* needed to draft the contract.
	or
	Dan told Bill that *Bill* needed to draft the contract.

b. Implied References

Pronouns must refer to a specific stated noun in the same sentence or the previous sentence, not to a word that is implied in the sentence.

Incorrect Implied Reference	Correct Specific Reference
After the verdict was rendered, the attorney thanked *them*.	After the *jurors* rendered a verdict, the attorney thanked *them*.

c. Vague References

The pronouns *it, this, that,* and *which* are often used in a vague manner. These pronouns must refer to one specific noun.

Confusing	Revised
If you put your hand on the banister, it will get wet.	If you put your hand on the banister, *your hand* [or *the banister*] will get wet.
The expert witness always arrives on time and is well dressed. This is important.	The expert witness always arrives on time and is well dressed. *Punctuality* [or *dressing well*] is important.
Steve took out his pen and signed the will. He then put it back in his briefcase.	Steve took out his pen and signed the will. He then put *the pen* [or *the will*] back in his briefcase.

d. Indefinite Use of *It* and *They*

When using *it* or *they,* make sure that a definite noun has first been used.

Incorrect	Correct
In the case *Allen v. Burns*, it describes the doctrine of equivalents.	The case *Allen v. Burns* describes the doctrine of equivalents. It holds that . . .

4. Use of *Who* and *Whom*

Who and *whom* are used either in questions, as in *Who wrote the book?* or in subordinate clauses, as in *I am unsure who will represent the plaintiff.*

- In questions, use *who* for a subject and *whom* for an object. Use *who* whenever *I, he, she, we,* or *they* could be substituted for *who* and use *whom* whenever *me, him, her, us,* or *them* could be substituted for *whom.*

Correct Examples: *Who will be going to the trial?*

Explanation: In this question, *who* acts as the subject of the sentence.

Whom does the indictment name?

Explanation: In this question, the object of the sentence is *whom* and the subject is *indictment*.

■ In subordinate clauses, use *who* and *whoever* for all subjects, and use *whom* and *whomever* for all objects.

Correct Examples: *Give the document to whoever needs it.*

Explanation: In this sentence, *whoever* is the subject of the subordinate clause *whoever needs it.*

It was Judge Allen whom I saw.

Explanation: In this sentence, *whom* is the object of the subordinate clause *whom I saw.*

 Tip   # *Who* versus *Whom*: Remember *"m"* for *Whom*

In every use of *who* or *whom*, rephrase the question or subordinate clause and determine whether you would use *he* or *him* in its place. If *he* would be used, use *who*. If *him* would be used, use *whom*. Remember that the *"m"* in *him* matches up with the *"m"* in *whom*.

Example: **Who is calling?**

Test: Rewrite as *He is calling.* Replace *he* with *who*.

Example: **This is the man whom I mentioned earlier.**

Test: Rewrite as *I mentioned him earlier.* Replace *him* with *whom*.

---

5. Use of *That* and *Which*

That is used to introduce a restrictive clause (one that is necessary to the meaning of a sentence) and is not preceded by a comma. *Which* is nearly always used to introduce a nonrestrictive clause (a clause that is not necessary to the meaning of the sentence and that can be omitted without changing the meaning of the sentence). A *which* clause is usually preceded by a comma. Use *who* to refer to people and use *that* or *which* to refer to groups and things.

The use of *that* or *which* depends on the writer's intent. If the writer wishes to convey essential information, *that* should be used to introduce the information; if the writer intends to define, add to, or limit information, *which* should be used to introduce the information.

Example: *The corporation that was formed in Delaware has no assets.*

Explanation: The word *that* tells us which particular corporation has no assets. There may be several corporations that have no assets, but the writer is describing which particular corporation, namely, the one formed in Delaware (rather than others formed elsewhere), has no assets. Use *that*.

Example: *The contract that was modified was admitted into evidence.*

Explanation: The word *that* tells us essential information about which particular contract was admitted into evidence (namely, the one that was modified).

Example: *The car that was damaged in the collision was my car.*

Explanation: Elimination of the *that* clause causes the sentence to lose meaning. Use *that*.

Example: *The corporation, which was formed in Delaware, has no assets.*

Explanation: The phrase *which was formed in Delaware* provides additional information about the corporation, but it is not essential to the meaning of the sentence. The *which* clause is set off by commas because it acts as a parenthetical expression; it adds a fact about the only corporation being discussed. Use *which*.

Example: *The contract, which was modified, was admitted into evidence.*

Explanation: The phrase *which was modified* tells us a nonessential fact about the only contract being discussed.

Example: *My car, which was brand new, was damaged in the collision.*

Explanation: The *which* clause adds information, but it can be dropped and the sentence will still make sense. Use *which*.

Examples: *We may wish that the argument were true, but it is not, and that which we cannot deny, we should not deny.*

His summation sets the standard by which all others should be judged.

> **Explanation:** These two sentences are examples of the fact that the word *which* is not always preceded by a comma and *that which* is sometimes used to introduce a restrictive clause. The expressions *that which, in which, by which, of which,* and so forth are not preceded by commas.

Many writers are confused about the use of *that* and *which,* and you will likely see incorrect uses. Recognizing this confusion, many writing texts have relaxed the rules about the distinction between *that* and *which.* Nevertheless, because legal writing is so specific, try to remember to use *that* when you introduce essential information and *which* when you introduce nonessential information. See Chapter 2, Section C for additional information.

Tips → That or Which

To determine whether to start a clause with *that* or *which* consider these tips:

- If you can drop the clause and still retain the meaning of the sentence, use *which.* If you can't, use *that.*
- A clause beginning with *which* is usually set off by commas because it includes nonessential information.
- A clause beginning with *that* is not set off by commas.
- *That* introduces essential information; *which* seldom does.

6. Reflexive Pronouns

The reflexive pronouns are the *self* pronouns, namely, *myself, yourself, himself, herself, ourselves, yourselves,* and *themselves.* Reflexive pronouns usually reflect back on a subject, as in *She injured herself* or *He satisfied himself that the defendant was guilty.* Do not substitute a *self* pronoun for a personal pronoun (*I, me, he, him,* and so forth).

Incorrect	Correct
He won't give Lyndsey or myself his phone number.	He won't give Lyndsey or *me* his phone number.
The accident was witnessed by Mrs. Hendrix and himself.	The accident was witnessed by Mrs. Hendrix and *him.*
He issued a statement on behalf of his wife and him.	He issued a statement on behalf of his wife and *himself.*

Challenge Pronoun Use

Rewrite or select the correct pronoun.

- Her/she and James have docketed the trial date.
- It was me/I who prepared the lease.
- The contract was drafted by Megan and I/me/myself.
- Between you and I/me, Harry's conduct was inappropriate.
- Frank and him/he have left for the meeting.
- Patricia has instructed the expert and her/she not to respond to the question.
- The brief that/which was long was submitted after the deadline.
- The judge admonished the attorney, and he looked unhappy.
- After someone has argued a case, they/he or she often are/is relieved.
- A law student must study diligently if he or she/they want/wants to pass the bar exam.
- He is the attorney who/whom negotiated the settlement.
- She will depose the engineers, who/whom she will meet on Tuesday.
- Who/whom did the board appoint as their/its treasurer?

7. Gender-Linked Pronouns

Avoid using gender-linked pronouns. For example, the sentence *A nurse should always keep her thermometer handy* is objectionable because it suggests that nurses are always female. Similarly, the sentence *A judge must give his instructions to the jury* is likewise objectionable because it presupposes the judge is male.

a. Six Techniques for Gender-Neutral Language

There are several techniques that can be used to avoid offending readers:

(1) Change singular nouns to plural nouns. Changing singular nouns to plural nouns will force the singular pronoun *he* or *she* to be changed to a neutral plural pronoun, such as *they* or *their*.

> **Examples:** Nurses should always keep <u>their</u> thermometers handy.
>
> Judges must give <u>their</u> instructions to the jury.

(2) Rewrite the sentence to avoid using any pronoun. Many sentences can be rewritten so that no pronouns are used.

> **Examples:** A nurse should always keep a thermometer handy.
>
> A judge must give instructions to the jury.

(3) Use the noun *one*. In many instances, the pronoun *one* can be used. Note, however, that using *one* often results in a vague and stuffy sentence.

Examples: One should always keep one's thermometer handy.

One must give one's instructions to the jury.

(4) Use the pronoun *you*. In some situations, the pronoun *you* can be used. Thus, rather than writing *The applicant must provide his address*, write *You must provide your address*.

(5) Use *he or she*. In some instances, none of the techniques previously described will work smoothly. In those cases, consider using the phrase *he or she* throughout the document. The continued use of *he or she* throughout a long document, however, is often clumsy.

(6) Use *he* in transactional documents. If you are drafting a document such as a contract, you may use *he* throughout and at the end include a statement that the use of the masculine gender is deemed to include the feminine. This technique is appropriate for transactional documents such as contracts, leases, and so forth, but it is not appropriate for letters.

b. Constructions to Avoid

Although ensuring that language is gender-neutral is an admirable goal, there are some constructions that are disfavored and should be avoided.

- **Avoid *he/she*, *his/her*, and *s/he***
  Avoid using *he/she*. This construction creates an awkward appearance because slashes are seldom used in legal writing. Their use is noticeable and distracting to a reader. The combination *s/he* is even more noticeable and distracting and is unpronounceable.
- **Avoid alternating between *he* and *she***
  Avoid alternating between the pronouns *he* and *she* in a single document, especially in a single paragraph or section. This attempt to be fair and gender-inclusive is misguided and confusing and is disruptive to the flow of a project.

c. Letters

When addressing a letter to an individual whose gender is unknown, for example, a letter to the Secretary of State of Utah, check the Internet to see if you can determine whether the individual is a man or woman. If you cannot make that determination, address the letter as *Dear Sir or Madam*. Although the word *madam* is an archaic form of address, it is correct in such a situation. When both women and men will receive the letter, consider *Dear Ladies and Gentlemen*. Similarly, when you are responding to a letter written by an individual whose name is ambiguous, such as Terry L. Lowell, do some investigative work on the Internet or call the person's office and ask how the letter should be addressed. Rest assured, you will not be the first person confused by such a name. If contacting the person is not possible or practical, you could address the letter *Dear Terry, Dear Terry Lowell*, or *Dear Colleague*.

d. Closing Thoughts on Gender-Neutral Language

Correct gender-linked pronouns to avoid offending readers *if* you can do so without creating an awkward and distracting document. For example, the use of specially crafted words such as *personholes* (rather than *manholes*) is jarring and confusing to readers. Thus, it is still acceptable to use *he* or *him* when changing the pronouns or rewriting the sentence would result in clumsy and distracting writing.

8. Special Pronoun Situations

a. Use of *We* and *Us*

To determine whether *we* or *us* precedes a noun, select the pronoun that would be appropriate if there were no noun in the sentence.

Correct Example:	*We attorneys will not represent the corporation.*
Test:	*We will not represent the corporation.* (You would never write *Us will not represent the corporation.*)
Correct Example:	*The court refused to meet with us litigants.*
Test:	*The court refused to meet with us* (not *The court refused to meet with we*).

b. Comparisons with *Than* or *As*

Comparisons using the words *than* or *as* tend to be ambiguous because writers are often inclined to use incomplete constructions. Consider the sentence *Don likes these cookies more than me*. Because the word *cookies* is used as the object of the verb, the sentence means that Don likes the cookies more than he likes me. To reduce confusion, rewrite the sentence and add clarifying language.

Confusing	**Revised**
Don likes these cookies more than me.	Don likes these cookies more than he likes me.
	or
	Don likes these cookies more than I do.

c. Gerunds

A gerund is a verb form that ends in *-ing,* as in *writing* or *drafting.* A noun or pronoun that precedes a gerund should be in the possessive case (the case that indicates ownership, as in *our* book, *his* briefcase, *your* brief, and so forth).

Incorrect	Correct
The court approved of him giving the opening statement.	The court approved of *his* giving the opening statement.
I was unhappy with you addressing the jury.	I was unhappy with *your* addressing the jury.

9. Shifts in Pronouns

Maintain consistency in pronoun use in a sentence or section.

Inconsistent	Revised
All jurors must listen carefully or you may not understand the judge's instructions.	All jurors must listen carefully or they may not understand the judge's instructions.
One finds that when listening to oral argument, your mind wanders.	I find that when listening to oral argument, my mind wanders.

Challenge		Gender-Linked and Special Pronouns

Correct the following or select the right word.

- Each juror must affirm the verdict he reached.
- A counselor should maintain the confidentiality of her patients.
- He told me he was pleased by you/your drafting of the contract.
- An alibi may prevent his/him being accused of the crime.
- The decision by the appeals court was a setback for us/we appellants.
- David likes trial preparation more than me.

H. Conjunctions

A conjunction is a word that joins together words and groups of words.

1. Coordinating Conjunctions: *And, But, For, Nor, Or, So, Yet*

Coordinating conjunctions join elements of equal grammatical status, as in the statement *The attorney and the defendant arrived late,* in which the conjunction *and* joins two nouns. The coordinating conjunctions are *and, but, for, nor, or, so,* and *yet.*

Most traditional writers dislike the use of a coordinating conjunction at the beginning of a sentence, although this is becoming increasingly common, especially in newspapers and magazines. Whenever possible, avoid starting a sentence with a coordinating conjunction because it is likely to annoy and distract some readers. Moreover, it is likely to produce a sentence fragment, as in, *And also the transcript.* Thus avoid starting sentences with *and* or *but* except in very informal writing. In fact, some experts have commented that starting too many sentences with *and* or *but* sounds childish.

Disfavored	Revised
The court ruled in favor of the defendant. But the judgment was later reversed.	The court ruled in favor of the defendant, but the judgment was later reversed.
	or
	The court ruled in favor of the defendant, although the judgment was later reversed.

2. Correlative Conjunctions: *Both-And, Either-Or, Neither-Nor, Not Only-But Also, Whether-Or*

Correlative conjunctions are used in pairs so they work together and, like coordinating conjunctions, join elements that are of equal grammatical status. The correlative conjunctions are *both-and, either-or, neither-nor, not only-but also,* and *whether-or.*

There are three straightforward rules for ensuring correct verb selection with coordinating or correlative conjunctions:

- **If the subjects are singular words, use a singular verb.**
  (Correct Example: *Either Tom or Fred has jury duty.*)
- **If the subjects are plural words, use a plural verb.**
  (Correct Example: *Neither the plaintiffs nor the defendants were prepared for trial.*)

- **If the subject is made up of both singular and plural words, the verb must agree with the subject nearer to it.**
  (Correct Example: *Not only the plaintiff but also her attorneys <u>have</u> copies of the documents.*)

3. Subordinating Conjunctions

A subordinating conjunction is used to join a dependent clause (one that cannot stand by itself) to an independent clause (a main clause that can stand by itself). Some of the commonly used subordinating conjunctions are *after, although, because, before, once, since, unless, until, when, where,* and *while*. These conjunctions serve as smooth transitions in a sentence.

Correct Examples: *Although the plaintiff testified, she did so reluctantly.*

After a judgment is rendered in a case, it can then be appealed.

(Note that the phrases beginning with *although* and *after* are dependent; they cannot stand by themselves.)

Challenge Conjunction Junction

Punctuate correctly or select the correct word.

- The attorney made a persuasive argument. But the motion was denied.
- Neither the brief nor the motion was/were proofread.
- Either the attorneys or the client has/have discussed settlement of the case.
- The defense counsel argued the case. And she did so succinctly.
- She was not only well prepared but was professional in her demeanor.
- Either the bailiff or the court clerks has/have read the docket.

chapter 2

Punctuation

StyleLinks

www.gpoaccess.gov/stylemanual/index.html
Select Chapter 8 of the Government Printing Office *Style Manual* for information
and rules on punctuation.

http://owl.english.purdue.edu/handouts/grammar
Purdue University's Online Writing Lab offers excellent information on
punctuation, together with exercises and answer keys.

http://grammar.ccc.commnet.edu/grammar/marks/marks.htm
This site provides a thorough review of rules relating to punctuation.

www.grammarbook.com
Select "Punctuation and Capitalization" for a review of punctuation rules,
exercises, and answer keys.

A. Introduction

When you speak, you use pauses and changes in voice inflection as well as gestures to signal meaning to the listener. In writing, these signals are given through the use of punctuation. Punctuation makes writing more understandable to a reader. For example, a period instructs the reader that a complete thought or sentence is concluded. Without periods, all of a writing would be one incomprehensible sentence. Similarly, quotation marks signal to a reader that the exact words of another are being used.

Slight differences in punctuation may make great differences in meaning. For example, consider the alternate punctuation shown in the following trick sentences:

- Woman! Without her, man is nothing.
- Woman, without her man, is nothing.
- Mark said Lisa is smart.
- Mark, said Lisa, is smart.

This part of Section One discusses ending punctuation (periods, question marks, and exclamation points), commas, apostrophes, colons, semicolons, quotation marks, parentheses, and the less frequently used marks in legal writing, namely, dashes, hyphens, and slashes.

There is some variation in punctuation. Given the same paragraph, two writers may punctuate slightly differently from each other. Nevertheless, the basic rules of punctuation have remained relatively unchanged since about the mid-1880s. Although the newer, more modern approach to punctuation, often called *open punctuation*, uses fewer marks than the older approach (for example, many modern writers and most newspapers no longer use the serial comma discussed later), legal writing, like business writing, tends to be somewhat formal. Therefore, just as was recommended in the section in this Handbook on grammar, when in doubt, err on the side of caution and use the more conventional approach to punctuation rather than some unusual approach.

B. End Punctuation

There are three punctuation marks used to end a sentence: a period (.), a question mark (?), and an exclamation point (!).

No iron can pierce the heart with such force as a period put just at the right place.

Isaac Babel (1932)

1. Using Periods

A period is generally used to indicate the end of a complete sentence.

Use a Period	Correct Examples
to signal the end of a declaratory sentence.	*The deposition will be held on Tuesday.*
to signal the end of an indirect question (one that reports what a speaker said but does not use the speaker's exact words).	*The judge asked whether the witness needed a recess.*
after a mild command.	*Please leave.*
after some abbreviations.	*The meeting will be held at 9:00 a.m.*

Tips ➡ On Using Periods

- If a sentence ends with an abbreviation that includes a period, do not add another period.

    Incorrect: *The hearing is at 4:00 p.m..*

- If an abbreviation that ends with a period falls in the middle of a sentence, use normal punctuation after the period.

    Correct: *The hearing was to begin at 9:00 a.m., but the court reporter was late.*

- Acronyms (abbreviations that are pronounced as words, such as NATO and AIDS) are usually presented without periods.
- Many writers place two spaces after a period ending a sentence, but it is becoming more common to use just one space (because modern word processing programs automatically allow suitable spacing between letters).

---

2. Using Question Marks

Use a question mark after a direct question (but not after an indirect question).

Correct Examples

Who will be appointed as the arbitrator?

I asked, "Have all the exhibits been attached to the brief?"

He was effective, wasn't he?

The judge asked if the plaintiff was ready to proceed.

3. Using Exclamation Points

Exclamation points are used to emphasize an idea or statement. They are rarely used in legal writing except to show the exact words of a speaker. Exclamation points stand alone and are not used with any other punctuation mark except when they are part of a quotation.

Correct Examples

The witness screamed, "He hit me!"
What a disaster!

C. Commas

I was working on the proof of one of my poems all the morning and took out a comma. In the afternoon I put it back again.

Oscar Wilde

Commas (,) indicate brief pauses. They are considered the most troublesome of punctuation marks because of their many uses and because some of the rules regarding their use are discretionary and flexible whereas other rules are mandatory. Commas can be used to introduce, to separate, to enclose, and to show omissions.

1. Rules for Comma Use

There are thirteen rules to follow when using commas.

☐ **Rule One: Use a comma after the salutation of an informal letter and after the closing of any letter.**

Correct Examples

Dear Aunt Kay,

Sincerely,

☐ **Rule Two: Use a comma after the year in complete dates (month, day, and year) within a sentence and between the day of the week and the month (but not between a month and the year). Always place a comma after a full date when it appears within a sentence. Although writers often omit it, it is correct to place a comma after the year when a complete date is given.**

Correct Examples

The trial will begin on Monday, September 8, 2008, and will conclude in January 2009.

☐ **Rule Three: Use a comma between a city and a state and after an address when the address is written in a sentence. Do not place a comma before a zip code.**

Correct Example

The witness resides at 2345 Cedar Street, Cleveland, Ohio 92117, and has resided there since January.

☐ **Rule Four: Use a comma to separate digits in numbers of four or more digits.**

Correct Example

The transcript is 4,312 pages.

Note, however, *The Bluebook* Rule 6.2, which provides that commas should be used only in numbers containing five or more digits. Thus, according to the *Bluebook*, the sentence would read *The transcript is 4312 pages.* This style is disfavored by many writers and *ALWD*.

☐ **Rule Five: Use a comma to set off introductory material in a sentence. When the introductory phrase is short (fewer than three words), the comma may be omitted.**

Correct Examples

According to the plaintiff, the accident occurred on Park Avenue.

Unfortunately, the judge ruled against us.

After the trial, I will take a vacation.

First, the defendant entered Mrs. Harris's residence.

Although the witness was sick, she attended the hearing.

In June I will begin trial preparation.

☐ **Rule Six: Use commas to set off interruptive phrases or a transitional expression.**

Transitional expressions make connections between sentences or parts of sentences but are not essential to the meaning of a sentence. Transitional expressions include *additionally, clearly, for example, however,* and *therefore.* Transitional expressions that appear at the beginning of a sentence are followed by a comma.

Correct Examples

The jury, however, voted to acquit the defendant.

Research skills, for example, are critical for legal professionals.

The defendant, over the strenuous objection of his counsel, insisted on testifying.

Therefore, the motion was granted.

☐ **Rule Seven: Use a comma to separate two or more adjectives that equally describe the same word.**

Correct Example

Allison was a fearful, anxious witness.

Note that *and* could also be used to join these two parallel adjectives.

☐ **Rule Eight: Use a comma to separate a phrase that shows contrast or contradiction.**

Correct Example

It was the plaintiff, not the defendant, who failed to attend the hearing.

☐ **Rule Nine: Use commas to separate items in a series of three or more items.**

Although the final comma in a series (often called the *Oxford comma* or the *serial comma*) is optional in most writing, in legal writing it is required. For example, consider the following two sentences:

I leave all my property in equal shares to Jim, Helen, Tim, and Eva.

I leave all my property in equal shares to Jim, Helen, Tim and Eva.

In the first example, it is clear that each of the individuals will receive one-fourth of the estate. In the second example, it is arguable that the estate will be divided into thirds, with Jim and Helen each receiving one-third and the group composed of Tim and Eva sharing one-third.

Similarly, consider a book dedication that reportedly read *To my parents, the Pope and Mother Teresa*. Without the serial comma after *the Pope*, the sentence implies that the writer's parents are the Pope and Mother Teresa.

Because the omission of the last comma in a series can cause ambiguity, always include it to show readers that each item is separate.

Correct Examples

Ray asserted the defenses of waiver, estoppel, and acquiescence.

The court found the defendant's conduct was willful, reckless, and egregious.

☐ **Rule Ten: Use a comma to separate two independent clauses connected by a coordinating conjunction, such as *and*, *but*, *for*, *nor*, *or*, *so*, or *yet*.**

This rule is often violated. The comma is required after the coordinating conjunction if the clause that follows is independent, meaning one that has a subject and a verb and that can stand on its own. The comma may be omitted if the clause is short, generally five words or fewer. The comma is not needed after the coordinating conjunction if the clause that follows cannot stand on its own.

Incorrect Examples

Stan finished law school, and is looking for a job. (This sentence is a compound predicate, a sentence with one subject and two verbs. Do not use a comma with a compound predicate.)

The directors voted on the measure, and refused to reconsider it.

Correct Examples

Stan finished law school, and he is looking for a job. (This sentence is a compound sentence, a sentence with two independent clauses, each with a subject and predicate or verb. Use a comma after the coordinating conjunction.)

The directors voted on the measure, and they refused to reconsider it.

The plaintiff intended to amend the complaint, but the statute of limitations had expired.

The door closed and we left.

☐ **Rule Eleven: Use commas to enclose appositives.**

An appositive is a phrase that explains the noun it follows.

Correct Example

William Emery, the noted attorney, consulted on the case.

☐ **Rule Twelve: Use a comma before and after most quotations; use a comma before and after quotations beginning or ending with words such as** *he said,* *she stated,* **and so forth.**

Correct Examples

She said, "I need the report by noon."

"I need the report by noon," she said.

"The decision of the lower court is reversed," stated Judge Allen, "and the case is remanded to the lower court to proceed according to this decision."

☐ **Rule Thirteen: Use commas to set off nonrestrictive phrases, namely those including nonessential material.**

A nonrestrictive phrase is one that is not essential to the meaning of a sentence. It could be removed without impairing the meaning of a sentence. Commas are used to set off these nonessential phrases or clauses wherever they appear in a sentence. Nonrestrictive phrases are often introduced by the word *which.*

A restrictive phrase or clause identifies which of several possible things or people the clause refers to and thus limits or restricts the information previously given in a sentence. Restrictive phrases are essential to the meaning of a sentence and are not set off by commas. Restrictive phrases are often introduced by the word *that.* Generally, it is the writer's intent that determines whether a clause is essential or nonessential. See Chapter 1, Section G.5 for additional information.

Sentences with Restrictive Phrases

The corporation that was bankrupt merged with ABC Inc.

In this sentence, the information about the corporation's bankruptcy is included because it identifies which corporation merged with ABC Inc. (the bankrupt one). Thus, it is an essential or restrictive phrase and is not set off by commas.

The judge who issued the decision entered the courthouse.

This sentence indicates which of several judges entered the courthouse (namely, the one that issued the decision).

Sentences with Nonrestrictive Phrases

The corporation, which was bankrupt, merged with ABC Inc.

In this sentence, the writer is expressing the main thought that the corporation has merged. The fact that it was bankrupt is incidental to the meaning of the sentence. Thus, the information is introduced by *which* and is set off by commas.

The judge, who issued the decision, entered the courthouse.

This sentence simply notes an extra fact about the judge who entered the courthouse.

Sentences with Restrictive Phrases

The tenants who complained were evicted.

This sentence indicates that only some tenants were evicted. Other tenants (namely, those who did not complain) were not evicted.

Sentences with Nonrestrictive Phrases

The tenants, who complained, were evicted.

In this sentence, all of the tenants were evicted.

2. Comma Misuse

Do Not Use a Comma

between a subject and its verb.

between a verb and an indirect quotation.

after the words *include, like,* or *such as.*

after a coordinating conjunction.

before a dependent clause at the end of a sentence.

Incorrect Examples

The attorneys, drafted the brief.

The judge asked, whether the witness needed a recess.

The allegations include, fraud, breach of contract, and negligence.

The defendant agreed to go, and, the bailiff escorted her out of the room.

The attorney was late, and was rebuked by the judge for her tardiness.

Case Illustration: The Million Dollar Comma

A contract dispute in Canada has focused on what has been termed a "million dollar comma." A contract between cable company Rogers Communication and telephone company Bell Aliant provided that the agreement "shall continue In force for a period of five years from the date it is made, and thereafter for successive five-year terms, unless and until terminated by one year prior notice."

In 2005 Rogers was informed by Bell Aliant that the contract was being cancelled. Rogers contended that the contract could not be cancelled for five years; Bell Aliant claimed that the second comma in the sentence allowed for termination of the contract at any time, upon one year's notice. A Canadian regulator sided with Bell Aliant, stating that "based on the rules of punctuation," the comma in question allowed for termination at any time, so long as one year's notice was given. The regulator stated that the second comma should have been omitted if the contract was intended to last for five years.

The contract would have protected Rogers from rate increases; if the contract is cancelled, it may cost Rogers more than $2 million. At the time of the writing of this text, the case was unresolved. This case is a clear reminder to legal writers that the placement of a single comma can be critical.

See Figure 2-1 for Quick Reference: Comma Use.

Figure 2-1   Quick Reference: Comma Use

Rule: Use a Comma	Correct Example
after informal salutations and all closings in letters.	*Dear Henry,* *Best regards,*
between the day of the week and the date and between the date and year.	*The trial will begin on Tuesday, December 14, 2009.*
between elements of an address in a sentence.	*I live at 909 Beech Drive, Tampa, Florida 90923.*
after dates and addresses when they appear within sentences.	*July 18, 2008, was my first trial.*
in digits.	*The report was 16,190 pages.*
after introductory elements.	*In the present case, the plaintiff alleged fraud.*
to set off interruptive words and transitional expressions.	*His defense, however, was invalid.*
to separate parallel adjectives.	*Ellen was an organized, diligent worker.*
to separate contrasting elements.	*It was John Turner, not Jason Turner, who represented the plaintiff.*
between the items in a series of three or more items.	*To be patentable, an invention must be novel, useful, and nonobvious.*
before a coordinating conjunction that introduces an independent clause.	*The witness was late for the deposition, and the court imposed sanctions against her.*
to enclose appositive expressions.	*Judge Adams, the presiding judge, vacated the judgment.*
to introduce quotations.	*Judge Moreno ruled, "I hereby affirm the judgment."*
to set off nonessential information.	*The briefcase, a new one, was left in the courtroom.*

Tips ➡ On Restrictive and Nonrestrictive Elements

- If information is essential to the meaning of a sentence, it is restrictive, and it will not be introduced by a comma.
- If information is not essential to the meaning of a sentence, it is nonrestrictive, and it must be set off by commas.
- If information is introduced by the word *that*, it is restrictive and does not take a comma.
- If information is introduced by the word *which*, it is usually nonessential and will be set off by commas.

Challenge ❓ Punctuation

Punctuate the following sentences correctly, correct the punctuation errors, or indicate if the sentence is correct.

- The witness not her attorney failed to attend the hearing.
- The trial occurred in May, 2008.
- The witness was a tall distinguished gentleman.
- November 8 1980 is her birthday.
- In spring, I will begin school.
- Concluding the opinion Judge Bates wrote "The defendant abandoned the trademark."
- Concluding the opinion Judge Bates wrote that the defendant abandoned the trademark.
- Having strong research and writing skills, is essential for legal professionals.
- The exhibits include, pleadings, reports and surveys.
- The report which was prepared by the engineer was lengthy.
- The judge reviewed the document and he found several inconsistencies in it.
- The judge reviewed the document and found several inconsistencies in it.
- The witness however was contradicted by Dr. Ellis the expert.

D. Apostrophes

An apostrophe (') is used to show possession or ownership or to show omission of one or more letters, as in the contraction *don't*. Writers generally have little difficulty with contractions (except for *it's*), but the use of apostrophes to show possession, especially with regard to proper names, is often confusing.

1. Possessives

a. General Rules

There are three basic rules relating to using apostrophes to show ownership or possession.

☐ **Rule One: Add an apostrophe and an *s* ('s) to show possession for all singular nouns, even if the noun ends in *s*, *k*, *x*, or *z*.**

> **Correct Examples:**   *The girl's coat* (the coat of the girl)
> *The plaintiff's evidence* (the evidence of the plaintiff)
> *Charles's friend* (the friend of Charles)
> *Anyone's argument* (the argument of anyone)
> *Xerox's marketing plan* (the marketing plan of Xerox)
> *The witness's testimony* (the testimony of the witness)
> *My boss's birthday* (the birthday of my boss)
> *Texas's election* (the election of Texas)
> *Congress's intent* (the intent of Congress)

☐ **Rule Two: When a plural word ends in *s*, add only an apostrophe (') to show possession.**

> **Correct Examples:**   *The ten shareholders' agenda* (the agenda of the ten shareholders)
> *The workers' job benefits* (the job benefits of the workers)
> *The judges' hearings* (the hearings of the judges)
> *Our bosses' offices* (the offices of our bosses)

☐ **Rule Three: When a word is plural and does not already end in *s*, add an apostrophe and an *s* ('s) to show possession.**

> **Correct Examples:**   *The children's toys* (the toys of the children)
> *The mice's cages* (the cages of the mice)
> *The men's shoes* (the shoes of the men)

b. Proper Names

To form the plural of most family names or to show possession for most family names, follow the rules just given.

> **Correct Examples:**   *Ed Smith's pleadings were filed yesterday.*
> *The Smiths are giving a party next week.*
> *The Smiths' house is large.*

For names that end in a sounded *ch, s, sh, x,* or *z,* however, form the plural by adding *es* and then form the plural possessive by adding an apostrophe after the *es* (*es'*).

Correct Examples: *Tim Jones attended the conference.*
Ellen Lynch attended as well.
The Joneses are wealthy.
The Lynches bought a new car.
The Joneses' house is in Chicago.
The Lynches' new car is a Honda.

 Tip *Lucas' or Lucas's?*

Note that many grammar books permit the use of an apostrophe alone with a singular word ending in *s* when adding another *s* would make the word difficult to pronounce or look odd. Thus, you may see *Mr. Rogers' sweater* or *Lucas' book.* Nevertheless, the *Style Manual,* Strunk and White, and most conventional grammar books suggest the *'s,* as in *Mr. Rogers's sweater* or *Lucas's book.* This form is always correct.

---

c. Special Situations Involving Apostrophes

There are a few exceptions to the general rules given earlier.

■ **Joint Possession.** To show joint possession, add an apostrophe and an *s* (*'s*) to the last word.

Correct Examples: *Lewis and Clark's expedition began in 1804.*
My mother and father's house is large.

■ **Individual Possession.** Use an apostrophe and an *s* (*'s*) with each element to show possession for each.

Correct Example: *The plaintiff's and the defendant's opening statements were quite different from each other.*

■ **Ancient Proper Names.** Form the possessive of ancient proper names that end in *es, is,* and *us* by adding only an apostrophe (*'*).

Correct Examples: *Jesus' teachings*
Moses' laws

Note that it may be less awkward to reword such phrases, as in *the teachings of Jesus* and *the laws of Moses.*

- **Abstract Words.** Form the possessive of a few abstract words that end in an *s* or an *s* sound by adding an apostrophe (').

  Correct Examples: *For goodness' sake*
  For conscience' sake

- **Compound Words.** For compound terms such as *mother-in-law*, form the possessive by adding an apostrophe and an *s* ('s) to the last word.

  Correct Examples: *My sister-in-law's files*
  The attorney-at-law's billing statement

- **Units of Time and Measurement.** The possessive form of expressions of time and measurement is shown with an apostrophe and an *s* ('s).

  Correct Examples: *The tenant was given three weeks' notice to*
  vacate.
  The trial will begin in two hours' time.

- **Silent Letters.** If a non-English word ends with a silent *s* or *x*, form its possessive by using only an apostrophe, as in "This Chablis' taste is dry and fruity."

See Figure 2-2 for Quick Reference: Using Apostrophes to Show Possession.

Figure 2-2 Quick Reference: Using Apostrophes to Show Possession			
Singular	Singular Possessive	Plural	Plural Possessive
The pleading	The pleading's caption is wrong.	The pleadings were filed today.	The pleadings' allegations were consistent.
Henry James	Henry James's novel is long.	The Jameses were both famous.	The Jameses' books are challenging to read.
The woman	The woman's contract was amended.	The women were in court.	The women's documents contained errors.

2. Contractions

An apostrophe is used to show the omission of a letter or letters in a contraction. Other than in letters, contractions are rarely used in legal writing because they are viewed as informal words. In fact, some writing experts advise using contractions to reduce a stuffy tone in correspondence.

Correct Examples:
   don't   do not
   can't   cannot
   shouldn't should not

One common error is the misuse of the contraction *it's*. *It's* is a contraction for *it is* (or *it has*). The apostrophe is used to indicate that the letter *i* (or letters *ha*) has been omitted. To show the possessive of *it*, meaning *belonging to it*, use *its*. Only use *it's* when you mean to write *it is* (or, *it has*).

Correct Examples:
   It's a learned court that has the wisdom to reverse its decisions.
   The corporation held its annual meeting yesterday.
   It's the first day of the trial.

3. Numbers and Letters

There is some disagreement whether an apostrophe should be used to show the plural of a number or letter. The better practice and that of the *Style Manual* is to follow the general rules for forming plurals and to omit the apostrophe unless the result would be confusing.

Correct Examples:
   There are two Exhibit Bs.
   The audit showed all 9s.
   All of the IOUs have been paid.
   The LSATs are difficult.
   Be sure to dot your i's.

 Tips On Using Contractions

- Most spell-checkers cannot accurately catch errors in the use of *it's* and *its*. Thus, careful proofreading is essential.
- Don't confuse contractions (such as *didn't*) with the personal pronouns *yours, hers, his, theirs, ours, whose,* and *its*. Apostrophes are never used with these personal pronouns.

   Incorrect: *The file is her's.*

Challenge Apostrophes

Punctuate the following:

- Judy Davis acting award is a prized possession.
- The appellate courts record disclosed errors.
- The Iowa corporations audit was printed yesterday.
- The Iowa and Ohio corporations audits were printed yesterday.
- Mr. Higgins will has been prepared.
- Ms. Anthonys will has been prepared.
- The agenda included a discussion of womens rights.
- He was given one months salary as severance.
- He was given two months salary as severance.
- The four hostesses coats were missing.
- He will be the Marine Corps next Commandant.
- The attorney generals appointment was confirmed.
- Who's/Whose file is this?
- The companys annual report disclosed its/it's profits.

E. Colons

A colon (:) is usually used to signal that material follows. In sentences, a colon can only be used after an independent clause (one that can stand by itself).

Use a Colon	Examples
to introduce a list, especially after expressions such as *the following* or *as follows*.	*The defendant asserted the following three defenses: waiver; estoppel; and acquiescence.*
	(Note that the items in the list could also be separated by commas.)
to signal that clarifying information will follow.	*We have instituted a new policy: Goods may not be returned after ten days.*
to introduce a formal quotation (when the introduction is an independent clause).	*The court ruled against the defendant in unequivocal terms: "Liability is based upon this act of gross negligence."*
	(Note that most quotations may also be introduced by a comma.)
after salutations in formal letters.	*Dear Mr. Garcia:* *Dear Michael:*
to separate minutes from hours.	*The hearing ended at 5:30 p.m.*

On Using Colons

- Place one space after a colon.
- If the material following a colon is not a complete sentence, it should begin with a lowercase letter.
- If the material following a colon is a complete sentence, it may begin with either a capital letter or a lowercase letter. Many experts prefer to use a capital letter.

> **Correct:**   *The report produced one finding: The defendant was an ex-convict.*

- Do not use a colon after a verb or after a preposition.

> **Incorrect:**   *Entering the courtroom were: the judge, the marshal, and the bailiff.*
> *You will find the answer in: the case, the statute, or the transcript.*

- Do not use a colon after the expressions *for example, namely, including,* or *such as.*

> **Incorrect:**   *The contract dealt with issues such as: term of employment; employment duties; and stock option grants.*

- Place colons outside closing quotation marks.

F. Semicolons

A semicolon (;) is usually used to separate items of equal status, such as two independent clauses.

Use a Semicolon	Examples
to connect two independent but related clauses that are not joined by a coordinating conjunction.	*That was his final summation; it was strong and forceful.*
	(Note that this could be correctly presented as two sentences.)
between two independent clauses joined by a transitional word or phrase such as *however, for example,* or *therefore.*	*The defendant was not credible; therefore, the jury voted to convict her.*

Use a Semicolon	Examples
	The attorney argued persuasively; however, the judge overruled her.
to separate items in a list containing commas.	*Standing trial for embezzlement were Connie Rivers of Portland, Oregon; Samuel Walter of Seattle, Washington; and Susan Stone of Boise, Idaho.*
to separate items in a list introduced by a colon.	*The elements to be proved in an action for breach of contract are as follows: the existence of a contract; the unjustified breach of that contract by one party; and damages caused by that breach.*
	(Note that these items can also be separated by commas.)

G. Quotation Marks

Quotation marks usually indicate the exact words of a speaker and appear in double form (" ") or single form (' '). Additional information relating to quotations of legal authorities is provided in Appendix A.

Use Double Quotation Marks	Correct Examples
to indicate the exact words of a speaker.	*Patrick Henry said, "Give me liberty or give me death."*
	"The motion," said the judge, "is hereby granted."
to explain or emphasize a word.	*The author misspelled the word "appellant" in the brief.*
	The words "its" and "it's" are often confused.

Use Single Quotation Marks	Correct Example
to enclose a quotation within a quotation (and use a thin space to separate single and double quotation marks).	*"It was the jury foreman," said Betty, "who announced, 'The defendant is guilty.' "*

Quotation marks are not used for indirect quotations. An indirect quotation summarizes a person's words but does not quote the person directly.

Incorrect	**Correct Examples**
Upon entering the courtroom, the judge said that "she expected silence from the spectators."	*Upon entering the courtroom, the judge said that she expected silence from the spectators.*
	Upon entering the courtroom, the judge said, "I expect silence from the spectators."

Capitalize the first word of a direct quotation if it is a complete sentence but not if it is a sentence fragment.

Challenge Punctuation

Correctly punctuate the following:

- Are you familiar with the legal phrase "res ipsa loquitor?"
- The defendant said I plead not guilty.
- The plaintiff shouted That's the man who robbed me
- I was the court clerk said Sue and everyone knew it.
- She asked him if he would prepare the report
- The defendant stated I did provide an eviction notice however it was never received.
- We prepared the following exhibits the lease the amendment to the lease and the eviction notice.
- The will was witnessed by two witnesses: Therefore, it is valid.
- Lee prepared the complaint it included three counts.
- You will need supplies, such as: folders, labels and pens.
- Jake announced the verdict; the defendant is guilty.
- Kyle excels in: research, writing and interviewing.

H. Parentheses

Parentheses ( ) are generally used to enclose interruptions or explanations. The use of parentheses in legal citations is discussed in Appendix A.

Other Punctuation with Quotation Marks and the Use of Ellipses

- Periods and commas are always placed inside quotation marks.
- Semicolons and colons are always placed outside quotation marks.
- Question marks and exclamation points are placed inside quotation marks only if they are part of the quoted material.

  Correct Example: *"She's guilty!" yelled the foreman of the jury.*

- When a quotation is introduced by a signal phrase, such as *she said* or *he wrote*, follow the signal phrase with a comma and begin the quotation with a capital letter.

  Correct Example: *The bailiff said, "All rise."*

- If a quotation is interrupted by explanatory words, do not use a capital letter to start the second part of the quotation unless it begins a new sentence.

  Correct Examples: *"When the opening statements are complete,"*
  said the judge, "we will begin the trial."

  "Overruled," said the judge. "Proceed with
  your evidence."

- Use a thin space to separate single and double quotation marks. (See example in Section G.)
- When a quotation carries over from one paragraph to another, use double quotation marks at the beginning of each paragraph, but place the final double quotation marks at the end of the last paragraph only.
- Quotations of forty-nine or fewer words should be enclosed in quotation marks but not indented.
- Quotations of fifty or more words should be indented left and right, justified, and single-spaced. No outside quotation marks are used for these quotations, often called *block quotes*. The indentation of these longer quotes itself indicates a quotation. The citation for these block quotes appears at the left margin on the line following the block quotation.
- Indicate omissions in a quotation by an ellipsis (three periods separated by spaces and set off by a space before the first and after the last period).

  Correct Example: *"Punitive damages must be based upon . . .*
  actual damages."

- If the omitted matter includes the end of a sentence, add another period to the ellipsis (. . .).
- Do not use an ellipsis to begin a quotation; instead, use brackets, as in *"[E]very contract includes a covenant of good faith and fair dealing."*
- Use brackets [ ] to show changes in quotations, usually the addition of a word or letters.

  Correct Example: *"Punitive damages are based upon [actual]*
  damage[s]."

Use Parentheses	Correct Examples
to set off interruptions, explanations, or translations.	*His primary argument was res ipsa loquitur (a Latin phrase meaning "the thing speaks for itself").*
to direct the reader to other information.	*The plaintiff failed to allege materiality in the fraud cause of action. (Compl. ¶ 14.)*
to introduce defined terms or labels.	*The plaintiff, Southwest Avionics Industries ("SAI"), alleged fraud.*
to enclose numbers or dollar amounts.	*The settlement agreement was forty (40) pages.*

Other Punctuation with Parentheses

- Do not put a comma before a parenthetical item.
- If a parenthetical item falls within a sentence, do not capitalize the first word in the parenthetical item even if it is a complete sentence (unless the item begins with *I* or a proper noun).

  Correct: *The new partner (he arrived yesterday) will begin work on Monday.*

  Please return the signed contract by October 10, 2008 (Friday).

- If the parenthetical item does not fall within a sentence and is a separate sentence, it should begin with a capital letter and end with a period (or the appropriate punctuation), which should be placed within the parentheses.

  Correct: *Please return the signed contract by October 10, 2008. (This date is a Friday.)*

- Avoid having one set of parentheses follow another. Thus, the following use of parentheses should be avoided: *Your contract should be signed by Monday (September 2, 2008). (This date is Labor Day.)*

I. Other Punctuation Marks: Dashes, Hyphens, and Slashes

1. Using Dashes

Dashes create drama and draw a reader's attention. In general, however, they are considered too informal for legal writing, and, in most instances, other punctuation marks, such as commas, parentheses, or a colon, would be more appropriate.

There are two types of dashes. An em dash is as wide as a typesetter's *m* key and is used in most instances because it produces a more defined break. An em dash usually shows interruptions and is made by using two hyphens. It is the most commonly used dash, and there are no spaces before or after it. It may replace commas or parentheses to show interruptions, although it is less formal. An en dash is as wide as a typesetter's *n* key and is used primarily to show a span of time, as in *She was the substitute during the week of June 21–28* or *You must read pages 82–91 of the text.* An en dash is made by using one hyphen.

Use a Dash	Correct Examples
to indicate a break or interruption.	*The defendant—not his brother—testified.*
to reference certain legislation.	*The Sarbanes–Oxley Act was passed in 2002.*

2. Using Hyphens

Hyphens are used in compound words and to show divisions between words at the end of lines. Most word processors automatically divide words appropriately at the end of lines (or move the entire word to the next line). Nevertheless, if you need to divide a word at the end of a line of text, use a dictionary to determine where to make the break and make sure you do not divide a proper noun. Additional examples regarding using a hyphen in compound words are found in Chapter 3.

Use a Hyphen	Correct Examples
when two or more words act together to modify a noun.	*She is a well-known judge.*
	The would-be informant testified.
	Her employment-related injury was severe.
with the prefixes *all-, co-, ex-,* and *self-.*	*He is self-involved.*
	Her ex-husband attended the hearing.
with a prefix before a proper noun.	*The House Un-American Committee*
	The pro-Israeli faction
to prevent confusion.	*The status of the chicken coop will be reexamined by the co-op board on Tuesday.*
in certain awkward words.	*My mother-in-law was the runner-up.*

Use a Hyphen	Correct Examples
to divide compound numbers from twenty-one to ninety-nine.	*The defense called thirty-two witnesses.*
in fractions that are spelled out.	*Two-thirds approval is needed.*

3. Using Slashes

A slash is a diagonal line (often called a *virgule* or *solidus*) that usually shows options. Its meaning is *or* (not *and*). Thus, the sentence *The litigation class is pass/fail* means that one can pass the course or one can fail it. Similarly, the sentence *Billy Joel is the singer/composer of the song* means that Billy Joel is either the singer or the composer of the song, but not both. Although it may be wordier, it may be necessary to explain the meaning of such a sentence, by saying *Billy Joel is the singer and the composer of the song.* In general, the slash mark is considered ambiguous and should be avoided in legal writing. In particular, the constructions *and/or*, *he/she*, and *his/her* should be avoided. Slashes are acceptable to indicate dates in informal writing, as in *The hearing will be held on 8/12/08.* Slashes are also used in a particular business-related abbreviation, *d/b/a* (*doing business as*), as in the following correct example: *The defendant identified in the caption was Patricia Allen d/b/a Creative Catering of Philadelphia.*

Challenge   Parentheses, Hyphens, and Other Marks

Correct the following:

- All copartners must agree on the admission of a new partner.
- The defendant, Thomas Simmons (Simmons) denied the allegations of fraud. See Answer ¶ 5.
- She observed that anti American sentiment was on the rise.
- William H. Rehnquist served as Chief Justice from 1986–2005.
- He is a well respected judge who produces opinions that are well reasoned.

chapter 3

Spelling

 StyleLinks

www.gpoaccess.gov/stylemanual/index.html
Select Chapter 5 of the Government Printing Office *Style Manual* for thorough information about spelling.

http://.owl.english.purdue.edu/owl
Select "Spelling" for excellent information from Purdue University's Online Writing Lab.

www.sentex.net~mmcadams/spelling.html
This site offers a spelling test for frequently misspelled words.

www.spelling.hemscott.net
This site provides spelling worksheets and advice from an experienced English teacher.

www.dictionary.com
Check your spelling at this useful site, which also offers a thesaurus and spelling FAQs.

www.grammarbook.com
The *Blue Book of Grammar and Punctuation* offers tips and hints for spelling correctly. Select "Spelling."

http://dictionary.law.com
Law.Com offers a dictionary of legal words and phrases.

A. Introduction

Because English is not a phonetic language, many people have difficulty spelling. One of the most distressing results of misspelling is the effect produced in the mind of a reader. If the aim of writing is to inform or persuade a reader and the reader is confronted with spelling errors, any value a product may have could well be overshadowed by the misspellings. Readers of legal documents, such as clients, attorneys, and judges, tend to be highly critical and perfectionistic. When confronted with spelling errors, they may react by assuming that if you cannot be trusted to spell properly, you cannot be trusted to have conducted legal analysis properly. Thus, spelling errors cast doubt on more than your ability to spell by causing readers to question the correctness of your legal conclusions. At best, spelling errors make readers believe the writer is careless. At worst, they make readers question the writer's intelligence.

B. Strategies to Improve Spelling

Following are some tips and strategies to improve spelling.

1. Use a Dictionary

The only way to ensure that a word is spelled correctly is to use a dictionary. A legal dictionary, such as *Black's Legal Dictionary*, will include words used in legal settings, such as *rescission*, as well as Latin terms and phrases commonly used in the profession. Don't be afraid to write in your dictionary. Circle or highlight troublesome words. When you look up a word such as *canceled* in the dictionary, you may notice that you are first given the spelling *canceled* and then the alternate spelling *cancelled*. Usually, the entry given first is the preferred spelling, and you should use this form of the word. Similarly, use the commonly accepted spelling of a word rather than some foreign or exotic spelling. For example, use *behavior* rather than *behaviour*, which is the British spelling of the word. The website www.dictionary.com is an excellent source. Note that some dictionaries are descriptive (meaning that they merely explain how a word is presently used), and others are prescriptive (meaning that they tell you how a word should be used and provide advice and notes on usage).

2. Develop a "Hit List" of Commonly Misspelled Words

Many writers find that they routinely misspell the same words. Write the ten or fifteen words you most commonly misspell on an index card and keep it near your computer or writing area. Write the correct spelling only. Refer to the list frequently and note the words that you misspell most often so you can spend additional time on these. The effort that you take in considering these words and writing them out will help you learn their correct spellings. Once you learn the words on your list, develop another list with a new group of troublesome words.

3. Pronounce Your Words Carefully

If you make a concerted effort to pronounce *than* differently from *then* and *effect* differently from *affect*, your spelling will improve. It will be difficult for you to remember to spell *environment* correctly if you pronounce the word as *enviro-ment*.

4. Use Misspelled Words as Passwords

Use one of your frequently misspelled words as a password to access your email or ATM account. When you have mastered this word, change your password to another troublesome word.

5. Use Mnemonic Devices

Remember that the *princi*pal *of your school is your* pal to help you remember to spell the word *principal* (and not *principle*). Remember that the dessert treat after dinner has two *s*'s, just like a strawberry shortcake, whereas an arid, sandy desert has one *s*, just like the Sahara Desert. Remember to match up the *o* in the word *dome* with *capit*o*l* and that all other uses of the word are spelled *capital*.

6. Don't Rely Only on Your Spell-Checker

Use a spell-checker to help you catch some spelling errors but recognize its limitations, namely, that it will not signal incorrect usage. Thus, for example, if you write *principle* when you mean to write *principal*, the spell-checker will not flag the incorrect word as long as it is spelled correctly. The spell-checker is an aid to good writing, not a replacement for careful proofreading and editing. Use the "find and replace" feature to correct common errors automatically. For example, if you routinely type *Untied States* rather than *United States*, the find and replace feature will locate each occurrence of the error and replace it with the correct spelling.

7. Proofread Carefully

Be thorough in your review of your finished project and read through the last draft for spelling errors. In many instances, a misspelled word will not look "right" to you, and you can readily locate your errors. If you find it difficult to catch your own errors, ask a colleague or friend to proofread your project for spelling errors. Proofreading and editing are discussed further in Chapter 11.

8. Learn Some Spelling Rules

Many spelling rules are easy to remember. Following are some helpful rules, although there are exceptions to nearly every rule.

☐ **Rule One. Place *i* before *e*, except after *c*, and except when it sounds like ay, as in *neighbor* or *weigh*. This rule should help you remember the correct spelling of *receive* or *eight*. There are, however, many exceptions to this rule; for example, *weird*, *seize*, *leisure*, and *neither* do not conform to the rule.**

☐ **Rule Two.** When the endings *-ness* and *-ly* are added to a word, the spelling of the word remains the same. Thus, the words *gladness* and *finally* are spelled correctly. Note, however, the following exception: For words ending in *y*, such as *heavy*, change the *y* to *i* before a suffix, as in the word *heaviness*.

☐ **Rule Three.** Drop the final silent *e* before an ending or suffix that begins with a vowel.

Correct Examples

revise + ing = revising
argue + able = arguable
compose + ition = composition

☐ **Rule Four.** Keep the final silent *e* before an ending or suffix that begins with a consonant.

Correct Examples

state + ment = statement
care + less = careless
hope + ful = hopeful
sincere + ly = sincerely

☐ **Rule Five.** When adding a prefix to a word, the word remains the same.

Correct Examples

un + anticipated = unanticipated
mis + spell = misspell
non + disclosure = nondisclosure

☐ **Rule Six.** To determine if an ending of a word is spelled *-able* or *-ible*, follow these tips:

   ■ If the base of a word is itself a word, the ending *-able* is more commonly used, as in the following correct examples: *preferable, removable,* and *predictable*. Many more words end in *-able* than *-ible*.
   ■ If the base of a word is not a word, the ending *-ible* is more commonly used, as in the following correct examples: *admissible, permissible,* and *feasible*.
   ■ Words that end in *-ible* often have negative forms, such as *illegible* or *inedible*. Also, *-ible* is not used after vowels.

☐ **Rule Seven.** Words ending in *-ant, -ent, -ance,* and *-ence* follow no predictable pattern. Thus, you will likely need a dictionary to ensure the correct spelling of the following words although many of them sound nearly identical: *defendant, dependent, persistent,* and *resistant*.

☐ **Rule Eight.** Words ending with the sound of *seed* follow three rules:

   ■ Almost all words ending with the sound of *seed* end in *-cede*, as in *recede, intercede,* and *precede*.

■ Only one word ends in -*sede*: *supersede*.

■ Only three words end in -*ceed*: *succeed, exceed,* and *proceed*.

☐ **Rule Nine. Omit hyphens with most prefixes and suffixes. Although there are some exceptions, generally omit hyphens with prefixes, as in the correctly spelled words *reexamine* and *unannotated*, and with most suffixes, as in the correctly spelled words *childish* and *troublesome*. Hyphens are discussed further in the next section.**

Special Spelling Problems: Doubling Final Consonants and Forming Plurals

Doubling Final Consonants

Generally, the only words that double their consonants before a suffix beginning with a vowel (such as -*ed* or -*ing*) is added are those that satisfy the following criteria:

- They have only one syllable or are stressed on the last syllable;
- They have only one vowel in the only or last syllable; and
- They end in a single consonant.

    Examples: bag——→bagged——→bagging——→baggage
                              rob ——→robbed ——→robbing ——→robber
                              forgot→forgotten
                              begin →beginner →beginning

Forming Plurals

- Plurals are usually formed by adding an *s* to a noun, as in *plaintiffs, complaints,* and *judges*.
- If a singular word ends in a sibilant (*ch, s, ss, sh, x,* or *z*), form the plural by adding *es*, as in *taxes, bosses,* and *lunches*.
- Most words that end in a consonant followed by a *y* form the plural by changing the *y* to *i* and adding *es*, as in *baby/babies* and *proxy/proxies*.
- Most nouns that end in *f* or *fe* form plurals by changing the *f* to *v* and adding *s* or *es*, as in *life/lives* (but there are exceptions, as in *belief/beliefs*).
- Form the plural of a compound term by adding *s* to the most significant term, as in *attorneys general, mothers-in-law,* and *senators-elect*.
- When a singular noun ends in *o* preceded by a consonant, use a dictionary to verify the plural form because sometimes the plural is formed by adding an *s* and sometimes it is formed by adding *es*.

    Examples: tomato → tomatoes   hero ——→heroes
                            ego ——→ egos   memo →memos

C. Compound Words

A compound word is a word comprising two ideas or words, such as *able-bodied* or *courtroom*. Some compound words, such as *cyberspace*, are so new that they may not be found in dictionaries. Thus, spelling compound words correctly presents certain challenges.

There are generally three ways to spell compound words: as two separate words, as in *the attorney is well known*; as hyphenated words, as in *all-inclusive*; and as one word, as in *jetlag*. Generally, words tend to evolve from two words, to the hyphenated form, to one word. For example, the word *online* progressed from *on line*, to *on-line*, to the commonly accepted spelling *online*. Use the one-word form whenever possible. To be sure of the spelling and presentation of a compound word, use a dictionary. If the word is not listed, present it as two separate words.

There are few fixed rules regarding the spelling of compound words, but following are some general guidelines.

☐ **Rule One. Use a hyphen between a prefix and a proper noun or a word beginning with a capital letter.**

Correct Examples

anti-American
mid-December

☐ **Rule Two. Use a hyphen after the following prefixes: *all-, ex-, half-, quarter-, quasi-,* and *self-*.**

Correct Examples

all-inclusive
ex-president
quasi-contract
self-centered

☐ **Rule Three. Use a hyphen with the suffix *-elect*, as in *senator-elect Anderson*.**

☐ **Rule Four. Generally, omit a hyphen when a prefix ends in *e* or *o* and the base word begins with the same letter.**

Correct Examples

reexamine
coordinate
reevaluate
preexisting

There are several exceptions to this rule, most of which require the use of a hyphen to prevent words from being confused with each other.

Correct Examples

She can recover damages after she re-covers the sofa.

He bought a chicken coop, which he intends to keep in his New York City co-op.

Hal and Sue are co-owners of the building.

The witness has re-signed the will.

☐ **Rule Five. Hyphenate compounds for numbers from twenty-one to ninety-nine as in *forty-eight allegations* and *one hundred and twenty-first claim*.**

☐ **Rule Six. Hyphenate spelled-out fractions, as in *one-half* and *three-fourths*.**

☐ **Rule Seven. When a compound word acts as single modifier or adjective before a noun, hyphenate the words so that it is clear they are acting as a unit.**

Correct Examples

She is a well-respected judge.

We will prepare a follow-up brief.

The corporation's short-term profits are at risk.

☐ **Rule Eight. When a compound word follows a noun, omit the hyphen (because it no longer functions as an adjective). Similarly, words need not be hyphenated if they are not acting as a single modifier or adjective before a noun.**

Correct Examples

The judge is well respected.

We will follow up with a brief.

In the short term, the corporation's profits are at risk.

Challenge Spelling

Select the correct word:

- He has asked for the advice/advise of his attorney.
- Pam will present the argument/arguement to the judge.
- The court calender/calendar is crowded.
- Only relevant/relevent evidence may be admitted.
- She has claimed the attorney-client privelege/privilege.
- He has continued to harrass/harass the employee.
- The evidence is admissible/admissable.
- The maintenance/maintainance of the building is his duty.
- Her counsel/council is representing her in court.

D. Capitalization

She lived in capital letters.

Al Carmine (1985)
Eulogy for Marion Tanner, the model for Auntie Mame

StyleLinks

www.gpoaccess.gov/stylemanual/index.html
Select Chapters 3 and 4 of the Government Printing Office *Style Manual* for information about capitalization.

http://grammar.ccc.commnet.edu/grammar
Select "Capitalization" from the *Guide to Grammar & Writing* offered by Capital Community College.

1. General Capitalization Rules

Follow these rules when capitalizing:

Rule: Always Capitalize	Correct Examples
the pronoun *I*.	*I recognized the defendant.*
the first word in a sentence.	*File the brief this afternoon.*
the first word of a direct quotation if it is a complete sentence but not if it is a sentence fragment.	*The judge stated, "The evidence in this case is clearly contradictory." The judge stated that the evidence was "clearly contradictory."*
the first word following a colon if what follows the colon is a complete sentence.	*The brief contained the following error: It misidentified the reference to the court record.*
names of languages and specific courses but not general fields of study.	*I studied Spanish, sociology, and French. Next year I will take Algebra II and history.*
defined terms.	*Sandra Carias ("Tenant") will rent the premises at 123 Elm Street (the "Premises"). Tenant may take occupancy of the Premises on December 1, 2009.*
headings and titles (capitalize the initial word, the word following a colon, and all other words except articles and conjunctions).	*Battery: An Intentional Touching* *Insider Trading in Corporate Transactions*
proper nouns.	
■ names of people	*Allison M. Taylor*
■ geographical names and structures	*Lake Superior, Central Park, the Washington Monument*
■ regions (if designating a specific section of the country)	*I love the East and the Appalachian Trail.* *Head west until you see the courthouse in northern Virginia.*
■ days of the week, months, holidays, and historical events (but not seasons)	*Memorial Day is my favorite holiday because it signals the beginning of summer.* *The Great Depression was the most significant economic event of the twentieth century.*
■ government departments and agencies	*Department of Labor House of Representatives Congress* (but *congressional inquiry*)
■ specific organizations	*The American Medical Association lobbied against the bill.*

Rule: Always Capitalize

Correct Examples

■ titles (when used with the person's name and for important public figures)

He saw Representative Wilson on television.
The clerk is a staunch supporter of Vice President Cheney and the President.
The declaration was submitted by Professor Barnes.
Judge Andrews was the first federal judge appointed by Congress last fall.
The Secretary will state the policy of the EPA.

■ the word "president" when referring to the President of the United States

The President will address the nation today about his presidential veto.

■ names of schools and businesses

Walt Whitman High School
General Mills Co. files periodic reports with the Securities and Exchange Commission.

■ family titles that stand alone or are used with a name.

I asked Uncle Jim if Mother would like to attend her cousin's wedding.

Capital Ideas

Correct

Senator Kennedy
The South of France
Nike Corp.
Chief Financial Officer Smith
I asked Dad.
London Bridge
Ash Street
New York City
Democratic Party
Judge Lopez
The Department of Commerce
Battle of Bull Run
Fourth of July
Coach Saunders
Doctor Alvarez
Congress
Christianity
Governor McNenly
Georgetown University
The Federal Bureau of Investigation
Director Mueller

Correct

The senator testified today in Congress.
a southern flair
the company *or* the corporation
Smith, the chief financial officer
I asked my dad.
the famous bridge
the street near my home
the city of San Diego
a political party
Jan Lopez, a federal judge
a federal agency
a famous battle
fifth of July
the team coach
the admitting doctor
a congressional committee
a religion
Ted McNenly, the governor
an eastern school
The Bureau reported its results.
The Director of the FBI

For Using Capital Letters

- Avoid using all capital letters in a communication (unless they are used in headings). Text in all capital letters is difficult to read.
- Using all capital letters in email is viewed as shouting.
- Reproduce personal and company names exactly as the person or company does, including any punctuation.
- Capitalize *federal* only when it is the name of an agency as in *the Federal Reserve Board*. Do not capitalize *federal* when it is used as an adjective, as in *Fay Carson is a federal judge* or *Bob works for the federal government.*
- Although there is some disagreement about how to present words associated with the Internet, most dictionaries capitalize *Internet* and *World Wide Web* but not *website*. The word *email* is usually not capitalized and is often presented with a hyphen (e-mail).

2. Capitalization in Legal Documents

Following are some of the more common *Bluebook* and *ALWD* rules for capitalization in legal documents, such as court briefs and legal memoranda. See Appendix A for additional information on citation form.

Rules for Practitioners — Capitalize	Examples
Act (when referring to a specific act).	*The Sarbanes–Oxley Act was passed in 2002.*
Circuit (when using the word with a name or a number).	*The Ninth Circuit held otherwise* and this court agrees.
Code (only when referring to a specific code).	the 1954 Code, the Code of Federal Regulations *The code was enacted in 1954.*
Constitution.	
■ when referring to the U.S. Constitution	*the U.S. Constitution*
■ when referring to parts of the Constitution in text	*the Supremacy Clause, the First Amendment*
Court.	
■ when naming any court in full	*the Court of Appeals for the Sixth Circuit*
■ when referring to the United States Supreme Court or a state supreme court	*the Court's opinion in* Brown v. Board of Education

Rules for Practitioners — Capitalize	**Examples**
◼ when referring to the court in a document submitted to that court	*This Court is respectfully urged to grant the Motion.*

Federal.

◼ when the word it modifies is capitalized	*the Federal Drug Administration the federal budget*

Judge or Justice.

◼ when referring to a specific individual	*Judge Brown was the first federal judge appointed this year.*
◼ when referring to any Justice of the United States Supreme Court	*The dissent of the Justices was lengthy.*

Party designations (Plaintiff, Defendant, and so forth) when referring to the parties in the matter that is the subject of the document.	*Although the Defendant has moved to change venue in this case . . . In that 1989 case, the plaintiff alleged negligence.*

State or Commonwealth.

◼ when it is part of the full title of a state	*the State of Hawaii the Commonwealth of Virginia*
◼ when used as an adjective	*the State Inspector General*
◼ when the state is a party to litigation	*The State has requested the death penalty in this case.*

titles of court documents (for documents filed in that action but not when used in a generic manner).	*In his Second Amended Complaint, the Plaintiff alleged fraud. This is inconsistent with Plaintiff's responses to the interrogatories prepared by him earlier this month.*

E. Abbreviations

1. General Principles

An abbreviation is a shortened form of a word (such as *Corp.* for *Corporation*) or a symbol used in place of a word (such as using & for *and*). The following discussion relates to using abbreviations in textual matter, such as correspondence and legal memoranda. Using abbreviations in legal citations (for example, 123 A.L.R.3d 439) is discussed in Appendix A.

Generally, because legal writing is more formal than other types of writing, abbreviations are not commonly used, except when the abbreviation is extremely well known, such as using *a.m.* when indicating time or using *Dr.* for *Doctor*. To determine the correct abbreviation for a word, consult a dictionary or consult some of the online sources identified earlier. In particular, the U.S. Government Printing Office *Style Manual* is a well-respected authority; in fact, *ALWD* Rule 3.4 provides that for abbreviations for words not identified in *ALWD*, readers should use the *Style Manual*. *Bluebook* Rule 8 is the same.

Never start a sentence with a number, an abbreviation, or a symbol. Sentences start with complete words. The only exception to this rule is for years, as in *2008 was a record year for corporate profits*. This construction can look odd, so consider revising, as in *Corporate profits hit a record high in 2008*.

- **Periods in Abbreviations.** Most, but not all, abbreviations end with periods. Abbreviations composed of all capital letters and acronyms, such as *NAACP* or *AIDS*, do not generally include periods. *Bluebook* Rule 6.1 states that when an entity is commonly referred to in spoken language by its initials rather than by its full name (for example, *CIA* and *SEC*), such abbreviations may be used without periods in text and in case names. *ALWD* Rule 12.2 is similar.
- **Titles.** Use abbreviations for titles before and after proper names. If an abbreviation is used with a person's name, the name stands alone and is not accompanied by another abbreviation, such as *Ms.* or *Mr.*

Before Proper Name	**After Proper Name**
Dr. Eve Blake	Eve Blake, M.D. (not Ms. Eve Blake, M.D.)
Mr. Luis Santiago	Luis Santiago, Esq. (not Mr. Luis Santiago,
Sen. Edward Kennedy	Esq.)

- **Acronyms.** Use abbreviations (all capital letters and no periods) for most acronyms (an abbreviation that spells out a pronounceable word, such as *MADD* or *RICO*). In legal writing, it is customary to spell out a word or organization name in full the first time it is given, immediately indicate its abbreviation in parentheses, usually in quotation marks, and then use the abbreviation consistently thereafter.

  Correct Example: The National Organization for Women
  ("NOW") has chapters in all
  fifty states. The headquarters of
  NOW is in Washington, D.C.

- **United States.** Abbreviate *United States* as U.S. only when it is used as an adjective.

  Correct Example: The current U.S. policy provides an
  interesting overview of the trade
  position of the United States.

- **Days, Months, and Addresses.** Do not abbreviate parts of addresses or names of months and days when they are written in sentences. Such abbreviations are acceptable in tables and charts but disrupt the flow of a narrative presentation.

  Correct Example: The witness resided at 290 Forest Grove
  Drive, Dallas, Texas 90124 until
  Tuesday.

  Incorrect Example: The witness resided at 290 Forest Grove
  Dr., Dallas, TX 90124 until Tues.

- Note that *Bluebook* Table T.12 and *ALWD* Appendix 3 provide abbreviations for months of the year when they are used in citations.
- **Company Names.** Follow a company's or organization's preference for presentation of its name. Review the company's letterhead, its website, or official filings, and reproduce the name as shown. Thus, a review of the website maintained by Microsoft Corporation shows that it refers to itself as *Microsoft Corporation*. It would thus be inappropriate to refer to the company as *Microsoft Corp.* Use the punctuation the company uses, as in *Land O'Lakes, Inc.*
- **A.M. and P.M.** Use *a.m.* and *p.m.* only with specific numerals.

Correct Example: *The trial is scheduled for 9:30 a.m.*

Incorrect Example: *The trial is scheduled for 9:30 in the a.m.*

■ **Numerals.** Although most authorities, including the *Style Manual*, provide that words should be used for the numerals one through nine, and that figures are used for numerals 10 and greater, *The Bluebook* Rule 6.2(a) is quite different and requires legal writers to spell out the numerals zero to ninety-nine in text and in footnotes. *ALWD* Rule 4.2 is similar. *Bluebook* also provides that commas are used in numerals only when the numeral has five or more digits. This *Bluebook* rule is contrary to most style manuals and is ignored by most practitioners.

Style Manual Example: *The transcript was 4,230 pages.*

Bluebook Example: *The transcript was 4230 pages.*

ALWD Example: *The transcript was 4,230 pages.*

■ **Money.** According to *Bluebook* Rule 6.2(d), the dollar symbol ($) should be used whenever numerals or figures are used, and the words should be spelled out whenever numerals are spelled out. There is no space after the dollar symbol.

Bluebook Examples: *The filing fee is Twenty-Five Dollars.*
The filing fee is $350.

Note, however, that to ensure there are no errors in monetary amounts, most practitioners prefer to spell out any amount in words, and then show the figures in parentheses, as follows: *The judgment was entered for Forty Thousand and Twenty-One Dollars ($40,021)*. Because small numbers are easier to work with than large ones, spell out the words *million, billion,* and so forth, rather than using zeroes as in *The jury awarded $14 million to the plaintiff* (not *$14,000,000*).

■ **Percentages.** According to *Bluebook* Rule 6.2(d), the percent symbol (%) should be used whenever numerals or figures are used, and the word *percent* should be spelled out whenever numerals are spelled out. There is no space before the percent symbol.

Bluebook Examples: *The interest rate was twelve percent.*
Profits increased 126% this year.

■ **Ampersand.** The word *ampersand* is a corruption of the phrase *and per se and* and it is the name for the symbol (&) used in place of the word *and*. Do not use an ampersand symbol in writing. Use the symbol only when a company does in its presentation of its name and only in the names of cases in case citations according to citation rules (discussed in Appendix A).

- **Symbol for *At*.** The symbol @ should be used only in email addresses, not in the normal flow of text.

Challenge ?	Capitalization and Abbreviations

Correct the following:

To get to the ofcs. of Mr. Ian Nelson, Esq., go thru S. Martin St. and then head NE on Mass. Avenue. 100 yards North of this is the federal Communications Commission, which is a division of the Federal Government. Last Spring, the F.C.C. held 10 hearings relating to Congressional budget shortfalls & issued full decisions in 9 of those matters. Most of these hrgs. relate to US policy as formulated by the president.

2. Legal Abbreviations

Although abbreviations in citations are more fully discussed in Appendix A, following are some of the more common *Bluebook* and *ALWD* rules.

- *Bluebook:* Spell out the numerals zero to ninety-nine in text and in footnotes (as in *The complaint named eighty defendants, sixteen of which were corporations*). *ALWD*: ALWD notes that in the legal field, the convention is to spell out zero to ninety-nine and use numerals for higher numbers.
- *Bluebook:* Use commas in numerals only when the numeral has five or more digits (as in *4012* and *50,145*). *ALWD:* Insert a comma between the third and fourth digits (as in *4,012*).
- *Bluebook:* Spell out the words *section* and *paragraph* in text except when referring to a provision in the U.S. Code or a federal regulation. *ALWD:* Either use the symbols or spell out the words. The section symbol (§) and paragraph symbol (¶) are always followed by a space under both *Bluebook* and *ALWD* rules.

Bluebook **Example:**   *The provisions of 18 U.S.C. § 101 (2000) control, but section 52 of California's Penal Code provides additional guidelines.*

Tips ➡ On Using Numbers

- Spell out a number that begins a sentence.
- Spell out numbers up to 100, as in *sixty-four exhibits* (*Bluebook* and *ALWD* rule).
- A numeral's plural is formed by adding an *s*, as in *1990s*.
- Use numerals if you are referring to a section of a document, as in *The employer's duties are described in Paragraph 5.*
- Spell out indefinite expressions, as in *He is in his twenties.*
- Use numerals for statute references, as in *Title 17 of the United States Code* and *Chapter 11 bankruptcy petitions.*
- If one item in a series should be expressed as a numeral, use numerals for all of the items, as in *The documents were 18, 89, and 104 pages, respectively.*

Tips ➡ For Using Abbreviations

- When in doubt, spell it out.
- Never start a sentence with an abbreviation, a numeral, or a symbol. Thus, write *One hundred days after the incident, you must file your claim.*
- If a sentence ends with an abbreviation that includes a period, do not add another one.

    Incorrect: *The meeting will begin at 9:30 a.m..*

- Be consistent in the use of abbreviations. Once you have selected an abbreviation form, use it consistently throughout your project.
- Follow a company's preference for abbreviations in its name.
- Follow an individual's preference for the treatment of abbreviations such as *Jr.* and *Sr.*

Features of Effective Legal Writing and Organization

■ All well-written legal documents share the following features: They are accurate, clear, readable, concise, and well organized. Section Two provides a variety of strategies to ensure your writing meets these goals so that you communicate effectively to your reader, whether that reader is a client, colleague, adversary, or judge.

There are two things wrong with
almost all legal writing. One is its
style. The other is its content.
Fred Rodell,
Goodbye to Law Reviews,
23 Va. L. Rev. 38, 38 (1936)

chapter 4

Features of Effective Legal Writing

StyleLinks

www.plainlanguage.gov
This website, offered by a group of government volunteers, provides excellent information on plain writing as well as its major guidance document *Writing User-Friendly Documents.*

www.sec.gov/pdf/handbook/pdf
The Securities and Exchange Commission (SEC) offers its excellent publication *Plain English Handbook* with numerous examples and tips for producing understandable documents.

http://law.case.edu/faculty/friedman/raw/Writing%20Links, %208-17-00.html
RawData offers numerous links to websites that offer useful and practical information on legal writing.

A. Introduction

The cornerstone of the legal profession is communication—communication with a client, colleague, adverse party, or judge. In most cases the communication will be in written form. Even in those instances in which you communicate orally, you will often follow up with a written letter or memo to a file. Thus, effective legal writing is critical to success in the legal profession.

B. The Plain English Movement

One of the recurring criticisms of legal writing is that it is incomprehensible to the average reader because of its use of jargon, redundancies, and archaic words and phrases. The use of words and phrases such as *aforesaid* and *notwithstanding anything in the foregoing to the contrary* confuses and angers readers.

The increased activism of consumers frustrated with the inability to understand their insurance policies, mortgage documents, or car loan agreements led to the requirement in many states that certain documents be written in "plain English." In 1998 President Clinton signed a presidential memo requiring all federal agencies to use plain language for most of their written communications. The plain language initiative rests on three principles:

- Writing should be reader-oriented;
- Writing should use natural expressions, using commonly known and used words; and
- Documents should be visually appealing.

In fall 2007, Rep. Bruce Braley (D. Iowa) introduced legislation (H.R. 110-3548) that would require all government agencies to use "plain language," defined as "language that the intended audience can readily understand and use because it is clear, concise, well-organized, and follows other best practices of plain language writing." Government agencies would be authorized to follow the SEC's *Plain English Handbook* or the Federal Plain Language Guidelines. At the time of the writing of this text, the legislation had passed the House and had been referred to the Senate.

A number of agencies and governmental entities have adopted plain language techniques. For example, California revised its jury instructions in plain English so they would adequately communicate the law to jurors, and the Department of Veterans Affairs redrafted a standard form to make it clearer, resulting in a decrease in telephone calls about the form from 1,200 to 200 each year.

Writing in plain English so your reader understands you is not an easy task. Many legal concepts are complex and translating them into plain English is difficult. Similarly, some use of "legalese" such as Latin phrases may be unavoidable in certain instances. Nevertheless, well-written documents share the following features.

- They are accurate in every respect, including the "small" items, such as dates, addresses, and dollar amounts;
- They comply with American English rules of grammar, punctuation, and spelling;
- They use definite, concrete, and familiar language;
- They are organized in a manner that enhances comprehension;
- They avoid using double negatives;
- They omit surplus information and redundancy; and
- They enhance readability through attractive design and layout.

Highly respected and renowned financier Warren E. Buffett explains that when writing Berkshire Hathaway's annual report, he pretends he's talking to his sisters. Although highly intelligent, they are not accounting or financial experts. Mr. Buffett believes that he will be successful if they understand his writing. Similarly, United States Supreme Court Justice Stephen Breyer says that he tries to write his legal opinions so that they are understandable to high school students. Thus, legal writing need not be showy or pretentious. It need only be understood.

C. Accuracy

The difference between the right word and the almost right word is the difference between lightning and the lightning bug.

Attributed to Mark Twain

1. Introduction

The most important characteristic of legal writing is accuracy. Clients will rely on the information and opinions given to them by legal professionals. Judges, supervisors, administrators, and others must know the information provided to them is correct. Thus, being right is fundamental to effective legal writing. No amount of skillfully presented material can overcome a faulty statement.

Be accurate with regard not only to the "big" issues, such as legal conclusions and arguments, but also as to the "small" elements of a writing, such as names, dates, and dollar amounts. An error in the client's name or address will attract more attention than anything else in a document. Just as spelling errors cast doubt on your ability, so do accuracy errors have a disproportionately negative effect on the reader. The legal profession has become more adversarial in recent years and even clients (sometimes, especially clients) are quick to point out an error. Thus, because your audience is highly critical, you must be as accurate and precise as possible. Generally, other than inattention to detail, there are three causes for a lack of precision in legal writing: picking the wrong word, using a vague word, and selecting a word that has an unwanted connotation.

One notorious cause of imprecise writing is an overreliance on forms. Drafting a lease requires more than merely locating another lease in your office and then changing the names and addresses. When you use a form originally drafted for another client, proofread carefully to ensure that you do not import inappropriate language. Use the "find and replace" feature in your word processor to ensure the first client's name has been replaced with the second and that any references that might pertain only to the first client (such as the pronouns *he* or *him*) have been replaced with words and phrases appropriate for the second client.

2. Word Choice

The selection of an improper word will result in inaccuracy in your writing. Similarly, the use of qualifying language or words can cause unintended meanings. For example, no employee would be comforted by reading "There are no immediate plans to downsize your department." Although the writer may have intended to reassure the reader that his or her job was secure, the use of the qualifier *immediate* implies that there are plans to downsize; they simply are not immediate.

For accuracy, select the most descriptive and specific word possible. Descriptive words lend strength and vitality to your writing. Moreover, the selection of an incorrect word can be fatal in legal writing. An instruction to a defendant that a judgment *may* be paid will produce a far different result than an instruction that a judgment *must* be paid.

A number of words commonly used in legal writing cause trouble. Although many words and word pairs are discussed in the Glossary of Usage in Appendix F of this Handbook, a quick review of some words commonly confused or misused in legal writing follows:

- **And/or:** A number of courts have been called on to interpret the meaning of this expression. Although this expression is short, it is often unclear. For precision, instead of writing *the boys and/or the girls,* write *the boys or girls, or both.*
- **Argue:** Courts do not argue cases; lawyers do. Do not write *the court argued . . . .* Similarly, courts do not *contend, believe,* or *feel.* Conversely, courts *rule, decide, hold, state, conclude,* and so forth.
- **Compose/comprise.** *Compose* means *to make up,* as in *The brief is composed of three sections. Comprise* means *to include, contain,* or *consist of,* as in *The house comprises three wings.* Do not use the word *of* after the word *comprise.* It is as incorrect to write *The lawsuit is comprised of three counts* as it is to write *The lawsuit is included of three counts.*
- **Court:** The word *court* is singular, as in *the court has affirmed.* You may refer to a court by the name of its chief justice. Thus, when discussing *Brown v. Board of Education,* you may write *the Warren Court held that . . . .* A few legal writers object to references to a court by the name of a case and would thus frown upon *the Brown Court held that . . .* although such use is common in practice and frequently seen in court opinions themselves. In fact, the U.S. Supreme Court's Guide for Counsel in Cases to be argued before the Court specifically instructs attorneys, "[d]o not refer to an opinion of the Court by saying: 'In Justice Ginsburg's opinion.' You should say: 'In the Court's opinion, written by Justice Ginsburg.'" Sup. Ct. Guide for Counsel, Part II, E.3.
- **Dicta:** *Dicta* is plural and refers to extraneous remarks made by a judge, as in *Justice Sanders has continually noted in dicta that . . . . Dictum* is singular and refers to a single remark or observation.

- **Fact, contention:** A *fact* is something that has occurred or can be verified. A *contention* is an allegation that something has occurred.
- **Find, hold:** When a court makes a *finding*, it has decided certain facts. When a court makes a pronouncement about a legal issue, it issues a *holding*.
- **Guilty, liable:** In a criminal case, a defendant is found guilty. In a civil case, a defendant is found liable for damages.
- **I, my, we, our, us:** Personal pronouns (*I, my, we, our, us*) are used only in legal correspondence. They are not used in documents submitted to courts or in legal memoranda. Thus, write *Petitioner will show*, not *We will show*.
- **Judgment:** In legal writing and in most American writings, spell as *judgment*. In Great Britain, the word is spelled *judgement*.
- **Memoranda, memorandum:** *Memoranda* is plural and refers to several documents whereas a *memorandum* is singular and refers to one document.
- **Motion:** A motion is an application made to a court requesting that the court issue an order in a pending case, such as a motion for change of venue. A lawyer *makes a motion* or *moves for summary judgment*.
- **Oral, verbal:** *Oral* means something spoken, as in *The plaintiff's oral testimony at trial was consistent with her earlier testimony*. *Verbal* means a communication in words and could refer to a written or a spoken communication. Be precise.
- **Overrule, reverse:** A court *overrules* prior decisions in its jurisdiction. For example, in 2004 a court could overrule a precedent from a 1960 case. A court *reverses* the very case before it. Thus, if a defendant is found guilty by the trial court and appeals the decision, and the appellate court agrees with the defendant's reasoning, it will *reverse* the improper decision from the court below.
- **Prescribe, proscribe:** *Prescribe* means to order, as in *The doctor prescribed medication*. *Proscribe* means to prohibit, as in *Iowa law proscribes falsification of documents*.

Case Illustration: The Meaning of the Word *Between*

Case: *LeFeavre v. Pennington*, 230 S.W.2d 46 (Ark. 1950)

Facts: The Arkansas Supreme Court was called upon to interpret a will that read "The Bal. to be divided equally between all of our nephews and nieces on my wife's side and my niece, Nathalee Pennington." There were twenty-two nieces and nephews on the wife's side, and they contended that the property should be distributed equally among all of the beneficiaries so that each would receive one twenty-third.

Holding: The court divided the property into two equal shares, stating that the use of the word *between* showed that the testator intended to divide the property in two equal shares; had the testator intended otherwise, the word *among* would have been used.

3. Vague Words

To ensure accuracy in your writing, use concrete and descriptive words. Avoid vague and abstract words such as *matter, development, situation,* and *problem,* which provide little, if any, information to a reader. Thus, sentences beginning *Regarding this matter* or *Regarding the former issue* offer no guidance to the reader as to what *this matter* or *issue* might be. A better approach is to write *Regarding your lease.*

Similarly, avoid using words such as *above* or *herein.* For example, if in an agreement you use the words *as described above* in paragraph twelve, the reader does not know where in the previous eleven paragraphs the information was discussed. State, *as described in paragraph 4(b).*

Abstract words such as *justice* or *fairness* may be confusing because they mean different things to different people. Thus, be careful in the use of such words and consider selecting concrete nouns in their place.

Sometimes vagueness is caused by a lack of specificity. Will a reader understand a statement that *the plaintiff was injured* or that *the temperature in the employee lounge is too cold?* Why not write *the plaintiff suffered a broken leg* or *the temperature in the employee lounge is 65 degrees Fahrenheit?* Write *in 2007* rather than *recently.*

The words *it* and *this* are often used in an indefinite manner. Consider the following:

> The court ruled the defendant should be granted probation. This enables the defendant to participate in a work release program.

The word *this* could refer either to the court's ruling or to the defendant's probation. When using *it* or *this,* you should repeat the word that *it* or *this* refers to, as in the following:

> The court ruled the defendant should be granted probation. Probation will enable the defendant to participate in a work release program.

▶ **Tip: Use the "find and replace" feature on your word processor to locate sentences beginning with *It is, There is,* or *There are.* Sentences beginning with these words tend to be vague and ambiguous.**

Vague Examples	Revised Examples
There is copyright infringement when a copyrighted work is reproduced without the owner's permission.	Copyright infringement occurs when a copyrighted work is reproduced without the owner's permission.
It says in the case that the legislation is not retroactive.	The case states that the legislation is not retroactive.
The former cause of action was dismissed.	The negligence cause of action was dismissed.

Some Vague Words	
● aspect	● resource
● concept	● syndrome
● element	● system
● factor	● utility
● operation	● variable
● process	

4. Intentional Vagueness

In some cases, you may wish to be intentionally vague. For example, in ordering the desegregation of public schools, the U.S. Supreme Court stated that the task should proceed *with all deliberate speed. Brown v. Bd. of Educ.*, 349 U.S. 294, 301 (1955). Many experts believe the selection of this expression was itself deliberate, reflecting the Court's reluctance to impose strict time limits for such a complex task.

Similarly, many legal agreements use a variety of terms that are intentionally vague. For example, settlement agreements routinely require the parties to act in *good faith* or to *meet and confer* in the event of a dispute. Custody agreements often allow for *reasonable visitation*. In such cases, the drafters have usually artfully selected these vague phrases so that the parties can resolve their disputes, with full knowledge that a court may later be called on to determine what is *reasonable* or whether actions were in *good faith*.

In sum, if there is vagueness in your writing, make sure it is intentional.

5. Word Connotation

Many words have more than one meaning. When you select a word, consider its connotation, or suggested meaning. There is a great difference, for example, in referring to an item as *cheap* rather than *affordable*. The word *cheap* connotes shoddy or low quality whereas *affordable* conveys either a neutral or desirable meaning. Consider the effect of telling someone that he or she is *stubborn* rather than *firm* or *blunt* rather than *candid*.

Certain words carry hostile or negative undertones and will immediately make a reader defensive or angry. For example, consider the following: *The judge who decided the sexual harassment case was young.* Although the statement may be true, the subtle message it conveys is that the judge was so young and inexperienced that the decision was likely incorrect. Use a dictionary and a thesaurus to ensure that you have selected the appropriate word.

Consider the following word pairs and note that using a word on the left may unintentionally convey the meaning on the right.

Word	Possible Connotation
old, elderly	feeble, infirm, incompetent
proud	vain
venerable, established	old, outmoded
late (with a payment)	delinquent
long, lasting	endless
neat, organized	obsessive, compulsive
enthusiastic	hyperactive, manic
cautious	timid
simple	unintelligent
delay	hinder, obstruct

6. Special Word Problems: Made-Up Words, Slang and Colloquial Expressions, and Offensive Language

When writers begin to write as they would speak, there are usually three problems with the words they select: The words may be made-up, slang or colloquial expressions, or offensive.

a. Made-Up Words and Phrases

If the aim of writing is to communicate, how can a reader understand words that don't exist? Although you may have heard of, used, and even written some made-up or coined words such as *dialogued, Borked,* or *liaising,* these "words" are not generally found in most dictionaries because they are not yet recognized words in English. Similarly, the use of the suffix *-wise* has created a host of coined words, such as *taxwise* and *revenuewise.* Our conversation and writing are often influenced by business and technology terms. Thus, a number of terms, such as *cutting edge, synergy,* and *empower* are overused. Do not write *We need to <u>interface</u> to resolve the litigation* when you mean *meet.* Do not use *impact* as a verb. Write *His credit history will affect his ability to obtain a loan* (not *His credit history will <u>impact</u> his ability to obtain a loan*). Although English is an evolving language, do not use a word before it has evolved into an entry in a standard dictionary.

Words and Expressions to Avoid	Substitutions
an *impactful* exhibit	a dramatic exhibit
incentivize the employees	encourage or motivate the employees
We *efforted* the project.	We worked on the project.
We were *tasked* with finding a solution.	We were asked (or requested) to find a solution.

Words and Expressions to Avoid	Substitutions
Gift your clients with this pen.	Give your clients this pen.
We should meet and *strategize* a solution.	We should meet to find a solution.
John is Carol's *mentee*.	Carol is John's mentor.
We should *dialogue* about the case.	We should discuss the case.
We should *concretize* our plans.	We should finalize our plans.

Made-Up and Overused Words and Phrases: Conference Room Bingo

One game circulating on the Internet (see www.jokeindex.com) demonstrates the pervasiveness of made-up or overused business expressions and challenges attendees to note how often the following words or phrases are spoken in a meeting. The game of "conference room bingo" is won when all of the listed words have been used in the meeting.

- synergy
- bottom line
- revisit
- bandwidth
- out of the loop
- proactive
- think outside the box
- push the edge of the envelope
- touch base
- game plan
- leverage
- fast track
- mindset
- win-win
- empower
- user-friendly
- get closure

b. Slang and Colloquial Expressions

Slang is informal language, often used by a particular group. Although slang may be dramatic and forceful when spoken, it is too flippant for any formal writing (unless reporting the exact words of a speaker). Colloquial language is common everyday language, and it is inappropriate for legal writing. Generally, avoid any words marked as *inf* (for *informal*) or *coll* (for *colloquial*) in a dictionary.

Slang or Colloquial	Revised
The plaintiff was ripped off.	*The plaintiff was defrauded.*
The premises had heavy-duty defects.	*The premises had significant defects.*

Slang or Colloquial	Revised
The plaintiff got used to the pain.	The plaintiff became accustomed to the pain.
The parties began to get along.	The parties began to cooperate.
The doctor did not measure up to the standard of care.	The doctor did not satisfy the standard of care. (or The doctor breached the standard of care.)
The plaintiff is entitled to get the documents.	The plaintiff is entitled to obtain the documents.

Somewhat similar to slang and colloquial expressions are *idioms*, phrases the meaning of which cannot be understood from the ordinary meaning of the words, as in the use of the phrase *give in* to mean *surrender* or *yield*. Many legal idioms are confusing because of the prepositions used with them. For example, are you *enjoined from* taking action or are you *enjoined to* take action? Both are correct. Once you have some experience in reading cases and legal materials, you will have a better understanding of legal idioms. Some common idioms used in legal writing are listed on page 84 of this chapter.

c. Offensive Language

Language can be offensive because it is sexist or biased or suggests stereotypes. Avoid references to personal characteristics, such as sex, race, or disability. Offensive language distracts from the message and focuses attention on the writer. It is sometimes so jarring that any underlying message is lost entirely. The use of gender-linked pronouns is also discussed in Chapter 1. Following are some examples of sexist words and expressions and suggested replacements.

Sexist Language	Revised
A judge should issue his decision promptly.	Judges should issue their decisions promptly.
	A judge should issue a decision promptly.
Mr. Carr and Barbara Carr attended.	Mr. and Mrs. Carr attended.
businessman	business executives, managers
chairman	chairperson, chair, head, presiding officer
congressman	congressperson, congressional representative
draftsman	drafter

Sexist Language	Revised
foreman	supervisor
layman	layperson
male nurse	nurse
man-hours	worker hours, work hours
man and wife	man and woman, husband and wife
mankind	humanity, people
newsman	reporter
woman lawyer, woman judge	lawyer, judge
workman	worker (especially in reference to workers' compensation)

Use common sense and sensitivity when describing people and try to use the term that the group prefers. For example, since the 1992 Rehabilitation Act Amendments, the use of the word *handicapped* has been largely replaced by the word *disabled*. The use of the word *mongoloid* has been replaced by *Down syndrome*. Use *hearing impaired* rather than *deaf*. Use *mentally ill* rather than *insane* (unless the word *insane* is used in its strict legal sense, as defined by a case or statute), and use *mentally impaired* rather than *retarded*.

Avoid outmoded and pejorative expressions such as *Chinese fire drill, Indian giver, Mexican standoff,* or *Protestant work ethic*. The racial designation used to describe African Americans has changed from *colored*, to *Negro*, to the current uses of *black* and *African American*. At present, there are significant disputes regarding the use of the words *Hispanic* and *Latino* with some individuals strongly preferring one term and others preferring the other. A similar dispute exists regarding the terms *American Indian* and *Native American*. Consider using the Internet and viewing the websites of organizations such as the NAACP or the National Congress of American Indians for guidance. Consider using a specific term such as *Seminole* rather than *Indian* or *Japanese* rather than *Asian*.

Consider whether it is necessary to describe a person in terms of race, religion, or sex at all. In many instances, a description of a person is simply not relevant. For example, writing that *Justice O'Connor was a well-respected female jurist* implies that Justice O'Connor is well respected even though she is a woman. Write instead that *Justice O'Connor was a well-respected jurist*.

In sum, be sensitive when describing people, select neutral language whenever possible, but don't be so politically correct that you describe a short witness as someone who is *vertically challenged*.

Challenge Word Choice

Select the correct word or rewrite to improve meaning.

- Judges and their wives will attend the conference.
- He will file a claim for workmen's compensation.
- An engineer should promptly prepare his reports.
- We will need to engage with Susan later this week.
- After the meeting, Ben was asked to own the action.
- Jeff doesn't have enough bandwidth to handle the case.
- Let's diary that for next week when we can surface the issue to the board.
- Francie prepared both memoranda/memorandums.
- The court believed/held that the will was invalid.
- The company plans to monetize its assets.
- The condominium complex is richly amenetized.

D. Clarity

Words, like glass, obscure when they do not aid vision.

Joseph Joubert, *Pensees* (1842)

The second feature of effective legal writing is clarity, namely, ensuring that your project is easily understood by the reader. Your writing style should be invisible. It is bad writing that is noticeable. Because legal writings are read not for pleasure, but for function, readers expect you to make your point clearly and quickly.

The three primary legal writing flaws that obscure clarity are elegant variation, the overuse of negatives, and improper word order.

Common Idioms in Legal Writing

Following are some common idioms or expressions seen in legal writing with the correct preposition given.

- Abide by a ruling; abide in a house
- Abstain from taking action
- Accede to demands
- According to the case; in accord with the case
- Acquiesce in a reorganization plan

(continued)

Common Idioms in Legal Writing

- Agree on a resolution; agree to the demands; agree with a person
- Angry with the witness (not angry *at*)
- Appeal to a court (not appeal *at* a court); appeal by the plaintiff
- Compare with the previous case; compare to a summer's day (metaphorical use)
- Comply with the demands (not comply *to*)
- Concur with the defendant's interpretation; concur in the majority opinion
- Damages of $50,000; damages for negligence; damages in the libel case; damages from the defendant
- Defrauded into buying the house; defrauded by the defendant's action
- Demand on the debtor; demand for money
- Depart from a previous ruling
- Different from (not different *than*)
- Disclaimer of a warranty; disclaimer by the seller; disclaimer in the contract
- Discovery of documents; discovery by the plaintiff; discovery under the Rules of Civil Procedure
- Dissent in this case; dissent from the majority opinion
- Enjoined from taking further action (meaning *prohibited*); enjoined to take further action (meaning *compelled*)
- Inadmissible into (or *as*) evidence; inadmissible for the purpose of impeachment
- Insured against loss; insurance on the property; insurance for the business
- Intervene between the parties; intervene in a dispute or case
- Irrelevant to the case
- Judgment of the court; judgment for the plaintiff; judgment against the defendant; judgment in the case
- Lawyer for the plaintiff; lawyer with (or *at* or *of*) the firm
- Opposed to the proposal
- Party to (or *in*) a lawsuit
- Plead to the charge of murder; plead for mercy; plead in response to the complaint
- Proxy for Ellen; proxy to vote on Ellen's behalf
- Ratification of a contract; ratification by a party
- Related to the issue
- Released from a debt; released into custody; released by the court
- Relevant to the issue
- Remand to a lower court; remand by (or *from*) a higher court; remanded for further proceedings
- Stipulation by the plaintiff; stipulation of facts

1. Elegant Variation or the Slender Yellow Fruit Syndrome

Elegant variation refers to the practice of substituting one term for another in a document to avoid repetition of a term. Writers are often reluctant to repeat a term, believing that repetition of a term is boring or unsophisticated. Unfortunately, selecting alternate terms creates the impression that something entirely different is intended. Consider the following sentence:

> *Four of the defendant's witnesses were women, whereas all of the plaintiff's witnesses were ladies.*

In an attempt not to repeat the word *women*, the writer conveys something entirely different about the two groups of witnesses.

In her excellent book *Woe Is I*, author Patricia T. O'Conner notes that editors frequently call this practice the Slender Yellow Fruit Syndrome: "It is best explained by example: *Freddie was offered an apple and a banana, and he chose the slender yellow fruit.*"

Elegant variation is deadly in legal writing. For example, if you are reading a document that continually refers to the owner of property as the *landlord* and then suddenly refers to the *lessor*, you would be correct to assume that the newly introduced *lessor* is not the same individual as the previously described *landlord*.

Be cautious about varying words and terms used in legal writings. Although you may believe that selecting alternative terms shows your extensive vocabulary and lends interest to the document, you unintentionally may be creating the impression that there is a reason that different terms have been selected and that there is a legal distinction to be drawn based on this variation.

In particular, once you have given a label to an individual, use the term consistently. For example, assume that the introduction to a document refers to *the buyer, Patrick L. Moore ("Moore")*. You have now created a defined term. Every later reference to the individual must be to *Moore*. Referring to the individual as *buyer* or *Mr. Moore* is inappropriate. Use the "find and replace" feature of your word processor to ensure terms are used consistently.

Illustration: No Elegant Variation

Note the repetition in Sir Winston Churchill's speech about Dunkirk, delivered in 1940. There is little, if any, elegant variation. Rather, each repetition of the word *fight* makes for a stronger and more forceful statement.

> [W]e shall not flag or fail. We shall go on to the end. We shall fight in France, we shall fight on the seas and oceans, we shall fight with growing confidence and growing strength in the air, we shall defend our Island, whatever the cost may be, we shall fight on the beaches, we shall fight on the landing grounds. We shall fight in the fields and in the streets, we shall fight in the hills; we shall never surrender.

Challenge ? Elegant Variation

Rewrite the following statements.

- The noncompetition agreement was signed on June 10. The executed covenant prohibiting competition was then filed with the court.
- The company has alleged breach of a software license agreement. The plaintiff specifically claimed that the agreement permitting use of the software was invalid.
- The corporation's board of directors called an annual meeting in May. The company managers submitted financial reports at this convention.
- The applicant must submit an application for employment by July 30. A candidate's failure to submit a résumé is grounds for disqualification.
- The purchaser must deposit the purchase price with the seller within thirty days. If the buyer fails to deposit the purchase price within one month the vendor may terminate the contract.

2. Negatives

The overuse of negatives is often confusing to readers. Although statutes are often set forth in negative fashion by describing what is prohibited, using more than two negative words in a sentence usually forces the reader to stop and think through what has been said. The phrase *not unlikely* must be translated to *probable*. The phrase *not unimportant* must be converted to *important*. In fact, these are examples of *litotes*, expressions that make an assertion by denying their opposite, as in *not unmindful*. Legal writing is prone to the use of these expressions.

Consider the following statement from a recent U.S. Supreme Court decision: "But given the fact that the District Court found that the 32 months required by TRPA to formulate the 1984 Regional Plan was not unreasonable, we could not possibly conclude that every delay of over one year is constitutionally unacceptable." *Tahoe-Sierra Preservation Council v. Tahoe Reg'l Planning Agency*, 535 U.S. 302, 341-43 (2002).

A reader would likely need to read the statement several times to make sense of it. Anytime the reader is interrupted from reading the project, your message is weakened. As a writer, your task is to ensure that a reader proceeds smoothly through the document without needing to stop and puzzle over phrases. For example, the statement *No individual shall be prohibited from refusing to submit to a Breathalyzer examination* is confusing. It requires a reader to consider three negative words: *no, prohibited,* and *refusing*.

In drafting projects, keep in mind that there are many more negative words than the obvious ones *no, none,* or *never*. Many words function in a negative fashion, such as *deny, except, limit, preclude, refuse, void,* and so forth. Although it is impossible to purge your writing of all negative terms, you should carefully scrutinize your writing to ensure that you have not used too many negative words that obscure your meaning.

The other disadvantages of using negative words are that they are not as forceful as affirmative expressions and they are generally wordier than affirmative expressions. For example, it is more effective and shorter to say *the plaintiff was late for her deposition* than *the plaintiff failed to timely appear for her deposition*. To give strength and vitality to your writing, and to enhance clarity, use affirmative and positive terms.

Challenge Negative Expressions

Rewrite the following negative expressions.

● We are not unfamiliar with the concept of copyright infringement.
● We are reluctant to say that we do not disagree with you.
● Vote for no more than one candidate for the board of directors.
● We do not deny that scandalous trademarks are ineligible for federal registration.
● You should not forget to deny the allegations of the complaint.

Substitutions for Negative Expressions

Consider replacing negative phrases or compounds with a single word that means the same thing.

Negative Compound	Single Word
not able	unable
not accept	reject
not certain	uncertain
not unlike	similar
does not have	lacks
does not include	excludes, omits
not often	rarely, infrequently
not . . . unless	only if
not . . . except	only if
not . . . until	only when
did not recall	forgot
did not comply with	violated

Source: From *Plain English Handbook*, www.sec.gov.

Case Illustrations: Tied Up in Nots

Consider the following clunkers from various court opinions:

- "This principle is so well established that no parent should expect that a termination of amounts designated spousal support but in fact needed to augment an insufficient child support award insures against an upward modification of child support after the spousal support ends." *In re Marriage of Catalano*, 251 Cal. Rptr. 370, 375 (Ct. App. 1988).
- "In an appropriate case, there is no reason why courts, on a motion to dismiss, could not identify a response as not 'clearly unreasonable' as a matter of law." *Davis v. Monroe County Bd. of Educ.*, 526 U.S. 629, 649 (1999).

Backward ran the sentences until reeled the mind.

Wolcott Gibbs (about the style of *Time* magazine)

3. Word Order

The most common sentence structure in the English language is the placement of the subject first, the verb second, and the object third. Thus, the sentence *The defenant attacked the victim* is phrased in this standard way. Although the thought can certainly be expressed in another way (such as *The victim was attacked by the defendant*), readers typically anticipate that sentences will follow the expected pattern of subject, verb, and object. Place your main thought or message at the beginning of your sentence.

Although you may not want to structure every sentence in a project in the same fashion, excessive variation from the expected sentence structure may cause confusion and lack of clarity. Just as you should avoid exotic spellings of words because they draw attention to your writing rather than your message, avoid unusual sentence structure.

Vary from the anticipated sentence structure of subject, verb, and object when you want to draw attention to a thought. Thus, if you have a point you want to emphasize, vary the way it is structured. This technique will create interest. For example, consider the following two sentences:

Ordinary Structure:	*My first trial was the most memorable event of my career.*
Inverted Structure:	*The most memorable event of my career was my first trial.*

Note how the second example builds interest and creates drama.

Keep this technique in mind if you need to "bury" a weak portion of an argument. Phrase it in the manner commonly anticipated by readers because this will draw the least amount of attention to it.

One of the other benefits of using "normal" sentence structure is that you will automatically phrase your thoughts in the active voice. When you vary from the anticipated order in sentences, the result is often conversion to the passive voice, which creates a weaker (and often longer) sentence.

Case Illustrations: The Risks of Poor Writing

Courts are becoming increasingly impatient with poorly written briefs. In one recent case, *In re King*, No. 05-56485-C, 2006 U.S. Bankr. WL 581256 (Bankr. W.D. Tex. Feb. 21, 2006), the court noted that it could determine neither the substance of the defendant's legal argument nor the relief requested by the defendant. The court therefore denied the defendant's motion "for being incomprehensible." Thus, poor writing can result in an adverse ruling for a client. Similarly, in *United States v. Devine*, 787 F.2d 1086, 1089 (7th Cir. 1986), the court affirmed a defendant's conviction for a variety of reasons, including the poor quality of the defendant's brief, noting that "the brief was desultory in nature; in general a poorly written product with numerous typographical errors. It was obviously never edited by a caring professional. As a panel of judges already overburdened with cases and paper, we find it insulting to have to dutifully comb through a brief which even its author found little reason to give such attention. We condemn this type of shoddy professionalism."

E. Readability

Because the subject matter discussed in legal writing is often complex, and frequently boring, you need to make your project as readable as possible. Clients will be unfamiliar with legal topics. Judges and other legal professionals will be too busy to struggle through a complex and pompous document. Remember that the more complicated a topic is, the greater the need is for readability.

Readability Tests

Several readability formulas can be used to determine the readability of a project. One of the best known tests is the Flesch Reading Ease Formula, which determines readability by using a calculation based on the average sentence length and average number of syllables in words. Reading tests, however, tend to rely on surface or technical characteristics and cannot test coherence; average sentence length and average syllables per word are indirect predictors of the readability and comprehensibility of a writing.

Microsoft Word users can evaluate their projects against the Flesch Reading Ease scale and against the Flesch-Kinkaid Grade Level scale (which identifies the grade level of a writing). To activate this feature, follow these steps:

- Go to the "Tools" menu and select "Options."
- Select "Spelling and Grammar."
- Check "Show readability statistics" and then select "OK."

To run the test on a document you write, select "Tools" and then "Spelling and Grammar." A dialog box will disclose the readability scores.

To enhance readability:

1. Prefer the Active Voice

The quickest fix for plodding documents is the use of the active voice. The active voice focuses attention on the subject of the sentence that performs or causes certain action. The active voice is consistent with standard English sentence structure of subject, verb, and object and is more forceful than the passive voice, which makes the subject of the sentence the recipient of the action.

The passive voice focuses attention on the object of the action by placing it first and relegating the subject or actor of the sentence to an inferior position.

Passive Voice	Active Voice
A meeting was held by the corporation.	The corporation held its meeting.
An argument for acquittal was made by the defendant's attorney.	The defendant's attorney argued for acquittal.
Testimony was given by the doctor that the patient consented to the operation.	The doctor testified that the patient consented to the operation.
The policy was announced by the committee.	The committee announced the policy.

Note that in these passive constructions the person or the thing doing the action is introduced with the word *by*. This is a tip that you have shifted into the passive voice. Similarly, sentences in which no actor is named are passive, such as *The judge was informed that the juror was sick.* You can readily spot sentences in the passive voice because they will always combine some form of the verb *to be* (*am, are, been, is, was, were,* and so forth) with a verb in the past tense (as in *was announced*).

The active voice is stronger and more forceful than the passive voice. For example, consider the well-known NIKE Inc. slogan JUST DO IT®. What would be the effect of the slogan if it were phrased, DOING IT SHOULD BE DONE BY YOU?

Similarly, what if Rev. Martin Luther King, Jr. had said, "A dream was had by me" rather than the powerful "I have a dream"?

Additionally, readers comprehend a sentence in the active voice more quickly because it follows the way they normally process information. They do not have to search through the sentence looking for the actor or subject. Finally, another advantage of using the active voice is that it usually produces shorter sentences.

There are situations, however, in which the passive voice may be preferable. Generally, use passive voice when the thing being acted on is more important than the actor, when the actor is obvious, or when you wish to deflect attention from the actor. For example, assume your law firm represents a defendant accused of fraud. Instead of stating *The defendant deposited checks in his bank account*, you could write *Checks were deposited in the defendant's bank account*. This use of the passive voice shifts the focus away from the defendant. The reader is informed of what occurred but not who did it. In fact, some experts refer to this approach as using *weasel words* because there is no indication as to who is responsible for an act. The classic illustration of a weasel statement is seen in the recent statement of a politician accused of wrongdoing who stated, *Mistakes were made* rather than *I made a mistake*. What better way to deflect responsibility than to have a sentence with no one in it?

▶ **Tip: Most word processors have a feature that will flag the use of passive voice. This feature is a useful guide but can be distracting.**

Challenge ? Word Order and Active Voice

Rewrite the following:

- He demanded a jury trial on Monday.
- Preparing the request for the production of documents was a difficult task for Beth.
- It was foggy on the date the accident occurred.
- An extension of time was requested.
- Abandonment of trademarks has been thoroughly discussed by the Second Circuit Court of Appeals.
- An invitation to the defendant to enter into settlement negotiations was issued by the plaintiff.
- The budget and the compensation report were approved by the board of directors.

2. Use Lists

Another way to enhance readability is to use lists when discussing complex matters. Lists not only enable readers to comprehend information quickly, they also create visual drama and interest because they are usually numbered or bulleted and set apart from the rest of the text. Lists (sometimes called *tabulation*) are especially helpful for setting forth the elements of a cause of action, components of a definition, and so forth.

Lists can be structured in several ways, but to increase interest:

- Set the list off from the rest of your narrative by spaces above and below the list;
- Indent your list;
- Identify the items in your list with numbers, letters, or "bullets" (which can be formulated automatically by most word processors); and
- Punctuate correctly by putting a semicolon after each item except the last item and include *or* or *and* before the last item.

Most lists are introduced by a phrase such as *the following* and a colon. Each component in the list must fit grammatically with the words in front of the colon.

Not all lists need to be indented. If the list is short, perhaps a series of three or four words, you may separate each item from the next by a comma, and include the list as part of your narrative text. You may also insert parenthetical numbers before each item.

Correct Example: *The employee is required to perform the following duties: (1) supervise department meetings, (2) audit the company's financial records, and (3) attend monthly executive sessions.*

The grammatical structure of all the items in any list must be identical or parallel. Thus, if the first word in a list is a gerund (a verb form ending in *-ing* such as *preparing*), all of the following items must also begin with a gerund. Similarly, the items in the list must be either all complete sentences or all phrases. This type of consistency is called *parallel structure*. Note that each item in the preceding bulleted list begins with a verb (*set, indent, identify,* and *punctuate*).

Incorrect	**Correct**
The elements of a cause of action for breach of contract are as follows:	*The elements of a cause of action for breach of contract are as follows:*
- *an agreement;* - *a breach of that agreement by one party; and* - *the act of the breaching party must have caused damage.*	- *an agreement;* - *a breach of that agreement by one party; and* - *damage caused by the act of the breaching party.*

Parallel structure is discussed further next.

3. Use Parallel Structure

I came, I saw, I conquered.

Words attributed to Julius Caesar by Plutarch

StyleLinks

http://owl.english.purdue.edu/handouts/grammar/g_parallel.html
Purdue University's Online Writing Lab offers excellent information on parallel form.

http://grammar.ccc.commnet.edu/grammar/parallelism.htm
This *Guide to Grammar & Writing* provides instruction on using parallel structure as well as quizzes to test your knowledge.

a. Introduction

Consider the following revision of Caesar's words: *I came, then I was seeing, after which I engaged in conquering.* The original statement is a striking example of parallelism or parallel structure, matching grammatical structures through the use of the same pronoun followed by simple verbs in the past tense. Parallelism requires ensuring that ideas or elements in a sentence are presented in similar or parallel form, so that adjectives are paralleled by adjectives, nouns by nouns, gerunds by gerunds, and so forth. Thus, the sentence *The attorney alleged fraud and negligence* is parallel because it uses a noun and then another noun. The sentence *The defendant's conduct was reckless, willful, and malicious* is parallel because all words describing the defendant's conduct are adjectives.

Nonparallel	Correct
The speakers were exhausted, drained, and needed food.	*The speakers were exhausted, drained, and hungry.*
The board of directors will invest the money to provide shareholders with income, protection of their assets, and achieving tax benefits.	*The board of directors will invest the money <u>to provide</u> shareholders with income, <u>to protect</u> their assets, and <u>to achieve</u> tax benefits.*

Not only is parallel structure a grammatical requirement, it also is an opportunity to achieve balance and effect in writing. Consider the following two quotations, each of which uses parallel structure to deliver a compelling message.

[A]sk not what your country can do for you—ask what you can do for your country.

President John F. Kennedy (1961)

We will not tire, we will not falter, and we will not fail.

President George W. Bush (2001)

There are four particular situations that require you to ensure parallel structure: when using coordinating conjunctions, when using correlative conjunctions, when making comparisons, and when using lists and headings.

b. Coordinating Conjunctions

The coordinating conjunctions *and, but, for, or, nor, so,* and *yet* always indicate a need for parallelism. Phrases linked by any of these words must be parallel in structure.

Nonparallel	Revised
The system is capable of retrieving records, processing data, and communication with the server.	*The system is capable of retrieving records, processing data, and communicating with the server.*
Ted loves reading, writing, and research.	*Ted loves to read, write, and research.* or *Ted loves reading, writing, and researching.*

c. Correlative Conjunctions

Correlative conjunctions (pairs of words that connect elements such as *either-or, neither-nor,* and *not only-but also*) require elements in parallel form. The grammatical structure following the second part of the correlative conjunction (for example, the word *or* when using *either-or*) should mimic the structure following the first part. Make sure that any element you repeat is placed after the first part of the correlative conjunction (for example, after *either* when using *either-or*).

Nonparallel	Parallel
I will act as either a mediator or as an arbitrator.	*I will act either as a mediator or as an arbitrator.*
Jackie expects not only to be offered the job but also she expects to be well paid.	*Jackie expects not only to be offered the job but also to be well paid.*

d. Comparisons

Use correct parallel structure when making comparisons using the words *than* or *as.*

Nonparallel	Parallel
The exhibits in the first trial were more effective than the second trial.	*The exhibits in the first trial were more effective than the exhibits in the second trial.*
It is more important to write the brief than arguing it.	*It is more important to write the brief than argue it.*
My appellate brief is shorter than her.	*My appellate brief is shorter than hers.*

e. Lists and Headings

When making lists, using headings, or placing items in a series, make sure the structure is parallel. Presentation must be parallel or consistent as well so that if the first heading in a document or item in a list is a complete sentence, later ones shoud also be full sentences. Similarly, if the first heading or item is a clause, later ones should also be clauses. Faulty parallel structure is often seen in résumés when applicants describe their job experience.

Nonparallel	**Parallel**
My experience includes:	*My experience includes:*
▪ *drafting documents;*	▪ *draf<u>ting</u> documents;*
▪ *assisting in trial preparation; and*	▪ *assis<u>ting</u> in trial preparation; and*
▪ *preparation of pleadings.*	▪ *prepar<u>ing</u> pleadings.*

 Tips ➡ # On Using Parallel Structure

● It is not significant what grammatical structure you use for a series, list, or group of headings as long as the use is consistent:

Examples: *prepare, assist, write*

prepared, assisted, wrote

preparing, assisting, writing

● When you introduce items or elements with an article (*a, an, the*), a preposition (such as *to*), or a pronoun (*his, her*), the introductory word may either appear before the first item only or be repeated before each item.

Nonparallel	**Parallel**
She wanted to hike, swim, and to run.	*She wanted <u>to</u> hike, swim, and run.*
	or
	She wanted <u>to</u> hike, <u>to</u> swim, and <u>to</u> run.

● To check for parallel structure:

○ Examine words that appear on either side of the words *and* and *or*;
○ Put words and phrases in columns to make sure they match in their structure;
○ Read aloud and listen to the rhythm and sounds of elements to ensure they sound the same; and
○ Consider introducing each element with the same word, such as *by*, as in

You can increase profits <u>by</u> cutting costs, <u>by</u> consolidating operations, or <u>by</u> reducing overhead.

Challenge Parallel Structure

Correct the following:

- Our litigation plan is to take the expert's deposition, request documents, and interviewing of witnesses.
- There are other factors considered by the court: the nature of the display; the source of financial support for the display; and courts may consider the duration of the display.
- Her duties are to provide records, attend meetings, and to prepare minutes.
- This is a matter not for discussion but action.
- Either Susan must plead guilty or stand for trial.
- The most important parts of your project are the beginning and the end.

4. Avoid Nominalizations

StyleLinks

www.temple.edu/writingctr/student_resources/nominalizations.htm
This site provides a brief overview of nominalizations as well as examples of and remedies for nominalizations.

A nominalization occurs when you take a verb or adjective and turn it into a noun. Although a nominalization itself is technically correct, overuse of nominalizations drains your writing of forcefulness and makes it read as if written by a bureaucrat.

Nominalizations	Examples with Verbs
The defendant made an _argument._	The defendant argued.
The court issued a _decision_ in the case.	The court decided the case.
The judge provided an _explanation_ of the order.	The judge explained the order.
We will give _consideration_ to our options.	We will consider our options.

As you can see, nominalizations not only take strong verbs and convert them into dull nouns, they also tend to add wordiness to sentences. Although not all nominalizations can be avoided, their repeated use will render your writing unimaginative.

▶ **Tip: To avoid nominalizations, use the active voice and watch for words that end in -*ion*, -*ent*, and -*ant*.**

5. Avoid Legalese

The language of the law must not be foreign to the ears of those who are to obey it.

Learned Hand, *The Spirit of Liberty* (1959)

StyleLinks

www.law.ucla.edu/volokh/legalese.htm
This site, called *Eschew, Evade, and/or Eradicate Legalese*, by Professor Eugene Volokh of UCLA, provides a thorough list of archaic and stuffy legal terms together with suggested replacements.

www.partyofthefirstpart.com/index.html
The website "The Party of the First Part" gives humorous examples of legalese along with suggestions on how to avoid legalese in your writing.

a. Introduction

Jargon is the specialized language of a profession. The type of jargon used in the legal profession is called *legalese*. Legalese displays the following features:

- Archaic words, such as *opine* and *beseech*;
- Redundancies, such as *unless and until*;
- Legal terms of art and Latin expressions, such as *collateral estoppel* and *ab initio*.

The use of legalese frustrates readers and results in incomprehensible writing. Some critics have suggested that there are two reasons legalese is used: to enhance the prestige of the writer and to keep the reader in the dark. In other instances, legalese or inflated language is used by newcomers to the profession in the mistaken belief that they need to write "like lawyers." As a number of experts have noted, however, good legal writing is simply good writing.

Confine your use of Latin to those phrases and words that are readily understood. If possible, use the English translation for the term, such as replacing *ex contractu* with *from the contract*. In other instances, Latin phrases are used as signals of well-known concepts or as terms of art, as in phrases such as *res judicata, habeas corpus,* and so forth. These terms will pose no problems for legal readers. If you are unsure whether the reader will understand a term, provide a brief definition, as in *The review board will examine the issues de novo (afresh) when it meets on Tuesday.*

Consistent with the trend toward plain English, try to avoid using legal jargon. Often archaic or jargon-filled phrases can be omitted entirely or replaced with more familiar terms.

Jargon	Revised
THIS AGREEMENT is made and entered into this fourth day of May 2008, by and between ABC Inc. (hereinafter referred to as "Landlord") and Susan Adams (hereinafter referred to as "Tenant") regarding the premises and covenants hereinafter set forth.	This Lease is entered into May 4, 2008, between ABC Inc. ("Landlord") and Susan Adams ("Tenant") regarding the following facts.

The omission or replacement of archaic words and phrases with familiar ones not only enhances readability but also results in a more concise writing.

You may not be able to omit all of the legalese you would like, particularly when drafting wills, deeds, contracts, and other legal documents that have more rigid structures. These documents are often drafted in accord with standard forms and long-standing conventions. Nevertheless, you can easily omit most legalese from correspondence with clients, internal office memos, and documents filed with courts. For example, the phrases *enclosed please find* or *enclosed herewith is* are often used in letters that enclose other documents. Although there is nothing grammatically wrong with these expressions, they are examples of legalese. If something is enclosed, won't the reader find it? Simply use the phrase *enclosed is* followed by a description of the item enclosed.

If you are using unfamiliar legal terms or Latin phrases, be sure to give a brief but unobtrusive definition for your reader. A client will be completely bewildered by a letter informing him or her that *the doctrine of laches precludes your claim.* Rewrite as follows:

The doctrine of laches (an unreasonable and prejudicial delay) precludes your claim.

Although the insertion of a definition or explanatory phrase produces a longer document, the effect of enhanced readability is well worth the extra words.

Even if a document is prepared for another legal professional who will likely be familiar with the Latin phrase or legal term, add the definition because it often serves as a smooth transition for any reader. Readers experienced with the terms will not be offended by your inclusion of an explanation and will readily skip over it. Other less experienced readers, such as a law clerk or a client receiving a copy of the writing, will be greatly assisted by the "translation" you provide.

b. Indirect Writing

One form of legalese is indirect writing. In some cases, legal professionals are reluctant to give bad news and adopt a broad, vague manner of writing. Although legal writing should not be blunt, it must be accurate, and the use of indirect language or euphemisms obscures meaning. Be direct without being insensitive or engaging in doublespeak. In the world of doublespeak, employees are never fired, they are *dehired, laid off, rightsized,* or *downsized.* There is no failure, only *incomplete success.* There are no tax increases, only *revenue enhancements.* There are no salespersons sending you spam, there are *relationship managers* delivering their *direct marketing messages.* Be wary of such indirection in others' writing, and do not use it in your own.

c. Pretentious Writing

Persons who reside and dwell in silicone-based habitats should cease and desist from hurling compact mineral material.

In other words, people who live in glass houses shouldn't throw stones. Legalese often takes the form of showy or pretentious writing meant to impress the reader. This style of elaborate writing annoys readers. Adopt a writing style that focuses on the reader's comprehension rather than showing off your vocabulary or knowledge.

Pretentious	Revised
Until such time as we promulgate the revised Employee Handbook pursuant to the decision of the company, the currently existing manual relating to and setting forth employee policies should continue to be utilized.	*Use the current Employee Handbook until the revised handbook is issued.*

Consider the following pretentious statement by a district court: "A dismissal is appropriate where the complaint is a labyrinthian prolixity of unrelated and vituperative charges that defie[s] comprehension and the amended complaint fails to cure prolixity and incomprehensibility." *Thomson v. Olson,* 866 F. Supp. 1267, 1270 (D.N.D. 1994). Strive to make sure your reading is understood.

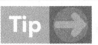 **Tip** → Curing Legalese

Consider the following suggestions to cure legalese.

Instead of This	Substitute
ab initio	from the beginning
albeit	although
antecedent to	before
apprise	inform
arguendo	for the sake of argument
assent	agree
bona fide effort	a good faith effort
case at bar	this case
case of first impression	novel question
commence	start; begin
concerning the matter of	about
contiguous to	next to
conveyance	transfer
elucidate	explain
et al.	and others (persons)
evidences (as in the document *evidences*)	shows
execute (as in *execute* the will)	sign
firstly, secondly	first, second
forthwith	now; immediately
hence	thus
herein	here; in this document
in reference to; in regard to	regarding; about
instant case	this case
inter alia	among other things
in the event that	if
I opine that	it is my opinion; I believe
pray	ask, demand, request
remainder; residue	rest
said (as in *said* document)	omit *said* or use *this*
subsequent to	after
terminate	end
to wit	namely
viz.	namely; that is to say

Tip ➡ Some Archaic Word Forms

Note that almost any word with *-forth (henceforth, forthwith), -in (therein, wherein), -at (thereat, whereat), -upon (whereupon), -as (whereas), -by (thereby, whereby), -here (herein, hereinafter)* and other similar prefixes and suffixes qualifies as legalese and should be avoided. In most instances, replacement with a modern word is easy. Thus, *thereafter* becomes *from then on,* *hereinabove* becomes *above,* and so forth.

Challenge Legalese

Rewrite the following:

- Pursuant to your request of the seventeenth of July, 2008, enclosed herewith please find the proof of service you requested.
- In the instant case, plaintiff has alleged and averred that the contractual agreement is void ab initio.
- Concerning the matter of your will, we respectfully request that you forthwith execute said will and deliver it to this office at your earliest convenience.
- We are in accord with your previous report albeit we have opined that it includes some inaccurate statements and averments.
- Classroom managers have objected to decreases in budgetary funding as well as negative advancement within their ranks.
- Many impoverished people experience food insecurity.
- I am returning herewith the settlement agreement, the same having been fully and duly executed by the plaintiff.

6. Keep Subjects and Verbs Close Together

To make sense of any sentence, a reader needs a subject and a verb. Thus, readers tend to look for these first when reading. Legal writing is known for creating huge gaps between the subject of a sentence and its verb. When too many words intervene between the subject and the verb, readers no longer remember what the sentence is about by the time they locate the verb. They are then forced to backtrack and hunt for the subject. Moreover, when subjects and verbs are placed far apart there is a greater chance that they will not agree in number.

Although you need not immediately follow every subject in every sentence with a verb, avoid large gaps between these two parts of a sentence. Statutes are especially notorious for separating subjects and verbs by long word strings.

There are two ways to remedy a large gap between a subject and a verb:

- Take the words that intervene between the subject and verb and make them into their own sentence; or
- Rewrite the sentence, moving the intervening words either to the beginning or to the end of the sentence.

Before	After
The partnership, an entity organized and existing under Missouri law and formed after the passage of the Missouri General Partnership Act, is composed of Adams, Baker, and Carr.	*The partnership is composed of Adams, Baker, and Carr. It is an entity organized and existing under Missouri law and was formed after the passage of the Missouri General Partnership Act.*

Challenge ❓ Keeping Subjects and Verbs Close

Rewrite the following:

- The lease, which included a variety of provisions for early termination as well as covenants relating to habitability, was signed on July 10, 2008.
- Mrs. Jacobs, the defendant whose deposition was taken earlier this month and whose testimony was inconsistent with that of her husband, has filed a counterclaim.

7. Use Forceful Words

Because legal writing is formal, writers often tend to adopt an emotionless, pallid tone in their writing. Although your writing should not read like a romance novel, the use of vivid and forceful words will not only keep your readers interested but also will aid in converting them to your viewpoint.

Emphasis cannot be obtained by merely underlining or italicizing words or phrases or by adding a modifier such as *very* or *hardly*. You need to select a word forceful enough to carry the meaning you desire. Avoiding nominalizations (see Section E.4 of this chapter) will produce stronger verbs. Use a thesaurus or dictionary to help you select words that are vivid and strong.

Weak	Forceful
The defendant said he knew where the witness was located.	*The defendant boasted that he knew where the witness was secreted.*
Mr. Fowell misrepresented the condition of the premises.	*Mr. Fowell lied about the condition of the premises.*
very sad	*sorrowful*

Weak	Forceful
not allowed	*forbidden, prohibited*
disagree with	*contradict*
acknowledge guilt	*confess*
could not believe	*was incredulous*
withdraw a statement	*recant*
material misrepresentation of fact	*lie*

Conversely, do not take a concrete word, which is strong in and of itself, and dilute it, such as by converting *improbable* to *somewhat unlikely* or *rapid* to *very fast*. Note that some words stand on their own and cannot be limited, such as *unique*, which means the only one of its kind. Something cannot be *quite unique* or *rather unique*.

8. Repeat Strong Words and Phrases

Although you want to avoid redundancy in legal writing, there are certain strategies in which repetition can add emphasis to your writing. The repetition of a key word or phrase creates interest and adds drama to writing. Review Sir Winston Churchill's speech about Dunkirk in Section D.1 of this chapter for an especially compelling example of the effective use of repetition. Consider also the following statement:

> The defendant misled the plaintiff. He misled her by promising the premises were quiet. He misled her by promising the premises were habitable. He misled her by promising the premises were safe.

Each repetition of the words *misled* and *promising* builds on the previous reference. When you use this technique, be sure to structure the sentence so you end with the strongest element, as in the following example:

> She was a diligent worker. She was a loyal friend. She was a loving mother.

9. Vary the Length of Sentences

Short sentences are easier to understand than long, complex sentences. Nevertheless, you do not want a project filled with sentences of approximately the same length. Such a writing would be tedious to read.

Just as you may occasionally want to vary the pattern of your sentences from the standard sentence order (subject-verb-object) to add interest, vary the length of your sentences to enhance readability. For example, a short sentence such as *He accepted* is concise and powerful. Generally, sentences that exceed three lines are too long for most readers. On the other hand, you do not want a writing filled only with short sentences. Such a project would have a choppy and abrupt tone and would read like a telegram.

Choppy Sentence	Revised
The landlord sent her the rent statement. She refused to pay. He sued her for the back rent. A jury trial was held. The jury ruled for the tenant.	*The landlord sent her the rent statement. She refused to pay and was sued by the landlord for the back rent. A jury trial was held, and the jury ruled for the tenant.*

10. Use Effective Transitions

StyleLinks

www.unc.edu/depts/wcweb/handouts/transitions.html
The Writing Center of the University of North Carolina offers excellent information on the use of transitional expressions.

http://owl.english.purdue.edu/owl/resources/574/01
The Online Writing Lab at Purdue University offers a useful list of common transitional words and expressions.

To move smoothly from one sentence, paragraph, or idea to another, use a transition word or phrase. Without transitions, sentences and paragraphs would be isolated and would lack links to each other. Transitions connect what you have said with what will follow and lend cohesiveness to your document.

Transitions can appear within sentences, between paragraphs, and between sections of a document. Transitions within sentences tend to be single words, such as *however* and *although*. Transitions between paragraphs show the logical relationship of one paragraph to another. These transitions may be words, phrases, or sentences. For example, a paragraph that begins with the phrase *In contrast* tells the reader that the paragraph to follow is different from the preceding paragraph. Make sure that each paragraph is logically tied to the one before it and the one after it. Transitions also help readers anticipate information. Thus, the sentence *There are two tests to determine insolvency* sets the stage for analysis and discussion of the two tests.

Most writers tend to rely on the same transition words. Two of the favorites are *however* and *therefore*. If you find yourself continually introducing sentences and paragraphs with the same words, examine your project and try to find other transitions to lend variety and interest to your writing.

If readers or instructors note that your writing seems abrupt or choppy or if they question how your ideas or sections are related, these are signals that you may need to work on your transitions.

See Figure 4-1 for some effective transitions.

11. Avoid Shifts in Tense

The basic tense of a verb can be past, present, or future, as in *I wrote the brief, I write the brief*, and *I will write the brief*. One of the most jarring faults in legal writing is an improper shift in tense. When a discussion begins in one tense and abruptly shifts without reason to another, readers are confused. Generally, the verb form in the first phrase or sentence establishes the tense for the rest of the phrase or sentences in a paragraph. The tenses of verbs should shift only when they reflect actual changes in time as in *After I write the brief I will file it with the court.*

Figure 4-1	Common Transition Words and Phrases		
To Introduce	**To Show Contrast**	**To Show Similarity**	**To Restate**
in general	although	equally important	in other words
initially	but	in the same way	more simply put
primarily	conversely	just as	to clarify
to	however	likewise	
	in contrast	similarly	
	nevertheless		
	on the contrary		
	on the other hand		
	yet		
To Emphasize	**To Show Additions**	**To Show Examples**	**To Show Sequence**
certainly	additionally	for example	first, second,
definitely	again	for instance	third, etc.
indeed	also	in fact	following this
in fact	besides	namely	next
undeniably	furthermore	specifically	previously
	in addition	that is	subsequently
	moreover	to illustrate	then
To Summarize	**To Show Conclusions**		
finally	accordingly		
in brief	as a result		
in conclusion	because		
in summary	consequently		
to conclude	inasmuch as		
to summarize	therefore		
	thus		

Challenge Transition Words

Rewrite the following to make them smoother:

- The corporation held its annual meeting. First, proxies were tabulated. Then votes were cast. Three directors were elected. They were elected by a plurality of votes. The shareholders then voted to adjourn the meeting. The next meeting will be held in May.
- Copyright protects many types of works. Some of these works are literary, musical, and artistic works. For example, poems, songs, and paintings are protected. No copyright notice is needed for protection of a work. The work is protected from the time of its creation. Infringement of a copyrighted work may give rise to damages. An action for infringement may be brought in federal court.

Incorrect Tense Shift:	*The court <u>held</u> that corporate promoters are liable unless they are expressly released from lease obligations. The court also <u>analyzes</u> the personal liability of promoters as joint venturers.*
Consistent Tense:	*The court <u>held</u> that corporate promoters are liable unless they are expressly released from lease obligations. The court also <u>analyzed</u> the personal liability of promoters as joint venturers.*
Correct Tense Shift:	*The promoter <u>has argued</u> that he should be released from the lease agreement. Plaintiff <u>will show</u> that this argument is not supported by Ohio law.*

There are three basic rules for using tense in legal writing:

☐ **Rule One: Use the past tense to describe events that occurred in the past.**

When discussing events that occurred in the past, use the past tense. Shift from this only when facts are developing or may occur in the future.

Correct Example: *A corporation <u>issued</u> a type of stock that <u>had</u> only the right to vote and no right to dividends. The owners of the stock <u>brought</u> a class action and <u>alleged</u> that the stock <u>deprived</u> them of an economic interest of ownership and <u>was</u> therefore invalid.*

☐ **Rule Two: Use the past tense to describe what a court did in a case.**

When discussing published case law, discuss the facts of the case, its procedural background, and the court's reasoning in the past tense.

Correct Example: *In <u>Stroh v. Blackhawk Holding Co.,</u> 272 N.E.2d 1 (Ill. 1971), the lower court <u>held</u> that the class of stock was valid. The case <u>was appealed</u> to the Illinois Supreme Court, which <u>affirmed</u> the lower court's decision. The court <u>analyzed</u> the Illinois statutes and the articles of incorporation and <u>concluded</u> that both <u>allowed</u> the corporation to deny dividend rights so long as voting rights <u>were</u> not limited or denied.*

☐ **Rule Three: Use the present tense when discussing current legal rules and principles, whether they are found in statutes, cases, or other legal authorities.**

Correct Example: *Illinois statutes and the articles of incorporation <u>allow</u> stock to be divided into classes with various preferences so long as voting rights <u>are</u> not prohibited.*

Challenge   Shifts in Verb Tense

Rewrite the following:

- In that case, the court upheld the lower court's determination that the scene endorsed a message that is secular.
- Vice-President Diaz mentioned the board's previous decision to award bonuses to employees and comments that any further compensation is unwarranted.
- The defendant assaults the victim, who died as a result of the attack.
- Identifying the documents was straightforward. Most are authored by the employee, leaving only a few that were authored by the employer.

F. Conciseness

Vigorous writing is concise.

William Strunk Jr., *The Elements of Style* (1918)

StyleLinks

http://owl.english.purdue.edu/handouts/general/gl_concise.html
Purdue University's Online Writing Lab offers excellent information and exercises on writing concisely.

http://grammar.ccc.commnet.edu/grammar/concise.htm
This *Guide to Grammar & Writing* provides a thorough review of methods to achieve conciseness in writing as well as a variety of quizzes.

www.bartleby.com
Select "Strunk's Elements of Style" Section II.13 for tips on omitting needless words.

1. Introduction

The length of a project does not necessarily indicate its quality. Some of the most compelling and well-known writings are the briefest. For example, the Gettysburg Address has 286 words; yet, just one federal statute relating to Medicare has more than 700 words.

Although almost all writers agree in principle that conciseness (being brief but meaningful) is an admirable goal in legal writing, conciseness is not easily accomplished. Many of us have difficulty abandoning our own words. Moreover, the topics discussed in legal documents are often complex, requiring thoughtful analysis. Finally, over-review of a document causes increased length. Each professional who works on a project will feel a need to improve a writing, generally by adding to it, changing *now* to *at the present time* and *if* to *in the event that*. Documents also grow in length because of the ease of word processing, which allows legal writers to take a previously drafted document and continually tinker with it, adding extra words and sections with a click of a keystroke.

Although judges complain about lawyers' inability to write succinctly, some writing experts suggest that judges themselves contribute to the mass of legal publication by writing longer opinions, with more footnotes, and more separate opinions.

Some of the writing strategies previously discussed will help achieve conciseness. Recall that using active voice and eliminating nominalizations will produce a more concise project.

Be merciless. Your reader's time is at a premium, and you cannot afford to frustrate the reader with redundancy and long-winded phrases. Additionally, more and more courts are imposing page limits and word count limits for submissions. Documents that exceed the stated requirements are rejected. Thus, failure to be brief may be legal malpractice.

2. Omit Needless Words

There are numerous phrases in English that we use simply by habit. Many of these can be eliminated or reduced to a more concise word or phrase. Careful writing and revising will help you eliminate extra words. Ask yourself if you absolutely need a phrase and whether there is an effective substitute for it. Many commonly used possessives can be replaced by single words with no loss of meaning. For example, use apostrophes rather than prepositions for some expressions, as in *plaintiff's allegations* rather than *allegations of the plaintiff*. In particular, avoid constructions that include more than one preposition, such as *in regard to*. Use *regarding*. See Figure 4-2 for examples of wordy phrases.

Figure 4-2   Some Wordy Phrases

Long-Winded Phrases	Substitutions
after the conclusion of	after
all of	all
any and all	any *or* all
as a result of	consequently, therefore
as to whether	when
at such time as	now
at the present time	whether
despite the fact that	because
due to the fact that	although
for the purpose of	for, to
in accordance with	by, under
in addition to	additionally
in connection with	about, regarding
in order to	if
in the event that	to
it is often the case that	often, frequently
prior to	before
pursuant to	under, according
subsequent to	after
whether or not	whether
with reference to *or* with regard to	regarding, concerning
with the exception of	except

The word *the* is often needed and cannot be omitted. For example, write *The trademark owner licensed the mark to the company* rather than *Trademark owner licensed the mark to company*. Eliminating *the* results in a choppy, telegram-like tone.

▶ **Tip: Watch for phrases including both the and of, as in the amount of or the case of. In many instances, the entire phrase can be deleted.**

Empty Words	Revision
The plaintiff was awarded damages *in the amount* of $50,000.	The plaintiff was awarded damages of $50,000.

▶ **Tip: To reduce sentence length, consider using citations by themselves rather than in introductory phrases, such as the court held . . . .**

Wordy	Revision
The California Supreme Court held in *Allen v. Carr*, 909 P.2d 14, 16 (Cal. 1990), that landlords must give written notice to tenants before evicting them.	Landlords must give written notice to tenants before evicting them. *Allen v. Carr*, 909 P.2d 14, 16 (Cal. 1990).

3. Avoid "Throat-Clearing" Introductions

"Throat-clearing" refers to introductions that are mere preludes for the main topic to follow. Writers often feel compelled to warm up readers by preparing them for the main idea rather than simply presenting the idea.

Throat-Clearing Phrases	Substitutions
In this regard it is important to recall that . . .	Recall, remember
The first issue to be considered is . . .	First
Attention should also be called to the fact that . . .	[none—state the fact]
It is interesting to note that . . .	Note
The fact of the matter is that . . .	[none—state the fact]

Other overused introductory words are *clearly* and *obviously*. Writers often add *clearly* before introducing a conclusion, believing that this word will lend persuasive force. To paraphrase a famous jurist, adding the word *clearly* to a sentence won't make it clear; and if the sentence is clear, you don't need the word *clearly*.

The word *obviously* should be avoided for the same reason as *clearly*. Moreover, *obviously* carries a hostile meaning. By introducing a sentence or topic with *obviously* you signal to readers that you believe they lack the capacity to understand the meaning of the sentence on their own.

4. Avoid Redundancy

A common criticism of legal writing is that those in the legal profession are enamored of redundancy. They cannot merely say *null*. They must say *null and void and of no legal force or effect*. Is all this needed? If something is null, isn't it void? If it is void, can it have legal effect?

The reason legal writing is so prone to word doubling (and tripling) lies in the history of our language. English has its roots in Latin and French as well as in the language of the Celts and the Anglo-Saxons. Often word pairings were used to ensure that readers would understand phrases regardless of their background or station in life. Thus, the French word *peace* joined with the Latin word *quiet*. These redundant doublings have persisted long after their need. Their use today is often the result of habit rather than necessity.

If you find yourself using these "stock" redundancies, stop and ask whether one word is sufficient. Make sure that each word in a writing performs a function.

Some word pairs are more than redundant; they are unintentionally silly. Consider the following:

> basic fundamentals
> close proximity
> cooperate together
> current status
> final result
> past history
> personal opinion
> previous experience
> small in size
> vitally necessary

Common Redundancies

acknowledge and agree	give, devise, and bequeath
alter, change, or modify	grant and convey
buy or purchase	keep and maintain
cease and desist	made and entered into
consented and agreed	null and void and of no legal effect
covenant, warrant, and represent	order and direct
due and owing	own or possess
each and every	refuse and fail
false and untrue	release, remise, and discharge
force or effect	right, title, and interest
free and clear	terms and conditions
full and complete	true and correct
	unless and until

Challenge Conciseness

Select a more concise word or phrase for the following:

- In the above-referenced matter
- Completely unanimous
- We are in receipt of
- Situated in the vicinity of
- Aware of the fact that
- Institute
- In excess of
- Advance planning
- Future plans
- Postpone until later
- For the duration of
- In the event that

Rewrite the following:

Minutes of Board of Directors' Meeting

The Board of Directors of ABC Inc. (the "Corporation") held a meeting on July 1, 2008, at twelve noon. The purpose of holding the meeting was to discuss and consider extending the employment contracts and agreements of Thomas Simmons ("Simmons") and Kara Andrews ("Andrews").

The Board is cognizant of the fact that Simmons and Andrews have fulfilled and effectuated all of the terms and conditions of their agreements. In addition to the foregoing, the employees have demonstrated commitment and devotion to the Corporation and its goals, purposes, and vision.

After due discussion and consideration, it was the consensus of opinion of the Board that the employment agreements for Simmons and Andrews should be extended for a duration of two years. Vice-President Beth Harris shall commence preparation of the respective extensions of the employment contracts and give and submit them to the Board upon their final completion for approval by the Board of Directors.

The President of the Corporation then announced that he would summarize briefly the Corporation's financial performance during the course of the past calendar quarter. The President announced that there is no doubt but that the Corporation's performance has met and exceeded all financial and monetary expectations. This success is attributable to the commencement of the Corporation's newly implemented computer accounting systems. Subsequent to the implementation of this system, the Corporation experienced demonstrable and significant cost savings. Subsequent to the presentation of this report, the President announced an adjournment of the meeting.

5. Avoid Repetition

Once you have stated your contention or communicated the information you need to communicate, stop. Many writers believe they should make every point three times by telling the reader what the project will say, saying it, and then reminding the reader of what was said.

There is no place in legal writing for such needless repetition. The only exception to the rule of avoiding repeating your argument is that in a long document, readers often appreciate a separate conclusion, which briefly and concisely summarizes the analysis.

Tips ➡ To Achieve Conciseness

- Use active voice.

  Passive: The case was decided by the jury.

  Revised: The jury decided the case.

- Change nominalization to verbs.

  Nominalization: The attorney made an objection to the question.

  Revised: The attorney objected to the question.

- Change unneeded *that*, *which*, and *who* clauses into phrases.

  Wordy: The brief, which was recently filed . . .

  Revised: The recently filed brief . . .

  Wordy: The attorney who is representing the plaintiff . . .

  Revised: The plaintiff's attorney . . .

- Watch sentences beginning with *It is*, *There is*, or *There are*. These introductory phrases can often be eliminated.

  Wordy: It is the judge who issues the order.

  Revised: The judge issues the order.

  Wordy: There are three elements that must be proved.

  Revised: Three elements must be proved.

- Sometimes the word *that* is necessary. Let clarity guide you. For example, *He knew her testimony was scheduled* is as clear as *He knew that her testimony was scheduled*. On the other hand, consider the sentence *The judge stated on Friday the case would be dismissed*. A *that* is needed for clarity, as in *The judge stated that on Friday the case would be dismissed* or *The judge stated on Friday that the case would be dismissed*.

> Writing is an exploration. You start
> from nothing and learn as you go.
> E.L. Doctorow

chapter 5

Organization and the Writing Process

StyleLinks

http://writingcenter.tamu.edu/content/category/12/46/77
Texas A & M University offers a variety of handouts on getting started, freewriting, and the writing process.

www.writing.ku.edu/students/guides.shtml
The University of Kansas offers several writing guides with information on prewriting steps and outlines.

http://owl.english.purdue.edu/handouts/index2.html#pwrg
Purdue University's Online Writing Lab offers strategies on coping with writing anxiety, tips for starting writing, and tips for developing outlines.

http://grammar.ccc.commnet.edu/grammar
Select "Freewriting," "Outlining," or "Clustering" for information and examples of writing outlines and organizational techniques.

www.alanmacfarlane.com/savage/typewriter.pdf
Author Alan MacFarlane provides an essay on writing methods with thoughts on writing in longhand, typing, and freewriting.

A. Introduction

A writing project must be well organized so that its reader can quickly find the information needed. Readers who are bombarded with a jumble of thoughts and impressions will often abandon a project. Thus, every writing project needs a coherent structure. There are a number of outlining techniques you can use to achieve internal organization.

Once you have decided on a basic plan for the entire project, you can then focus on its major sections, the beginning, middle, and end, and then consider where to place information that should be emphasized and information that should be minimized.

Finally, some methods of writing are faster and more efficient than others, and some techniques writers engage in during the writing process, such as micro-editing, are often time wasters.

B. Order and Internal Organization

1. Outlines

Just as you would never begin a car trip to a far-off destination without a road map, you should never begin a writing project without some idea of how to approach it. A project that is poorly organized not only fails to inform or persuade the reader, it may so frustrate the reader that it will not be read.

The best system for organizing a writing is to use an outline. Although the most complete outline includes full sentences or topics divided into headings and subheadings, an outline need not be so formal. The looseleaf notebook containing the notes you took while researching or the index cards containing notes of your research results are working outlines. By shuffling the index cards or the pages in your notebook, you are outlining, that is, organizing your approach to your writing. Some word processing programs include software for outlining and taking notes. Take your laptop to the library so your note taking is speedy.

It is not the format of the outline that is important; the mere existence of any type of outline forces you to consider and organize the structure of your writing. The outline should disclose the basic sections of your project and the order in which they will be addressed.

Following are some common methods of outlining that do not involve a formal outline (one with Roman numbers, formal headings, and so forth). Preparing an outline will not only help you achieve order in your writing but also serve as an effective prewriting technique to break writer's block.

a. Brainstorming and Freewriting

If the notes taken during research are not helpful in preparing an outline, simply jot down on paper in list form all the words and phrases you can think of that relate to your project. Keep writing and listing the entries; do not worry about organizing these entries yet. This outlining technique is usually called *brainstorming*, and it is similar to word association. After you have finished listing every topic you can think of, carefully examine the list and then group related items together. After you have settled on these rough groupings, decide the order in which the groups should be discussed, and then assign a label or title to each group. Writers often discover that their list provides ideas for the structure of the project. Keep your list handy as you write your first draft; you may discover other ideas that should be included in the project.

Somewhat similar to brainstorming is *freewriting*, a technique that is usually used to break writer's block. Freewriting involves setting a timer and writing or typing as fast as you can for ten to fifteen minutes. Do not worry about spelling, grammar, or usage. Just write sentence after sentence about your project without stopping. This nonstop writing will prevent you from editing your thoughts and rejecting ideas. Examine your freewriting sample to see if you gain any insight about how to organize your project.

b. Clustering and Tree Diagrams

Clustering is a visual method of outlining that enables writers to see the relationships among parts of a project. Place a circle or "nucleus" in the middle of a blank page of paper. Place the key word or topic of your project (for example, *statute of limitations*) in the nucleus. Now write a related topic or issue nearby. Encircle it and draw a line back to your nucleus. Continue by either branching out from the nucleus or the new circle. Trust your instincts to select new words and topics and continue linking new ideas to older ones. The final product should look like a spider web. Another similar visual approach is to use a "tree diagram" with the most important idea placed at the left margin and ideas and details becoming more specific as the branches extend outward to the right. Cluster and tree diagram outlines are nonlinear approaches to outlining and are visual methods that are attractive to many writers. In many instances, writers can tell by quickly glancing at their cluster or tree that certain sections and ideas are underdeveloped and need additional analysis.

c. Story Telling

Talk to a friend or colleague about your project. Pretend you are being interviewed. Start at the beginning by saying, "I am preparing a motion for change of venue. The facts of the case are . . . . " As you "tell the story" of your project, some organizational patterns should emerge. Don't censor yourself, and allow yourself to ramble a bit. Keep a notepad nearby, and write down ideas as you are speaking. Your notes are then a preliminary outline. Consider challenging yourself to tell the story of your project in three to five sentences. Because most of us are more comfortable talking than writing, talking it out is a good strategy for many projects.

d. Percolating

Try to allow some "down time" before you begin writing so that ideas percolate and bubble up to the surface. Nearly all writers have experienced an "a-ha" moment while showering or driving that gives them a great idea for a project. Keep your notepad handy so you can capture these ideas.

e. Reverse Outlining

One organizing technique recommended by many experts is reverse outlining, which involves creating an outline of what you have already written (rather than creating an outline before you write). A reverse outline allows you to review your organization and your content. To reverse outline, take your first draft and in the margin next to each paragraph (or on a separate sheet of paper) make notes about the main point of each paragraph. Use only a word or brief phrase. Then examine your list of topics, which is now an outline of your project. For example, your reverse outline for one section of a project may look like the following:

Paragraph 1:   Introduction to Business Judgment Rule

Paragraph 2:   Purpose of Business Judgment Rule

Paragraph 3:   Discussion of Facts of Case

Paragraph 4:   Examples of Directors' Breaches of Duty, Reliance on Experts, Defenses

Paragraph 5:   History and Purpose of Business Judgment Rule

Paragraph 6:   Application of Business Judgment Rule

Paragraph 7:   Conclusion

Review your outline and note any repetitious paragraphs or paragraphs that are out of sequence. For example, in the outline just shown, the information in Paragraph 5 should likely be omitted or combined with the information in either Paragraph 1 or 2. Similarly, Paragraph 4 seems to have too many topics, suggesting that this paragraph should be broken up into at least two or possibly three paragraphs. If you have trouble summing up a paragraph in a single word or brief phrase, this is likely a signal that the paragraph contains too many unrelated ideas. In contrast, if you have difficulty finding any word or phrase to summarize your paragraph, this is likely a signal that your paragraph has no unifying theme or point. Perhaps the entire paragraph can be omitted. Consider whether each paragraph leads logically into the next and whether your paragraphs are in the right order.

After you revise and edit your reverse outline, return to your project and ask yourself the following critical question: Does each paragraph support the main thrust of my argument? In other words, does each paragraph support my thesis statement? (See Section 3.b below and Chapter 7 for discussion of thesis statements.) Make sure you have proven what you have promised the reader.

2. The Paper Chase: Using the Legal Authorities

In many instances, by the time you are ready to write, you have reams of paper. You have photocopies or printouts of pertinent statutes, cases, law review articles, and other legal authorities. Using these materials in a planned fashion will bring coherence to your project. You might use colored sticky notes and assign a color to each section of your project. For example, if you intend to discuss elements of a contract first and breach of the contract second, flag all the cases, statutes, and other documents that deal with elements of a contract with a yellow sticky note and all the documents that discuss breach of contract with an orange sticky note, and so forth. Colored marker pens can be used the same way to highlight favorable and unfavorable authorities.

This is similar to the U.S. Supreme Court rules requiring different types of briefs to have different color covers (for example, light blue for briefs on the merits for petitioners and light red for briefs in response to these). The briefs are then instantly recognizable to the Justices. If you use colored sticky notes or flags, as you begin writing you will have an instant visual outline, making it easy for you to group related arguments together. Consider using sticky notes or flags that convey conventional messages: green for authorities that support your position, red for authorities that are contrary to your position, and yellow for authorities that you haven't yet decided to include. Similarly, within each authority you can use different colored highlighters to mark sections that correspond with parts of your argument. Don't censor yourself: Record your impressions and rank the authorities by marking documents and cases with grades of A, B, C, D, and F to indicate their level of helpfulness. When taking notes, indicate whether the material is a quotation or is paraphrased and indicate the complete citation(s). This investment of time will pay off later when you write your document.

3. An Overview of Most Writing Projects

Although letters to clients differ vastly from documents submitted to courts and although each particular type of legal writing is discussed in Section Three of this text, there are some elements and strategies common to all legal documents.

a. Introductory Section

All documents start with some form of introductory section. The beginning section of any project is important because it sets the tone for the project. This section also sets the stage for the information to follow. Almost all documents begin with a review of the facts on which the document is based. Discuss past facts in the past tense unless they are still developing. Most introductions formulate the central issue that the project will analyze. Present general information and define any terms that will appear later in the document. Because readers are impatient to get to the bottom line, consider putting the most important information first. The SEC's *Plain English Handbook* notes that it is hard for readers to understand details unless they have first been given the big picture and compares an introductory section to working on a jigsaw puzzle: It is nearly impossible to put together a jigsaw puzzle without first seeing a picture of the completed puzzle. Thus, individual pieces of information are more helpful to readers if the readers understand how the pieces fit into the overall project. It is possible that the introductory section will be dictated by the nature of the document. For example, most opinion letters start with a recitation of the facts on which they are based. Many court documents begin with a preliminary or threshold issue the court must resolve before other issues can be addressed. In any event, remember that there should be no information introduced in this section that is not later analyzed and discussed.

b. Middle Sections and Paragraphs

(1) Some General Thoughts. Use paragraphs to break up a discussion into units that are easy to read. Group related information together to identify and eliminate repetitious information. Readers will expect that each of your paragraphs relates to one distinct idea and will also expect that the first sentence of your paragraph will indicate what will follow. This signaling type of sentence is usually called the topic sentence. The sentences that follow should be logically connected to each other. In a sense, each paragraph is a mini-project because most paragraphs will begin with a topic sentence, explore and analyze the idea introduced by the topic sentence, and then wrap up. You can see that such an approach is a mirror image of any project, with its beginning, middle, and end. Readers should be able to read the topic sentence in each paragraph and understand the thrust of the paragraph. Some readers may read only the first sentence of each paragraph. Your project should be written such that these first sentences, read alone, carry the reader through the project.

Each section of your project should include a thesis statement, an assertive sentence or two that provides a framework for the discussion to follow and states the main point you are making. All sentences that follow elaborate the point you made in your thesis statement and flow from it. Review each paragraph to ensure that every sentence in the paragraph falls under the umbrella of your thesis statement. (See Figure 7-1 for more information on drafting thesis statements.)

(2) Paragraph Length. Avoid paragraphs that are too long. How long is too long? Most readers have difficulty with paragraphs that cover more than half a page. Not only does the mind crave a break from a long discussion, so does the eye. Remember the visual effect of your writing and create a document that is pleasing to the eye. If your project contains several paragraphs that are more than half a page, find a place to break the information into shorter paragraphs. Although most writers have been taught that every paragraph needs at least three sentences, don't adopt such a rigid and formulaic approach to your writing. Let the subject matter guide you. Too many short paragraphs will look choppy and incomplete, but on occasion you may want to use a one- or two-sentence paragraph for emphasis and visual effect.

(3) Moving Between Ideas. To move smoothly from one sentence, paragraph, or idea to another, use a transition word, phrase, or sentence. Without transitions, ideas would appear unconnected, and there would be a telegram-like appearance and sound to the writing. Transitions connect what you have said with what will follow and lead readers logically from one idea to the next. Review the material on transition words and expressions in Section E.10 of Chapter 4 and use some variety in your transitional expressions. Word patterns such as *first, second,* and so forth also serve to link ideas. Review each paragraph of your project. In the margin of your draft, summarize in a word or key phrase the topic of the paragraph. Then review only these words or phrases to ensure that the development of your argument or project is logical and that each paragraph leads smoothly into the next. Do not end a paragraph with a mere restatement of your topic sentence. For example, if your paragraph begins *Sexual harassment in the workplace is prohibited under 42 U.S.C. § 2000e (2000),* the last sentence should not read *Therefore, as stated earlier, such sexual harassment is prohibited under 42 U.S.C. § 2000e (2000).* A better conclusion would read *Therefore, because Defendant's conduct was unwelcome to the Plaintiff and created a hostile work environment, 42 U.S.C. § 2000(e) has been violated.*

c. Conclusions

Some documents, such as court briefs, call for formal conclusions, whereas others, such as letters, end with traditional "call me if you have any questions" sentences. If your document includes a formal conclusion, review it for two possible defects: Make sure that it does not introduce any information or idea that has not been previously discussed, and make sure that it doesn't simply repeat the central issue you formulated in the introduction. Leave the reader with a strong impression.

 Tip → # Don't Begin at the Beginning

If you have difficulty writing your introductory paragraphs in a project, save them until the end. On many occasions, you will not have a clear idea what your project will say until you have finished writing it. At that time you may be better able to write an effective thesis statement or introductory section.

---

4. Using Position and Voice for Emphasis

In nearly every persuasive writing project, for example, briefs submitted to a court, there are stronger points and then points writers wish they did not have to mention. Use the location or placement of the information as well as voice to draw your reader's attention to the more compelling parts of your argument and to minimize the effect of "negative" or weak sections of your project. There are four strategies to follow:

a. Start and End Strong

The most prominent parts of a writing are its beginning and its ending. Readers tend to begin projects with enthusiasm, lose interest in the middle, and then become more attentive again when the end is in sight. Therefore, put your strongest arguments and information at the beginning and ending of your projects, your paragraphs, and your sentences.

b. Bury Negative Information

Address negative or weak spots in the middle of your project, in the middle of your paragraphs, and in the middle of your sentences. These locations attract the least attention and may even be overlooked. Be very careful when including these unfavorable portions of your writing because a careless spelling error or typo will immediately draw your reader's attention. Remember that the persuasive writing style used in briefs differs from the objective style used in legal memoranda. As is discussed in Chapter 7, in such objective projects, the writer must disclose possible weaknesses in the case. Consequently, in these writings, you will not bury negative information but will give it as much emphasis as positive information.

c. Use Passive Voice

Because active voice is much stronger and more forceful than passive voice, consider using passive voice in discussing information you wish to minimize. Review the following two sentences:

> **Active Voice:**   *The defendant intentionally sold a house with known defects to the plaintiff.*
>
> **Passive Voice:**   *The house was sold to the plaintiff.*

You can readily see that the plaintiff would prefer the first version whereas the defendant would prefer the second. By using the passive voice you deflect attention away from the actor (the defendant) and onto the object of the action (the sale of the house). Note how the use of the passive voice in the second sentence eliminates any reference whatsoever to the defendant.

d. Avoid Forceful Language

The techniques described in Section E.7 of Chapter 4 for making writing vivid, such as selecting descriptive and concrete words and avoiding nominalizations, should not be used when discussing negative information. Although providing detail is helpful in describing favorable facts and issues, consider discussing unfavorable facts and issues in a more general fashion.

5. Avoid Micro-Editing During the Drafting Stage

No matter what kind of document you draft, consider the following strategy: Avoid micro-editing during the writing process. Agonizing over the choice of each word and continually rephrasing sentences may be a waste of time and energy if you later decide to omit a section. Do not interpret this suggestion to mean that no revisions should be done during the writing process. It is both helpful and necessary to revise throughout the writing process. Do not, however, write your initial draft expecting that it will be the same as the final version. Insert reminders to yourself in the draft, such as "work on this" or "revise," to remind you that further work needs to be done in a certain section. When writing, if you cannot decide between two ways of expressing an idea, include them both and decide later which version to keep.

Challenge ❓ Position and Voice

Rewrite the following for the defendant:

- The defendant failed to approve the figures as he was contractually required to do.
- The defendant attacked the plaintiff.
- Although corporate profits permit, the defendant corporation has not declared a dividend in two years.
- In violation of the employment agreement, the defendant employer has failed to pay sales commissions to the plaintiff.
- The defendant doctor negligently operated on the plaintiff.

C. Methods of Writing

There are three primary methods used for the actual writing process: writing by hand, dictating, and writing on a word processor. Each offers some advantages.

1. Writing by Hand

Many writers are comfortable writing in longhand. As you would expect, writing in longhand is the most time-consuming method of writing. Despite this, projects written in longhand often need less revising than projects dictated or composed on a word processor. Some experts believe that the neurological process that directs thought, through fingers, is highly sophisticated and that those who write in longhand learn to express their thoughts clearly and completely. Some writers use a combination of techniques and write delicate or complex sections in longhand so they can test for tone and accuracy and then compose other parts of the project on a word processor.

2. Dictating

Using a dictation machine is a very speedy method of writing. It can take some time, however, to shed self-consciousness when you dictate. Consider using a mini-outline when you first begin to dictate and follow it as you dictate. With time and practice, you will acquire skill at dictating together with a certain mental discipline enabling you rapidly and effectively to organize your thoughts. This skill in orally expressing complex thoughts may translate into ease and confidence in public speaking as well. Enhanced competence in oral presentation is one of the hidden benefits of dictating.

If you dictate, you will need to insert punctuation and paragraphing so the transcriber knows how to prepare the document. Similarly, you will need to spell certain words.

The popularity of dictating in law practice has waned significantly in recent years as writers have become more familiar with composing using a word processor. Nevertheless, dictating remains an effective and efficient way to draft for many writers.

3. Using a Word Processor

The most popular method of writing today is composing using a word processor. Although this method is very speedy and allows considerable flexibility in changing the placement of sections, writers tend to spend excessive time revising as they go along. Your project need not be perfect with the first draft. Your initial draft should focus on including the major issues and arguments that need to be addressed. Resist the temptation to engage in small-scale editing as you draft on a word processor. Allow your first draft to flow smoothly, and then devote effort to revision later.

If you use a word processor, consider the following:

- Save your versions frequently. Save every five to ten minutes. Most computers have functions that allow you to select how frequently the document will be saved.
- To ensure that you don't lose important information, back up your versions on disks, frequently print paper copies of the document in case the disk is corrupted, and email your document to your personal email account or to a friend for safekeeping.
- Use the features of your word processor to help you. Consider using the "track changes" feature to show changes between drafts. With a single keystroke, you can then accept (or reject) all changes. This feature, called *redlining*, is used when legal professionals negotiate the form and content of a document because it allows each to see at a glance the changes made by the other.
- Recognize that viewing the project one screen at a time allows you to see only a "slice" of the document. Thus, headings and other items may become inconsistent. You will need to review a hard copy of your project to check for consistency in the presentation of such items.

Tips → For Getting Started

A writer keeps surprising himself . . . he doesn't know what he is saying until he sees it on the page.

Thomas Williams

For some writers, getting started is the most difficult part of a project. Consider the following strategies to break writer's block:

- **Write Something.** Write anything. Just get started. Don't assume you have to start with the beginning. Begin with the part of the project with which you are most comfortable, whether it is the statement of facts, the part of the project that is the strongest, or the conclusion. The mere act of writing any section of the project will jar a writer's block. Consider freewriting, as discussed in Section B.1 of this chapter.
- **Start with the Easiest Task.** If the project has several elements, start with the easiest portion, even if it is merely photocopying the exhibits, checking citation form, or preparing the table of authorities. At least you will have made some progress.
- **Tell a Story.** Just as story telling is a good organization technique, it is a good technique for getting started. Speak about the project to a friend or colleague (or close your office door and pretend to do so). This may suggest ideas on how to begin writing.
- **Set Goals.** Tell yourself that the statement of facts must be completed by noon. Challenge yourself to complete a certain task within one hour. Make sure the goals are reasonable, however, so that you don't set yourself up for disappointment.
- **Bargain with Yourself.** Consider making a bargain with yourself that you will work for only ten minutes on the project. Work as hard as you can, and at the end of ten minutes, give yourself permission to quit. You may well find that you've created some momentum, and you may decide to work a bit longer, making a bigger dent in your project.
- **Go Public.** Announce a "drop dead" date to a supervisor by saying, "This will be on your desk by Tuesday." You will now be committed to a deadline.
- **Keep Going.** If you draw a blank, just keep going. Move to another section and come back to the difficult spot later. If you think of two alternative ways of phrasing things, write them both, and remove one later. Mark these sections with sticky notes if writing in longhand and with "xx" or some other signal if you are word processing. You can use the "find and replace" feature to locate these troublesome passages later. Don't worry about getting it perfect; just get it done.

(continued)

Tips ➡ For Getting Started

- **Minimize Disruptions.** Work in a place conducive to working. Put your calls on hold, close your office door, move to the library, and avoid email. If you are disrupted, leave a sticky note on your computer screen to remind yourself what you wanted to next address, or type a quick line into the draft about what you expect to do next.
- **Avoid Self-Censoring.** One of the biggest stumbling blocks to writing is that writers become so self-conscious they cannot go forward. Don't worry at this stage that something will sound awkward, unsophisticated, or silly. Similarly, don't worry about spelling and grammar, and so forth. You can clean up all these problems during the revision process.

sectionthree

Legal Documents, Legal Conventions, and Common Legal Writing Blunders

■ **Section Three** of the Handbook describes the most commonly prepared documents in law practice: letters, memoranda, court briefs, pleadings, and transactional documents. Several tips and strategies for preparing these very different documents are given and sample documents are provided. This section also discusses some of the standard customs and practices seen in legal writing and some of the common faults made by beginning legal writers.

> Letters have to pass two tests before they can be classified as good: They must express the personality both of the writer and of the recipient.
>
> E.M. Forster (1934)

chapter 6

Legal Correspondence

StyleLinks

www.writing-business-letters.com
This site provides information on writing formal business letters with checklists and links to numerous other resources.

http://ualr.edu/cmbarger/WritersResources.HTM#Letters
Professor Coleen Barger provides links to sites offering advice on preparing business and legal letters.

http://www.michbar.org/journal/article.cfm?articleID=449&volumeID=33
The *Michigan Bar Journal* offers advice on writing client letters.

A. The Elements of a Letter

1. Introduction

Although you will write different types of letters, there are certain "basics" that are common to all legal correspondence. The elements of legal correspondence are similar to those of general business letters. Many law firms have practice guides and templates specifying the format for all firm letters. Following are the standard components of legal correspondence.

a. Letterhead

Law firms, government offices and agencies, and corporations all use special stationery, called *letterhead*, that identifies the office by name, address, telephone and facsimile numbers, website address, and other relevant information. The information is usually at the top of the page but it is sometimes located at the bottom or along the left side of the page. Law firms with a few attorneys list all attorneys on the letterhead; law firms with several attorneys usually issue personalized letterhead to each attorney with his or her own name and email address. Use letterhead for all correspondence associated with your firm or company. Letterhead is used only for the first page of a letter. The remaining pages match the color and quality of the letterhead page but are not imprinted with the letterhead information. When drafting a letter, be sure to remember how much space the letterhead will take up in the final version.

b. Date

Every item of correspondence must include a date, written out in full by month, day, and year (for example, *August 12, 2008*). Do not use abbreviations or numbers, as in *7/22/08*. The date is usually centered three lines below the letterhead, although it is occasionally placed at the left margin. Because the dates in legal matters are critical, be sure the date given is the date the letter is actually mailed or sent, rather than the date of an earlier draft.

c. Special Notations

If your correspondence will be sent to the recipient by any means other than first class mail, indicate such as follows: *Hand Delivered*, or *Registered Mail*, or *By Facsimile*. This notation should be placed at the left margin two lines below the date and two lines above the address. Similarly, any other special notations (often called *legends*), such as *Attorney-Client Communication—Privileged and Confidential*, should appear before the inside address.

d. Inside Address

The name and address of the recipient should appear two lines below the date or any special notations. Always follow the addressee's or organization's preferences for spelling, capitalization, and punctuation. Review the company's letterhead, written materials, or website to ensure accuracy. Include titles, if appropriate, such as Hillary Young, M.D., Jose Moreno, Esq., or Mr. Gary F. Kimball, Executive Vice-President. For female recipients, use *Ms.* unless directed otherwise. The form *Mrs. William Trainor* is acceptable only in social letters. Use *Ms. Madelyn G. Trainor* in business and legal letters. See Figure 6-1 for sample inside addresses.

e. Reference or Subject Notation

The reference notation indicates the subject matter of the correspondence. The notation may refer to the title of a case, the topic to be discussed in the letter, or a file or claim number. The reference notation gives the reader an immediate snapshot of what is to be discussed and also helps you later if you need to locate a letter you previously wrote. The reference notation (abbreviated as *Re:*) is usually placed two lines below the inside address. It is placed either at the left margin or indented five spaces. As a courtesy to your reader, include his or her file or reference number if you know it, following your own reference notation.

Some sample reference notations follow:

Re: *Cochran v. Templeton Auto, Inc.*
     San Diego Superior Court Case No. 08-1324

Re: Estate of Phillips
     Our File: TM-1205
     Your File: 90126-CMM

Re: Remedies for Copyright Infringement

f. Salutation

The salutation, or greeting, is usually placed two lines below the reference notation. Unless you are well acquainted with the addressee, err on the side of formality and address the letter to Mr. Morales or Ms. Vance (rather than *Dear Mike* or

---

Figure 6-1 Sample Inside Addresses

Ms. Donna A. Higgins
2728 Belle Haven Drive
Alexandria, VA 22089

Janet R. Reynolds, Esq.
Allen, Calderson & Bell, L.L.P.
1776 K Street, N.W.
Washington, D.C. 20006-1819

Mr. Allen T. Navarro
Executive Vice-President
Falcon Enterprises, Inc.
1893 Bowen Street
Chicago, IL 18890-1467

Director of Human Resources
Whitney Management, Inc.
2900 Arlington Avenue
Irving, TX 75248-3189

Dear Jill). Again, unless you have been directed otherwise, address letters to females as *Ms*. Letters to an unknown recipient should be directed to *Dear Sir or Madam*. If you know a title, you may use that, as in *Dear Commissioner*. Some letters to unknown individuals are addressed *Dear Colleague*. Salutations in business and legal letters are usually followed by a colon (although it is becoming more common to see commas used, perhaps as a sign of increased informality). See Section G of Chapter 1 for additional information on addressing individuals. Although the use of the word *Dear* in a salutation may seem overly familiar, omitting it makes a letter seem abrupt. Once you have written the salutation, do not refer to the reader by name again in the letter. Thus, do not write, *You, Mrs. Dailey, should consider the following* . . . .

In one particularly odd construction, some letters are typed "Dear Mr. Brown" and then the author will use a pen to strike through this salutation and handwrite "Bill." Avoid this contrived way to show friendliness.

g. Body

The body of the letter begins two lines below the salutation. The body is the most critical part of your correspondence because it conveys your message. The first sentence and paragraph should set the stage for the rest of your letter by indicating the purpose of the letter. Use descriptive headings in a letter only if it is so long or complex that the reader will need signals as to the sections of the letter being discussed.

Business letters and legal correspondence are usually single-spaced and then double-spaced between paragraphs. Although the second and subsequent pages of a letter will not be on letterhead, they will contain a "header" as follows:

Mr. Allen T. Navarro
Page Two
August 12, 2008

h. Closing and Signature Block

Most letters close with statements such as the following:

- Please do not hesitate to call me if you have any questions.
- Thank you in advance for your cooperation and courtesy.
- If you have any questions or comments you may reach me at the number given above.

The complimentary closing is usually *Sincerely, Very truly yours, Best regards,* or something similar, followed by a comma. *Very truly yours* is generally regarded as more formal and is probably used less frequently than *Sincerely.* Don't agonize over the choice of the closing because most readers don't pay a great deal of attention to this portion of a letter. If the letter is addressed to a judge, representative, or senator, you typically would use the complimentary closing *Respectfully.* Capitalize the first letter in the complimentary closing and place it two lines below the last line in the body of the letter. The closing is usually centered (although it is placed at the left margin in a block-style letter, as discussed later).

Avoid informal or unusual closings such as *Affectionately,* or *Successfully yours.* Do not merge your complimentary closing with the last line of your letter. These merged closings were fashionable hundreds of years ago but have a stilted and archaic look. An example of a merged closing is as follows:

> *Thanking you for your attention, I remain,*
> *Yours very truly,*
> Samantha Bianco

If your name is not on the letterhead, type your title underneath your typed name so that the reader will know your position in the firm. Allow four lines between the complimentary close and your typed name, aligned, for your hand-written signature. This section of the letter is called the signature block. Some writers prefer to use blue ink for their signatures, so readers can easily tell the document is an original rather than a copy.

i.   Reference Initials, Enclosures, and Copies

Most letters indicate the author and typist by a reference as follows: *GAK/jal,* which would indicate that the author was Gregory A. Klein and the typist or word processor was Judith A. Lane. Using the form *gak:jal* is also common. These reference initials are placed at the left margin on the second line below the writer's name and title. If you prepared or typed your own letter, omit this section.

If you are enclosing something in a letter, indicate this with the word *Enclosure* or its abbreviation *Encl.* (or *Enclosures* or *Encls.* for more than one enclosure), placed at the left margin one line below the reference initials. Some writers list or identify the items enclosed. Avoid archaic expressions such as *enclosed herewith please find.* A simple *enclosed is* is sufficient. Other writers prefer to use the term *Attachments* when documents are physically attached to the letter.

Copies of the letter you write may be sent to others. For example, the client will routinely be provided with copies of letters sent about the client's case because this is a way of keeping the client informed of the progress of a case. To indicate the recipients of copies, use *cc:* followed by the names of those who will be receiving copies (in alphabetical order), placed at the left margin one line below the enclosure notation. Although *cc:* originally stood for *carbon copies,* which have universally been replaced by photocopies, the signal *cc:* remains in use and likely now stands for courtesy copies.

There may be instances in which you do not want the reader of your letter to know who will receive a copy of it. In such cases, simply sign your letter, mail it, and then mark the copies that will go to the unidentified individual (assume Mark Grayson) and that will be placed in the file *bcc: Mark Grayson.* This is a reference to *blind carbon copy.*

See Figure 6-2 for elements of letters.

Figure 6-2   Quick Reference: Elements of Letters

- **Letterhead:** The sender's name, address, and other pertinent information, usually centered
- **Date:** Centered three lines below letterhead with no abbreviations
- **Special Notations:** Indications of method of sending, privileges claimed, and so forth, at left margin, two lines below date
- **Inside Address:** Recipient's name and address, at left margin, two lines below special notations
- **Reference Notation:** Reference to case name, topic of letter, and so forth, at left margin, or indented five spaces, two lines below inside address (usually shown as "Re:")
- **Salutation:** Opening greeting, addressing all individuals as *Mr.* or *Ms.* unless directed otherwise and followed by a colon, placed two lines below reference notation
- **Body of Letter:** Begins two lines below salutation, single-spaced, with double-spacing between paragraphs, which may be indented five spaces or not indented
- **Complimentary Closing:** A closing phrase or word such as *Sincerely,* centered, appearing two lines below last line of body of letter
- **Signature Block:** Writer's name and title, aligned with complimentary close, four lines below complimentary close
- **Final Notations:** References to writer's and typist's initials, enclosures, and indications of those who will receive copies of letter, all appearing at left margin, beginning two lines below signature block, each appearing one line below the other

2. Format Considerations

The presentation and "look and feel" of a letter have an effect on its readability. Following are some items to consider when formatting a letter.

a. Size of Paper and Spacing

Letters are written on standard 8½" × 11" paper and are usually single-spaced and then double-spaced between component parts (for example, between the date and inside address, between the inside address and reference notation, between the reference notation and salutation, and between the body and the complimentary close) and between paragraphs.

b. Arrangement and Indenting

Some letters show no indentations for paragraphs because new paragraphs are clearly indicated by the double-spacing between paragraphs. This style is referred to as "block form" or "left justified." In block form, all elements of the letter, including the date and complimentary closing, begin at the left margin. This is the style commonly provided as a template by most word processing programs.

The more traditional approach is to indent five spaces for new paragraphs even though they are set apart from each other by double-spacing. This style is called "modified block form." Here the date, complimentary closing, and signature block are all centered.

c. Margins and Justification

When the right-hand margin is even and every line ends at the right at the same point (as in this text), this is referred to as "right justification" or "full justification." Such letters present a very crisp appearance. One drawback however, is that to ensure each line stops at the same spot, the computer will automatically re-adjust spacing, sometimes cramping some words, expanding others, and leaving "rivers" of white space running vertically through the body of the text. Reading studies show that fully justified documents are more difficult to read because the added spaces eliminate distinctive word spatial characteristics, which are needed to aid comprehension and ease of reading. Continuing improvements in word processing programs are eliminating these spacing problems. Nevertheless, some writers prefer the traditional "ragged edge" at the right margin, believing it makes the letter look less like a computer-generated form letter and more personalized. Most word processing programs now offer letter templates for business letters in which spacing and common closings are already included, allowing you to "fill in the blanks" of the form. Spacing is preset as well.

d. Widows and Orphans

Never allow a page to begin with the last line of a paragraph (called a "widow") or to end with a single line of a paragraph on the bottom of a page (called an "orphan"). Keep at least two lines of text together. Lonely lines present an unprofessional appearance. Many word processing programs have built-in features to eliminate widows and orphans.

e. Font and Typeface

Use 12-point type size for readability and use a standard typeface, such as Times New Roman or Courier. The Rules of the Supreme Court mandate type size of 12-point. Sup. Ct. R. 33. Fonts and typefaces are discussed further in Chapter 12.

B. The Audience and Tone for Legal Correspondence

I didn't have time to write a short letter, so I wrote a long one instead.
Usually attributed to Blaise Pascal

Unlike other legal writings, such as wills, pleadings, and court briefs, there is no rigid list of elements that must be included in a letter. Though all letters should, of course, contain the basics (date, salutation, body, and closing), you will be able to exercise creativity in letter writing based on the goal you seek to achieve in your letter. The tone you adopt and the order in which you elect to discuss items are at your discretion. To beginning legal writers this flexibility can be intimidating. Without a rigid format to follow, some writers become paralyzed.

Letters can be extremely effective tools. The first letter sent to a client or adversary often establishes the basis for a relationship. If your letter to adverse counsel is hostile and arrogant, you will be responded to in kind, and this will mark the tone of future communications. You never merely write; you write to someone. Thus, you need to do some planning and thinking before you write.

There are two critical questions to address before you begin a letter:

- Who will be reading this letter?
- What is the purpose of this letter?

The answer to the first question will set the tone for your letter, and the answer to the second question will tell you what type of letter you should write.

1. Who Will Be Reading This Letter?

The tone or style of your letter must be tailored to the reader. If the letter is directed to a layperson or a person inexperienced with litigation or the topic of the letter, you will need to explain the information you present in the most clear and complete fashion possible. If the letter is directed to another legal professional, you will know that your discussion of some matters need not be as detailed or elementary as for the lay reader.

If you find your letter is becoming stuffy and legalistic in style, there are three techniques you can use to warm up the tone and improve readability:

- **Use Personal Pronouns.** Using personal pronouns, especially *you*, does much to warm up a letter. Thus, rather than writing *Patentees have the right to sue for infringement of a patent*, write *As the holder of a patent, you have the right to sue for infringement*. A danger in addressing readers, however, is that it often causes a pronoun shift, as in the following: *When one alleges the alter ego doctrine, you generally try to prove a lack of corporate formalities*. In correspondence, check for pronoun shifts.

- **Use Contractions.** Although contractions are not commonly used in legal or business writing, their use in letters is more common because they tend to make letters more personal. For example, rather than writing *Patentees cannot obtain monetary damages more than six years after infringement,* write *You can't obtain money damages if infringement occurred more than six years ago.*
- **Use Headings.** Although headings are not commonly used in correspondence, you should include them in long or complex letters if they will aid comprehension. Headings provide visual relief and information cues for the reader in lengthy letters. Simple headings such as *Damages* and *Fraud* are sufficient.

Be especially careful when writing opposing parties or counsel. If you are too adversarial, you will set the stage for a mistrustful relationship in which all communications must be in writing and all communications will be marked with an overbearing tone. Rather than writing a letter merely to confirm an extension granted to you, use the opportunity to thank the party for the extension. Avoid writing letters when you're angry (or write the letter when you're angry, but don't send it). Watch your tone. Rather than write *you have failed to provide me with the exhibit,* write *I have not received the exhibit.* If you need to apologize, do so sincerely and without qualifications. Write *I am sorry for any inconvenience this may have caused* rather than writing *I am sorry you did not understand my correspondence.* When in doubt, ask a colleague to review your letter for its tone.

2. What Is the Purpose of This Letter?

Before you begin writing any letter, focus on the central purpose of the letter. Try to distill this to one or two sentences. For example, some purposes may be as follows:

- A client needs to know a deposition has been scheduled for next month.
- A debtor needs to understand that failure to repay a debt will result in litigation.
- A client needs advice as to whether a trademark has been abandoned.

These examples represent three basic types of legal correspondence: *general correspondence* or *informative letters, demand letters,* and *opinion letters.* Once you determine what type of letter you will be writing, the appropriate style will follow naturally.

C. Types of Letters

1. General Correspondence

General correspondence letters may include letters requesting information or responding to requests for information, cover letters that accompany documents, confirmation letters that confirm some agreement or arrangement reached with another, or status or report letters providing a report to a client or insurance company on the progress of a matter. Except for status letters, these letters are often brief and may be only one or two paragraphs in length.

Follow these guidelines in preparing general correspondence:

- Include the standard components of letters described previously.
- Comply with the elements of good legal writing, such as precision, clarity, and so forth. Watch the details: If you misspell the client's name or misstate a dollar figure or a date, this will attract more attention than the substance of the letter.
- When in doubt, send a confirming letter. Confirming letters keep the file complete and help establish the progress of a case. Always send a letter to adverse counsel to confirm dates, amounts, or any other matter, such as an extension of time to respond to interrogatories. Send a copy to the client.

The Royal We

Should letters be written in the *I/me* form or the *we/our* form? Should the author say *It is my* opinion or *It is our* opinion? It depends. Consider the following:

- If the letter is from a sole practitioner, it should always be written in the *I* form.
- If the letter is written on behalf of the entire firm or a company, the *we* form is usually used.
- Most law firms take the approach that legal opinion letters provide the opinion of the firm, not the individual writer, and therefore most opinion letters are written in the *we* form. The letter is then signed by a partner or member on behalf of the firm itself.
- Follow your firm or office practice.

☐ **Warning: Letters providing legal opinions or giving legal advice can only be signed by properly licensed attorneys.**

2. Demand Letters

Demand letters set forth a client's demands. The most common type of demand letter is a collection letter, which outlines the basis for a debt due to a client and demands that it be paid. Other demand letters, however, demand action rather than money, for example, a demand that a landlord repair a leaky roof or that a company cease using a trademark. Your tone should be firm and businesslike, not strident.

Consider the strategy underlying the demand letter. In some instances, sending a demand letter is a statutory requirement. For example, in some states, litigation may not be instituted in certain cases unless a notice of the claim is first sent to the potential defendant. The demand letter satisfies these requirements.

To eliminate any disputes as to whether the letter was received, send the letter by some verifiable type of delivery, such as registered mail.

The only portion of the letter that will differ from a general correspondence letter is the content of the body of the letter.

a. Elements of Demand Letters

Include the following elements in any demand letter:

- **Introduction.** The letter should begin with an identification of your firm or company and your role, such as *This firm represents Ms. June Matthews regarding her automobile accident of April 8, 2008.*
- **Recitation of Facts.** Include the facts underlying the client's claim. Because your aim is to motivate the reader to take some action, phrase the factual statement as persuasively as possible.
- **Demand.** State the client's demand as clearly as possible. If this is a collection letter, specify the exact amount due. If you are demanding that the recipient take some action, such as replacing an appliance, say so. If there are several components to your demand, you may wish to set them forth in a bulleted list.
- **Consequences of Noncompliance.** Tell the reader the consequences of not complying with the demand letter. These consequences may include litigation, stopping work on a project, eviction, or some other adverse action. Although most readers will be offended by heavy-handed threats, there is nothing wrong in plainly stating what will occur if the client's demands are not met.
- **Date of Compliance.** State clearly the deadline for compliance. Do not say *You must pay the sum of $10,000 immediately.* Specify an express date, such as *by close of business on May 15, 2008,* so the reader will know exactly when compliance is expected.

b. Some Common Pitfalls in Demand Letters

Demand letters fail to meet their objectives for a variety of reasons. Following are some of the more common failings in demand letters.

(1) Factual Pitfalls. Be sure you have all the relevant facts. If a client informs you that a debtor has breached a written contract, review the contract itself, rather than accepting the client's oral summary of it. A mistake in reciting the facts will result in an immediate response by the recipient pointing out the error, and any momentum you may have had, along with your credibility, will be lost. Consider sending a draft of the demand letter to the client for review and approval before sending the letter to the intended recipient.

(2) Legal Pitfalls. You cannot send a letter demanding money for breach of contract if enforcement of the contract and threatening litigation are barred by the statute of limitations or some other law. You must conduct some minimum amount of research to ensure that the client's claim is valid and enforceable.

☐ **Ethics Warnings**
  ○ **It is a violation of ethics codes to correspond with a person who is represented by counsel. Make sure the recipient is not represented by counsel before you send the letter.**
  ○ **It is unethical to threaten criminal prosecution if the recipient will not comply with the demand. Review your state's code of professional conduct.**
  ○ **Most states have consumer protection laws regulating demands for payments of certain types of debts. Research your state's consumer debt laws and the Fair Debt Collection Practices Act at 15 U.S.C. § 1692 (2000).**

(3) Inappropriate Tone and Content. The letter should be reasonable, firm, and businesslike. Overt threats and name-calling are not only inappropriate but also ineffective. There are two demand letter tactics that are notoriously ineffective: accusing the recipient of fraud and sending copies of the letter to others, such as to a debtor's employer or insurer. These tactics usually produce such outrage in the recipient that chances for settling the dispute amicably will vanish.

(4) Arguing the Case. A demand letter should not present all the evidence you would need to prevail at trial. The recipient will likely know some of the facts relating to the claim, and you need not provide copies of every item of correspondence and the name of every witness who supports the client's version of the matter. If the problem cannot be resolved by direct negotiation, you will have ample opportunity to argue the case during the litigation stage. Don't tip your hand at this juncture. Although a few legal authorities may be cited in some instances, routine collection and demand letters rarely include legal analysis.

(5) Failure to Follow Through. If you have told the recipient of the letter that legal action will be instituted by May 15 unless the amount of $10,000 is paid to the client, you must be prepared to follow through on that statement. Nothing jeopardizes credibility more than empty threats. If the client is unsure what action he or she intends to take if the demand is not met, you can create some "wiggle room" by writing one of the following:

  ▪ *We look forward to receiving your response to this letter by May 15;*
  ▪ *Please contact us to discuss this matter further; or*
  ▪ *Unless we receive a satisfactory response from you by May 15, we will take all appropriate legal action.*

Telling the recipient of the letter to make a counterproposal is a serious concession and invites the recipient to play "let's make a deal." See Figure 6-3 for a sample demand letter.

Figure 6-3   Sample Demand Letter

GREGORY & JOSEPHS, LLP
1300 B STREET
SUITE 1990
LOS ANGELES, CALIFORNIA 22010
(405) 766-1899

March 16, 2008

Mr. Peter M. Reynolds
Executive Vice President
Lowell Industries
3215 Fairmont Avenue
Kansas City, KS 19889

Re: Trademark TAXFILER
     U.S. Reg. No. 1,989,433

Dear Mr. Reynolds:

This law firm represents Strategy Systems, Inc. ("SSI"), the owner of U.S. Trademark Registration No. 1,989,433 for the mark TAXFILER used by SSI since 1990 in connection with a computer software program for the preparation of federal and state tax returns. A copy of SSI's registration certificate for TAXFILER is enclosed. This trademark is a valuable asset of SSI, which has spent considerable time and effort in establishing consumer recognition of this mark.

SSI recently became aware that Lowell Industries ("Lowell") began using the mark TAXFILE in January 2008 in connection with a computer software program for the preparation and electronic submission of federal tax returns. Lowell's use of TAXFILE for these goods is likely to cause confusion and mistake of the purchasing public as to the origin and source of the goods offered under the respective

Mr. Peter M. Reynolds
Page Two
March 16, 2008

marks, thereby causing damage to SSI. Consequently, Lowell's use of TAXFILE is an infringement of SSI's registered trademark TAXFILER.

SSI therefore demands that Lowell immediately cease using the mark TAXFILE or any other mark confusingly similar to SSI's mark and cease offering any goods bearing the mark TAXFILE.

Because this matter is of significant importance to SSI, we request that you respond to us in writing within ten days of the date of this letter to confirm your cessation of any further use of TAXFILE or any other mark confusingly similar to any of SSI's marks. Our client has instructed us to initiate an action for trademark infringement against Lowell if we do not hear from you within this time period.

We look forward to your timely reply.

Sincerely,

Ellen T. Gregory

ETG/ajj
Encl.
cc: Jay M. Romero

3. Opinion Letters and Their Elements

Letters offering legal advice or opinions can only be signed by attorneys. In some firms, opinion letters can be signed only by a partner after review by another partner or an opinions committee. In many law firms, the opinion letter is signed by a partner on behalf of the entire firm, signaling that the opinion is not provided by any single attorney but rather by the firm itself. Although opinion letters are usually sought by clients seeking advice on a particular matter, sometimes they are requested by a third party, such as an accountant who requires a legal opinion as to a mutual client's progress in litigation before the accountant prepares financial statements.

Opinion letters should contain the standard components of a letter (reference line, salutation, and so forth). Opinion letters should include a legend that they are subject to attorney-client privilege to protect them against later discovery. Opinion letters also share some features in common with research memoranda, although their analysis of legal authorities is more simplified, and they are usually written to a client rather than to another legal professional.

Opinion letters contain the following elements:

a. Date

Although all letters include dates, the date of an opinion letter is especially important because the opinion will relate to the status of the law on that date. Changes in the law after that date may well affect the correctness of the opinion.

b. Introductory Language

It is often a good idea to remind the client why the opinion is being provided. Such an introduction also establishes the scope of the letter by stating the issue that the letter will address. Consider the following introductions:

- *We enjoyed meeting you last week. As you requested, we have researched whether a trademark may be abandoned by nonuse.*
- *Pursuant to our telephone conversation of March 18, 2008, we have reviewed the issue . . .*
- *At your request . . .*
- *You have asked for our opinion whether . . .*

c. Review of Facts

An opinion letter should always set forth the facts on which it is based. Facts are usually given in a narrative (sentence-by-sentence) form rather than in numbered or bulleted list form. Including the facts gives the client the opportunity to correct you if you have misstated the facts. Even a minor factual error, such as in a date or dollar amount, can result in an incorrect opinion. Thus, include the facts so the reader understands that the accuracy of the opinion depends on the specific facts recited. Consider introducing the facts as follows:

- *You have informed us that you signed a written lease on April 30, 2008 . . .*
- *As we understand them, the facts are as follows: On June 24, 2008, you began using the CONFORM® mark . . .*

d. Opinion

The essence of an opinion letter is the advice given to the client. Clients are particularly interested in the "bottom line," and many writers immediately give their opinion or conclusion after reciting the facts. The conclusion is then followed by an explanation. This is an effective technique if the opinion you give is one that is fairly straightforward or will be welcome to the client. On the other hand, if you will be giving the client bad news, such as informing him or her that certain rights have been lost, you may want to lead the reader to this unfavorable news gradually. By explaining the law first, you will be preparing the reader for the unfavorable outcome, so by the time you give the bad news, the reader understands exactly why the outcome is unfavorable. See Figure 6-4. Consider introducing the conclusion as follows:

- *Based upon the facts you provided us and the applicable law in this state, it is our opinion that you may initiate an action for wrongful death against Douglas Sterling.*
- *We have concluded that you may bring an action for wrongful death against Douglas Sterling. Our conclusion is based upon the facts given above and our analysis of Ohio law.*

In any event, be sure your letter answers the client's specific question and is not an abstract discussion of general legal principles.

Figure 6-4   Bad News Bearers

In many instances, letter writers must deliver bad news to clients. In such an event, consider the following approaches:

- If you need to give a client unfavorable news, try to soften the approach by saying *success is extremely unlikely, the chances of a favorable outcome are remote at best,* or *cases similar to yours have been unsuccessful,* rather than a blunt *your case is entirely without merit.*
- Clearly deliver the bad news. Don't soften your approach so much that you haven't accurately conveyed your meaning. Readers often perceive what they want to, and there is no room for ambiguity in delivering unfavorable news to a client. Consider using phrases such as *We regret that the court dismissed your action* or *We are sorry to inform you that the insurance company has rejected your claim.*
- If possible, try to find an alternative avenue for the client, as follows:

  Because the statute of limitations has expired, you will not be able to bring an action against your neighbor for trespass. We would suggest, however, that you attempt to negotiate directly with your neighbor. If this approach is unsuccessful, contact your homeowners' insurance company because it may offer coverage for the damage done to your property.

e. Explanation of Opinion

This portion of the letter explains and summarizes the law on which the opinion is based. Because most opinion letters are written for laypersons who may not be familiar with the law, avoid detailed discussion of statutes and cases. It is usually sufficient to summarize the legal authorities in a general fashion. You should avoid giving citations to cases and statutes unless your reader is sufficiently knowledgeable to understand the citations. Similarly, do not merely retype the text of a statute or case; explain what the case or statute means for this particular matter. Consider the following:

- *Applicable case law provides . . .*
- *We have researched the pertinent statute that governs this matter. It provides . . .*
- *The legal authorities in this state are in agreement that . . .*

If this portion of the letter is long, you may use short headings and subheadings (such as "Damages") to divide your explanation into readable separate sections.

f. Recommendations

After you have explained the law that governs your conclusion, provide a recommendation to the client. Be sure that the recommendation is not unduly optimistic. Phrase advice as a probability rather than a certainty. Thus, write *A court would likely hold that* rather than *Your claim is undoubtedly valid.* Do not include any language that could be construed by the client as a guarantee of success. Conversely, make sure your letter provides an opinion. Wishy-washy phrases such as *It would seem that* or *We are inclined to think* do not tell the reader anything. Similarly, replace the phrase *We feel* with *We believe* or *It is our opinion that . . . .* It is acceptable to write *We recommend that [or we suggest that] you settle this case.*

g. Instructions

The last portion of an opinion letter is usually a direction to the client to contact the office or take some other action. For example, consider the following:

> *Because the statutes governing this matter require that a claim be submitted to the city within 100 days of the wrongful act, please contact us and provide us with your instructions. Failure to file the claim by* **May 1, 2008***, will bar any action against the city.*

If the recipient must take critical action by a certain date, place the date or instruction in bold type.

h. Protection Clauses

On occasion, you may not have all of the information you need to provide a complete opinion. For example, you may be awaiting a copy of a written employment agreement or other document. In such cases, protection clauses (sometimes called *savings* clauses) are used to explain that certain information is lacking or that the opinion may change depending on the information you receive. Similarly, think ahead and consider what defenses or arguments the other party may assert. Prepare your client to meet any challenges. Consider the following examples:

- *This opinion is based upon the facts you have provided us. Once we have had an opportunity to review the addendum to your lease, we will be better able to provide you with our opinion. Assuming the addendum does not materially alter the original lease, however, it is our opinion . . .*
- *While your employer may argue his business is not subject to the provisions of the Family Medical Leave Act, we believe such an argument is without merit because . . .*

See Figure 6-5 for a sample opinion letter.

Figure 6-5   Sample Opinion Letter

Taylor & Aldridge LLP
1401 New Hampshire Avenue, N.W.
Washington, D.C. 20005
(202) 455-1900

July 18, 2008

Privileged and Confidential

Mr. Anthony Fallon
President
WaveLength LLC
5644 Sunset Parkway
Arlington, VA 22201

Re: Monitoring of Employee Internet Use

Dear Mr. Fallon:

We enjoyed meeting you last week. As you requested, we have reviewed whether WaveLength LLC ("WaveLength") may monitor the Internet use of its employees, including their email transmissions.

We understand that WaveLength supervisors have observed employees using the Internet during business hours for nonbusiness uses, including shopping, browsing, and personal emailing. Access to the Internet is provided and paid for by WaveLength, and WaveLength owns the computers, laptops, and all electronic systems used by employees at the business premises.

WaveLength is concerned that nonbusiness use of the Internet reduces employee productivity, may subject the company to liability for copyright infringement if employees use the Internet to download software and music illegally, places the company at risk of importing computer viruses, and may subject the company to liability for harassment or defamation if employees engage in such activities using the company's computer systems.

We have reviewed both federal and state law relating to employer monitoring of employee Internet use. The key issues to examine when determining whether an employer may monitor employee Internet use and email messages are whether the employees have a reasonable expectation of privacy at the workplace, and, if so, whether the employer has a justifiable business reason to override that expectation of privacy.

Mr. Anthony Fallon
Page Two
July 18, 2008

Employers can justify surveillance of employees if employees are informed beforehand of such. Thus, if employers place their monitoring policies in employee handbooks or require employees to sign statements acknowledging the monitoring, such typically precludes employees from asserting that their privacy has been invaded because employees then have no reasonable expectation of privacy.

Accordingly, if WaveLength implements a carefully drafted Internet use policy, presents it to employees who must sign an acknowledgment of receipt of the policy, and consistently enforces the policy, WaveLength should be able to monitor employee Internet use without liability to its employees.

Due to the rapidly changing nature of the Internet, the law in this area continues to evolve, and we cannot predict what courts may do in the future. At present, however, if employees are informed of an Internet use and monitoring policy (which is consistently enforced), WaveLength may monitor its employees' Internet use.

Please feel free to call us if you have any questions or comments or if you would like assistance in drafting an Internet use policy.

Sincerely,

Taylor & Aldridge LLP

AMD:fpm

 For Successful Letter Writing

- Always write your letter with your intended audience in mind and think through your goals in sending the letter. Do you want to inform? Convince? Settle? Find out information? Deny? You will automatically achieve the correct style and tone.
- Avoid stuffy phrases, such as *Pursuant to your request of the seventeenth.*
- After you have finished drafting your letter, reread it, putting yourself in the reader's place. This will allow you to focus on whether the letter conveys the information it needs to, whether it will be readily understood by the reader, and whether the overall tone is appropriate.
- Start a file of sample letters you encounter that you believe are well written and adopt effective techniques you observe. Notice the way others order their paragraphs or conclude their letters and learn from them.
- Proofread one final time, paying special attention to names, dates, and numbers.

4. Electronic Communications

New forms of communication, namely, electronic communications, have arisen in the past several years, changing the way people communicate in the workplace. Although many of them are great timesavers, others may be traps for the unwary writer.

a. Communicating by Email

Email has become a common method of communication, both within the workplace and with clients. Email creates an air of informality, and the ease with which a message can be composed and sent causes countless errors. We have all heard stories of people who, much to their embarrassment, have mistakenly replied to an entire "list" rather than solely to the sender of a message. Many firms and offices have policies as to the types of communications that may be sent by email, and most include automatically inserted confidentiality notices at the conclusion of each email message.

Email is different from other written communications. Because it is nearly instantaneous, and the time between the sending of a message and receiving a response to it is so reduced, email is more informal and conversational than traditional paper communication. Thus, the communication style for email must be adjusted.

Although email sent to friends on an informal basis probably does not need to be rigorously checked for grammar and compliance with other usage rules, consider the following when using email in a business or office setting:

- Because email is often dashed off without a great deal of planning, it may result in brusque and abrupt communications. The reader will not be able to see your expression, gauge your body language, or hear any intonation. Thus, attempts at humor, irony, and sarcasm are often misperceived. Consider receiving a communication saying, *I resent your message.* You may be tempted to fire off a hostile response before you realize the writer meant to say *I re-sent your message.* When in doubt, leave it out.

- Understand that the recipient of your email may not use the same software and hardware that you do, and thus the formatting and "look and feel" of the message the recipient sees may appear quite different from what your screen shows. Formatting and visual appearance greatly affect readability.
- Spell-check all email and review it for accuracy. If necessary, print a hard copy of the message, proof it, correct it, and then send it. It is far better to be overly cautious than sloppy.
- Follow the same rules of courtesy and tone used in traditional communications. Ask yourself, *Would I say this in person?*
- Be a generous reader. Give the writer the benefit of the doubt and resist overreacting to an email communication that initially seems abrupt. The writer may have been trying to be brief.
- Avoid overusing email abbreviations (such as IMHO for *in my humble opinion*) in office settings. Similarly, don't use emoticons (emotional icons such as smiley faces) to convey meaning.
- Be brief and to the point. Many people receive a great number of email messages each day and won't bother to read a long, rambling communication.
- Never pass along inappropriate email at your workplace.
- Make the subject line specific. Let the recipient know at a glance what the message discusses. Do not overuse "urgent," and do not use either an overly long subject line or one that merges into the message.
- Control your own email inbox by adding the line *no need to respond* to your email message. This allows others the freedom not to reply to your emails.
- Understand that email is now specifically discoverable in litigation proceedings. Unless material is subject to attorney-client privilege, it may be discoverable. Be careful to maintain client confidentiality.
- Understand that once you send a message you have no control over its distribution and it may easily be sent to numerous others without your permission or even your knowledge.
- Do not assume that email is confidential. Generally, monitoring of email by employers is permissible if employers have notified employees that such monitoring may occur.
- Understand that email is not an effective forum for resolving disputes or for delicate situations in which tone of voice is important. Once a communication or "conversation" becomes even slightly confrontational, end the email and agree to meet in person or speak over the phone.

b. Communicating by Facsimile

Communicating by facsimile is so commonplace that many firms and offices use "real" mail (often called *snail mail*) only for more critical matters, such as opinions and status reports, or for sending documents that must be original. Check your firm or office policy as to documents that may be sent by facsimile. Most office fac-simile cover sheets include a confidentiality notice indicating that if someone receives the communication in error, he or she should return it to the sender. Such notices are used to preserve attorney-client confidentiality and privilege. Consider sending voluminous materials by mail or express delivery because even the best facsimile machines produce a copy that is less readable than an original. Either preprogram frequently called numbers into the facsimile machine or always double-check the facsimile number before pressing "send." Call the recipient and inform him or her that the document will be sent, especially if the document is confidential or the facsimile machine is in an open location or shared with others. Once the document is sent, it cannot be recalled.

c. Communicating by Telephone and Voice Mail

Although conference calls and voice mail can reduce the time you spend on communications and eliminate certain forms of written communications, there are some guidelines that will assist you:

- When participating in a conference call, treat it as a meeting and be prompt in dialing in to the conference number.
- Make sure that introductions are made for all participants and that all participants can hear each other.
- Always ask for permission before placing someone on a speakerphone.
- Always disclose that another is listening with you if you are on a speaker-phone.
- Do not leave overly long or rambling messages on voice mail.
- Clearly and slowly state your name and phone number on voice mail mes-sages. Repeat them at the end of your message for those unfamiliar with you so they do not have to replay the message to obtain your name and number. Spell your name if needed.
- Avoid using voice mail to "dodge" callers, evade bad news, and avoid speak-ing with the recipient. Nearly everyone will understand you deliberately called when you knew the person was not available.
- Keep notes for the file to confirm that you left (or received) a certain voice mail. Consider the following format: "M/M 9/16/08 re: corp. meeting date" (meaning that you left a message on the machine on September 16, 2008, regarding the date of the corporate meeting).
- Do not disclose confidential information over a car phone, cell phone, or on voice mail. Messages may be easily intercepted, and you do not know who may be listening.
- Check your office policy to see if cell phones can be used for business while you are driving. After a large law firm was sued in 2001 for an accident allegedly caused by one of its attorneys who was driving while using the cell phone for firm business, many firms now prohibit such use.

d. Communicating by Text Messaging

Text messaging (or *texting*) is the term used for sending short messages (usually fewer than 160 characters) from cell phones or personal digital assistants such as BlackBerrys. Texting has become increasingly popular. The language used when texting is called "text speak," and it is marked by often highly creative abbreviations and acronyms, such as PLZ (for *please*), UR (for *you are*), and DQMOT (for *don't quote me on this*). Many law firms distribute BlackBerrys to their professionals on the first day of work so that everyone can stay in touch at all times. If you text message anyone about a business-related matter, remember that although you may understand certain abbreviations, the recipient might not. Be sure your message is clear. When in doubt, write it out.

chapter 7

Legal Memoranda

StyleLinks

http://www.ualr.edu/cmbarger/SAMPLE_MEMO.HTML
Professor Coleen Barger's site provides a sample legal memorandum along with memo-writing tips.

http://sparkcharts.sparknotes.com/legal/legalwriting/section2.php
This site analyzes the elements of a legal memorandum and provides sample sections of legal memoranda.

A. Introduction

A legal memorandum or research memorandum is a research document designed to provide information about a case or matter. Memos are often written by paralegals or junior attorneys for more senior attorneys. You will be asked to research a question, and your answer will be provided in the form of a written memorandum or "memo." It is only by being completely knowledgeable about the strengths and weaknesses of a case that a fully informed decision can be made whether and how best to represent the client, prepare pleadings and motions, settle the case, proceed to trial, or appeal an adverse decision.

The memo is an internal document, meaning it is prepared for use within a law firm, corporation, or agency. Although a copy of the memo may be provided to a client, it is generally protected by the work product privilege and thus is not discoverable by an adverse party. Because it is not discoverable, its distinguishing characteristic is its objectivity.

Focus on the following three guidelines for effective memo writing:

1. Be Objective

The most difficult part of writing a memo is remaining neutral and objective. If you are not objective in pointing out weaknesses and flaws in the client's case, you do the client a disservice. Your goal is to explain the law, not to argue it. Force yourself to play devil's advocate. Role-play being a reporter. Approach the case as your adversary might and closely examine the authorities that appear unfavorable to your client.

2. Be Specific

If you are asked to determine whether a tenant may sublease rented property when the lease fails to address such an issue, focus on the specific question. You need not address the issue as if you were writing a textbook on the history of landlord-tenant relations. Because your memo will expressly state the issue it addresses, focus yourself by rereading the stated issue if you find yourself getting off track.

3. Be Thorough

The individual who assigns you the task wants a finished project, not a sheaf of notes or series of photocopied cases. Your job is to read and analyze the cases and other legal authorities, apply them to the facts of your case, and present this as a finished professional research memorandum together with recommendations or a prediction as to the likely outcome of the matter.

B. Format of Memoranda

Unlike documents filed in court, there is no one rigid format for an internal office memorandum. Some law firms, companies, and agencies have developed their own formats, and you should ask to review memos previously prepared because these will serve as a guide for you. The memo format provided in this Handbook is a very common and standard one. See Figure 7-4.

The components of a memo are each set off by their own headings, which are usually capitalized and centered. Memos are usually single-spaced with double-spacing between components, although double-spacing is common in many writing programs and firms. Always check with the person assigning the memo to see if there are any requirements for formatting the memo. Note that the first page of a memo will usually include the first three major elements: the issues, the answers, and the statement of facts. This presentation style allows a reader to review only a portion of the memo and yet comprehend a total view of the project. The reader does not have to search through the memo to understand the "bottom line." These three elements provide a snapshot of the client's case and putting them on the first page enables a reader to understand at a glance the strengths and weaknesses of the case.

1. Heading

The heading identifies the document, the person for whom the memo is prepared, the author and his or her position, the subject matter of the memo, and the date it is prepared. For ease of retrieval, the subject matter notation (the "Re:" line) should include some descriptive content, such as *Liability of General Partners* rather than merely a case name and file number.

2. Question(s) Presented

This section (also called *Issue(s)* or *Issue(s) Presented*) sets forth the legal issues the memo addresses. If the memo discusses more than one issue, number each one. Do not number a single issue. Most writers use a true question form, such as *Does a landlord have a duty to disclose to tenants information about crimes that have occurred at the leased premises?* Other writers use the "whether" form, as in *Whether landlords have a duty . . . .* Some attorneys dislike this form because questions that begin with the word *whether* result in incomplete sentences. Finally, some writers use the "under" form, as in <u>Under</u> *California Civil Code Section 3344, <u>does</u> a celebrity have a cause of action for violation of his right of publicity <u>when</u> his photograph is used in an advertisement without his permission?* This combination of *under, does/is,* and then *when* is a common way of forming issues.

Whichever form of question you use, be consistent and use the same format for all questions. The most important thing in drafting your questions or issues is to be specific. A question such as *What is a trademark license* is far too broad and unhelpful to a reader. Incorporate some facts from your case, as follows: *Is a trademark license valid if it imposes no duty on the licensee to monitor quality of the trademarked goods?* In many instances, language in a statute that governs the matter may provide ideas for phrasing the question. If there is more than one issue, list them in order of importance or the order in which they must be proven at trial.

3. Brief Answer(s)

This section of the memo briefly answers the questions you set forth, in the order you presented them (with the same numbering system you used for your questions). Try to avoid answers that merely repeat the question. Your answer should incorporate the reasons for your conclusions; thus, a one-word answer, such as *no*, is inappropriate. Keep your answers brief—no more than one or two sentences. Do not include formal supporting citations, although it is appropriate to write *Under California Civil Code Section 3344.1, a celebrity has a cause of action for violation of the right of publicity when his photograph or likeness is used for commercial purposes without his permission.*

4. Statement of Facts

The statement of facts may precede the issues or follow the brief answers. Either approach is common. Some readers prefer the facts to be given first so that they can make sense of the questions the memo will address. The statement of facts will be based on what you know about the case, what the client has said, and your review of the file. The factual statement must be objective; therefore, include facts unfavorable to the client's position, and do not tilt the facts in your favor. Include all facts and do not assume that a reader will know all the facts. In some instances, new attorneys may be assigned to the case and your memo may be the first source they review to become familiar with the case. Therefore, the statement of facts should be self-contained and not require reference to other sources. The most common approach in stating the facts is to present them in a chronological approach (in the order in which they occurred) and in a narrative style rather than in a bulleted list. Use the past tense unless facts are developing as you prepare the memo. If there is a dispute about certain facts, include both versions, as follows: *Although the tenant claims she provided written notice to the landlord of the leaky roof, the landlord disputes this.*

Do not include legal conclusions in your statement of facts. Thus, do not write *The partner breached his fiduciary duty by failing to disclose material information about the premises.* Write *The partner did not disclose that the premises were subject to an easement for a right of way.* The word *slapped* conveys a fact; the word *battered* conveys a legal conclusion. Remain neutral and objective in every part of your memo.

5. Analysis or Discussion

The heart of the memorandum is the analysis, or discussion, section. This portion of the memo provides an in-depth analysis of the issues presented. Cases, statutes, and other legal authorities will be discussed. Citations usually appear in the body of the memo rather than as footnotes, although practices vary.

Many experts recommend using a thesis statement (see Figure 7-1) as an introduction to the analysis section of a memorandum or other writing. This introductory statement serves to alert readers to the "big picture" that will be addressed in the memo and encapsulates your central argument. A thesis statement is especially helpful in complex projects or those that will address several issues or elements.

Consider using the IRAC or CRAC approach (see Figure 7-2) in your analysis of the legal authorities. Thus, provide the issue the memo will address or identify the conclusion, explain the legal rule that governs the issue, apply the legal rule to the facts of your case, and provide a brief conclusion.

Figure 7-1   Using a Thesis Statement

A *thesis statement* distills the central ideas and arguments in your project into one or two assertive sentences. It usually appears at the beginning of a project or issue to give focus and direction to the analysis to follow. It encapsulates the argument to follow. It responds to the central question, *My point is that . . . .* Nonlegal writers often like to build interest and allow readers to draw their own conclusions about characters and plots. Legal writers, on the other hand, must help their readers immediately understand the direction the analysis will take. Sometimes a thesis statement is called an *umbrella statement* because every part of the discussion to follow must fit beneath it. It directs both the writer and the reader by setting forth the rule that will be proved in the analysis to follow.

Although the thesis statement appears early in any discussion, in many instances, you will not be able to draft the statement until after all your research and analysis is complete. It is only then that you will know how to encapsulate your position in one or two sentences. Don't be concerned if you need to revise your thesis statement. It is possible that as you write your project you discover that your original thesis statement is not accurate; simply modify your thesis statement to reflect your argument. In fact, it may take several attempts to get the thesis statement just right.

A thesis statement is not the same as a topic. For example, a topic might be "liability for dog bites," and a thesis statement for this topic would be as follows:

> *Under California Civil Code Section 3342, the owner of a dog is liable for the damages suffered by anyone bitten by the dog while in a public place or lawfully in a private place, regardless of the prior viciousness of the dog.*

After providing this thesis statement, the writer should proceed to analyze the various elements of the statute (for example, showing that a party was the owner of the dog, that the victim was in a public place or lawfully on private property when he or she was bitten, and so forth).

Note the decisive nature and specificity of the preceding thesis statement. A much weaker thesis statement would be as follows: *The owners of dogs are generally liable for the behavior of their dogs.*

Similarly, a thesis statement is more assertive than a topic sentence, which generally merely announces the subject matter or theme of a paragraph to follow; a thesis statement, on the other hand, provides a specific conclusion.

Poor Thesis Statement	Better Thesis Statement
A material omission may constitute fraud.	*Failure to disclose significant defects relating to real estate sold to another is fraud.*

The thesis statement should be placed at or near the beginning of each argument or issue, and each issue should have its own forceful thesis statement. Later paragraphs may begin with topic sentences as you proceed to "prove" your thesis, much the way a scientist "proves" his or her hypothesis. Sometimes writers are reluctant to provide a thesis statement because thesis statements require a writer to commit to a position. You will need to shed this reluctance and state the conclusion you have reached about a subject.

Consider the following assertive and strong thesis statements:

- To state a cause of action for false advertising, the plaintiff must show that a statement is either literally false or implicitly untrue in that the statement is likely to deceive consumers.
- Jill Taylor, as a director of a corporation, will not be liable for mere errors in her business judgment so long as she had a reasonable basis for her decision and acted in good faith.
- To be enforceable, a noncompetition agreement must be reasonable as to its scope, duration, and geographic area.

In each case, the reader is given the applicable rule and a definitive preview of the analysis that will follow.

Thesis statements for legal memoranda will differ from thesis statements for persuasive documents, such as those submitted to courts. In a legal memorandum, the thesis statement will be neutral and explanatory; it will not advocate for a particular point of view. In contrast, when you prepare court briefs, your thesis statements will be strong and persuasive.

Example of Memo Thesis Statement:

To prevail in a copyright infringement action, a plaintiff must prove that he or she owns the copyright and that the defendant has impermissibly copied the work.

Example of Court Brief Thesis Statement:

The Defendant is liable for copyright infringement because the Plaintiff is the owner of the copyright in the book, and the Defendant has copied the Plaintiff's work without permission.

Figure 7-2 Methods of Legal Analysis

In discussing and analyzing authorities, many writers follow what is referred to as the "IRAC" method. The IRAC method is also a common approach used by students in answering essay examinations. IRAC is an acronym for Issue, Rule, Application or Analysis, and Conclusion. First, the issue is presented (*Does the Uniform Partnership Act govern a partnership that has no written agreement?*). Next, the rule or legal authority that governs the issue is explained. The cases and other legal authorities that provide the rule are discussed. Then the writer analyzes and applies the rule to the client's facts. The facts of the client's particular fact situation will be compared and contrasted with the cases and other authorities. After a thorough analysis, a conclusion is presented.

Other experts suggest a variation of IRAC, usually called "CRAC" (for Conclusion, Rule, Application, and Conclusion). In this type of analysis, the conclusion is given first, followed by the principal rule of law that supports the conclusion. The rule is explained and illustrated through analysis of cases and other legal authorities. The rule is then applied to the client's particular case, and the conclusion is restated.

Some writing experts dislike IRAC and CRAC because they believe these methods encourage a rigid and formulaic approach to writing. Others believe that IRAC is more useful for writing objective projects such as legal memoranda (because it requires the writer to state the issue in a neutral manner) and that CRAC (with its assertive conclusion given at the beginning) is more useful in persuasive writings such as court briefs. In any event, IRAC and CRAC may be useful tools to help you to remember to include certain elements when you analyze a legal problem.

Thus, although methods of analyzing cases vary, some techniques are common to all legal analysis:

- Analyze rather than merely summarize the legal authorities on which you rely. Describe the cases you rely on, giving sufficient facts from those cases so the reader may readily see how and why those cases apply to your case.
- Give the holding and the reasoning from the cases you rely on. Then compare and contrast the cases you rely on with the facts of your case.
- Convince the reader by applying the holding and reasoning from the cited authorities to your case. Complete the analysis by giving a conclusion. Don't force the reader to guess at a conclusion.
- When a case is so similar to the client's situation that it will be controlling, give more detail so the reader will understand the importance of the case.
- When cases are "against you," you may distinguish them from the client's situation in a variety of ways. You may argue that such cases are so dissimilar factually that they are inapplicable, that they are so old that they are no longer relevant, that they are decided by lower courts, or that the language that appears to be contrary to your position is dicta rather than a holding of the court. If these approaches do not work, you will either have to acknowledge the point or ask the court to overrule these prior decisions. Consider making a policy argument that the law should be changed.

Think back to the mathematics and chemistry courses you have taken. It was never sufficient to simply give an answer. The teacher always required that you show your work and demonstrate each and every step you took to get to your answer. The same is true in legal analysis. It is never sufficient to merely give a conclusion. You must show the reader how you arrived at the conclusion.

It is not enough to locate relevant authorities and then summarize them. Anyone can read a case and then restate its holding. You must analyze the authorities and discuss how and why they relate to your situation or case. This requires you to interweave and compare the facts of your case with the authorities on which you rely. Many beginning writers are reluctant to draw a conclusion. They simply summarize the authorities they have found and then move on to the next topic or issue. You will need to synthesize the authorities you discuss by comparing and contrasting them to each other and to your situation. Be sure to give some of the facts from the cases you rely on so readers can see how and why they apply to the client's situation. If a direct quotation is particularly apt, use it. Be careful, however, to ensure that your analysis consists of more than a series of quotations dropped into the memo. Explain their relevance to the client's problem. See "Tips for Using Quotations and Paraphrasing" and see Figures 7-1 and 7-2 for information on case analysis.

Use headings and subheadings throughout this section to serve as signposts to the reader that new topics are being introduced. A memo that consists of typewritten pages with no heading breaks is nearly unreadable. If you have difficulty composing headings and subheadings, review the headnotes in the cases you rely on for ideas (but remember not to quote from the headnotes). Finally, this section of the memo discusses what the legal authorities have to say and not your opinions. Therefore, use the third person only (*A court would likely find*) and not the first person (*I believe a court would find*).

Discuss the issues in the order in which you presented them in your issues or questions section, once again using the same numbering system you used for your questions and your brief answers.

If you find you may be drifting off track, reread your questions or issues presented. Ask yourself *Is this discussion directly responsive to the question I asked?* If not, it can likely be omitted.

6. Conclusion

The conclusion should be brief (probably no more than one paragraph) and should not include formal citations although it may indicate that a certain statute is applicable or inapplicable. In many ways, the conclusion will resemble your brief answer(s), although it will be in narrative form and will not be divided into numbered sections. If you cannot draw a conclusion because the authorities are in conflict, say so. If, during the course of your research and writing, you determine additional information is needed or other issues need analysis, create a new section for these matters called "Recommendations." The conclusion should not introduce any material that has not previously appeared in the body of the memo. See Figure 7-3 for examples of elements in a legal memorandum and Figure 7-4 for a sample legal memorandum.

For Using Quotations and Paraphrasing

Many beginning legal writers wonder when to use quotations, when to paraphrase, and when to attribute paraphrasing to legal authorities. Use the following guidelines:

- Use a quotation when what has been said is so articulate and apt that to paraphrase it would dilute its meaning, when the words of the quotation themselves are being analyzed in your writing, or when the author of the quotation is so well known that a quotation from this source would provide instant credibility.
- Avoid such long quotations that the reader's reaction is "please don't make me read this." Use quotations sparingly so that their effect is dramatic and they grab the reader's attention.
- Avoid using a quotation to begin discussion of an issue.
- There is nothing wrong with paraphrasing, which is putting someone else's ideas or words into your own language, so long as you properly attribute paraphrases to the source.
- To paraphrase, read the original source several times to make sure you understand it. Then use your own words to "reconstruct" the material without looking at it. Check your finished writing against the original to ensure you have not used too much of the original source's exact structure. Attribute the writing to the original source.
- Paraphrase when the original quotation is difficult to understand or would require so much restructuring (for example, with ellipses and brackets) that it would be distracting to the reader.
- Paraphrase when the quotation is so long that reproducing it in full would invite the reader to skip over it.
- Always provide a full citation, with a pinpoint cite to the particular page, for every quotation and paraphrase in your document.
- Avoid dumping quotations into projects without any analysis of how and why they apply to the client's case. Anyone can retype a case or legal authority.

Figure 7-3   Examples of Elements in a Legal Memorandum

Element	Poor	Better
Issue	Does the client have a cause of action for sexual harassment?	Under the Civil Rights Act of 1964, does harassment occur when a supervisor makes a single remark in the workplace, namely, "Hey, babe, you're hot"?
Brief Answer	No	Because courts consistently require that conduct be severe to constitute harassment, the single comment made in this case is highly unlikely to constitute harassment.
Facts	Grace Parks, the client, was subject to intolerable conduct in the workplace when a supervisor teased her by saying, "Hey, babe, you're hot." This comment was made in front of other employees and thoroughly humiliated Grace.	Grace Parks, the client, is an employee of ABC Inc. Two months ago, when Ms. Parks entered a conference room, her supervisor stated to her, in front of other employees, "Hey, babe, you're hot." Ms. Parks would like to know if this remark constitutes sexual harassment.
Discussion	A poor discussion will: – merely summarize cases and fail to include facts from cases relied on – rely on nonsimilar cases, such as those involving physical conduct and touching rather than oral remarks – lack objectivity and examine only cases in which harassment is found and ignore unfavorable cases – provide mere summaries of cases and fail to draw conclusions as to whether harassment is likely to be found	A better discussion will: – provide the text of governing statutes – discuss and analyze cases with similar fact problems, focusing on cases involving oral remarks rather than those involving only physical touching – discuss cases holding that a single remark can constitute harassment and compare and contrast these to client's case – analyze cases in depth
Conclusion	A poor conclusion will: – be overlong – include citations – introduce new material	A better conclusion will: – briefly summarize the major points of the memorandum

For Preparing Effective Legal Memoranda

- Do not number a single issue or question. If there is a *1* or an *a*, there must be a *2* or a *b* following it.
- Do not include formal citations in the Brief Answers or Conclusion sections.
- To eliminate unnecessary facts, reread your Statement of Facts after you have completed your first draft. If the Statement of Facts includes items not later mentioned in the Analysis section, those facts can probably be omitted.
- If each paragraph in your memo discusses a single case, this is a signal that you are merely summarizing cases rather than analyzing them.
- Retain symmetry in your memo. If there are three Questions, there should be three Brief Answers, and three main sections in the Analysis, each corresponding in number and order to the other.
- Use descriptive headings and subheadings. Thus, write *Elements of Fraud* rather than *Issue Two.*
- Review the beginning of each paragraph. If each starts with the same opening, for example, *In* Smith v. Jones, *the court held* . . . the project will have a choppy, stodgy style.
- Do not use first person pronouns. Avoid statements such as *The next case I found* or *I believe.*
- Identify parties in cases by their status (such as *plaintiff* or *defendant*) rather than by their names.

Figure 7-4   Sample Legal Memorandum

MEMORANDUM

To: James T. Younger, Esq.
From: Ellen T. Carpenter, Esq.
Re: Judith Davidson—Landlord's Liability for Criminal Acts of Third Parties
          Client Number: 0190-001
Date: August 10, 2008

==

ISSUE

Is a landlord who knows of violent criminal activity at and near its leased premises liable for a sexual assault on a tenant by a third party when it fails to warn the tenant of the prior criminal activity and fails to enhance security measures at the premises?

BRIEF ANSWER

Yes. Although a landlord is not an insurer of its tenants' safety, when a criminal attack is reasonably foreseeable, a landlord may be liable for injury to the tenant by a third party.

FACTS

Our client, Judith Davidson ("Davidson"), is a tenant at Brookside Gardens Apartments. Davidson signed a written lease for the premises on March 1, 2008, after the managing partner of the landlord, Jackson Property Management, LLP ("JPM"), showed Davidson the premises. Two months after Davidson moved into the premises, she was sexually assaulted by a nonresident, Kyle Reynolds, in the common area of the premises. Prior to the assault, JPM had been notified by the local police of increased criminal activity in the neighborhood near the premises and knew that two robberies and four physical assaults had occurred at Brookside Gardens in the six months before the attack on Davidson. JPM did not notify any tenants of these criminal activities and did not enhance any security measures at the premises.

DISCUSSION

1. Landlords Are Not Insurers of Their Tenants' Safety

Generally, in the absence of statutes or special relationships (such as parent and child), a private person has no duty to protect another from a criminal assault or from physical harm by another. Restatement (Second) of Torts § 315 (1965). Moreover, courts have usually held that landlords are not insurers of the safety of their tenants. Thus, the mere relationship of landlord and tenant does not impose on the landlord a duty to protect the tenant from the criminal activities of third person. Tracy A. Bateman & Susan Thomas, Annotation, *Landlord's Liability for Failure to Protect Tenant from Criminal Acts of Third Person*, 43 A.L.R.5th § 3 (1996). Nevertheless, landlords have been held liable for the criminal acts of third parties when the landlords have breached a contractual or statutory duty or when the criminal occurrence is reasonably foreseeable. *See, e.g., Tedder v. Raskin*, 728 S.W.2d 343, 350-51 (Tenn. Ct. App. 1987). In the present case, because there is no statute requiring JPM to protect its tenants and JPM had no contractual obligation to do so, the question is whether the sexual assault against Davidson was reasonably foreseeable under the circumstances.

2. A Landlord Is Liable for Reasonably Foreseeable Criminal Acts

In many instances, courts have refused to impose liability on landlords for crimes committed against tenants on the basis that the negligence or criminal conduct of a third party constituted an independent, intervening act that was the proximate cause of the tenant's injuries. *Feld v. Merriam*, 485 A.2d 742, 746 (Pa. 1984). More modern cases rely on traditional negligence principles in holding that a landlord's duty to exercise ordinary care to protect tenants against crimes by third parties extends to foreseeable criminal acts. *Days Inn of Am. v. Matt*, 454 S.E.2d 507, 508 (Ga. 1995).

Thus, the central question in this case is whether the assault on Davidson was reasonably foreseeable. As in other negligence actions, a plaintiff alleging that a landlord is liable for the criminal acts of third parties must prove that the landlord was on notice of a likelihood of danger to his or her tenants. The plaintiff must further prove that the landlord's failure to act after receiving notice sufficient to cause a reasonably prudent person to foresee the probability of harm is the proximate cause of the injury. To meet such a burden, the plaintiff tenant must show that the injury was a reasonably foreseeable probability and not merely a remote possibility. *Tedder*, 728 S.W.2d at 348-49.

Some courts have held that for a landlord to be subject to a duty of care to protect tenants from third-party criminal attacks, the injury to the tenant must be "substantially similar" in type to the previous criminal activities occurring on or near the premises such that a reasonable person would take ordinary precautions to protect his or her tenants against the risk posed by that type of activity. *See, e.g., Wojcik v. Windmill Lake Apts. Inc.*, 645 S.E.2d 1, 3 (Ga. Ct. App. 2007). In *Wojcik*, a pizza deliveryman was murdered by a nonresident at an apartment complex while delivering pizza. The court affirmed summary judgment in favor of the apartment owner, holding that although there was evidence that there were certain property crimes on the premises (such as vehicle break-ins), no murders had occurred at the complex. Thus, the landlord could not have reasonably anticipated the occurrence of the murder.

Similarly, prior property crimes (primarily, automobile thefts and vandalism in an apartment building garage) were insufficient to make the landlord reasonably anticipate that a violent sexual assault on a tenant might occur in the garage. *Doe v. Prudential-Bach/A.G. Spanos Realty Partners, L.P.*, 492 S.E.2d 865, 867 (Ga. 1997). Moreover, criminal incidents in the neighborhood surrounding a building were not sufficient to put a landlord on notice that a sexual assault of a tenant at the leased premises was foreseeable. *Rozhik v. 1600 Ocean Parkway Assocs.*, 617 N.Y.S.2d 535, 536 (App. Div. 1994).

3. Identical Criminal Activity Is Not Needed to Show Foreseeability

The crime committed by the third party need not be identical to prior criminal acts for a duty to rise on the part of the landlord. In *L.A.C. v. Ward*

Parkway Shopping Center Co., 75 S.W.3d 247, 256-57, 259 (Mo. 2002), the court held that a sexual assault of a female shopping mall customer was foreseeable where seventy-five violent crimes had occurred on the mall property in the three years preceding the attack (more than 60 percent of which involved female victims) and a security audit had noted that the area where the sexual assault occurred was frequented by unruly youths. Thus, although there was no evidence of an identical crime in an identical location, the mall owners and operators owed a duty to protect their customer from the sexual assault. The court specifically noted that foreseeability does not require identical crimes in identical locations. *Id.* at 259.

Other courts have permitted evidence of crimes in the neighborhood as bearing on the issue of foreseeability. *See, e.g., Holland v. Liedel*, 494 N.W.2d 772, 775 (Mich. Ct. App. 1992). In *Holland*, the court noted that of more significance than whether crimes had occurred previously at the premises was whether the premises as a whole were located in a high-crime area. *Id.* Similarly, several courts have endorsed the court's statement in *Paterson v. Deeb*, 472 So. 2d 1210, 1219 (Fla. Dis. Ct. App. 1985) that it was not willing to give a landlord "one free ride . . . and sacrifice the first victim's right to safety upon the altar of foreseeability by slavishly adhering to the now-discredited notion that at least one criminal assault must have occurred before the landlord can be held liable."

In *O'Hara v. Western Seven Trees Corp.*, 142 Cal. Rptr. 487, 490-91 (Ct. App. 1977), a tenant sued her landlord and others seeking damages for injuries suffered when she was raped in her apartment. The court held that her complaint stated a cause of action against the defendants because of their alleged negligence in failing to provide adequate security, in misrepresenting security measures in effect at the premises, and in failing to warn the tenant of the danger of rape where it was alleged that the defendants knew of rapes near the premises and had been given composite drawings of the suspect by the police.

In the present case, although there had been no prior sexual assaults on the premises, there had been numerous incidents of violent crime at the premises. The landlord had been informed of similar violent acts in the neighborhood by the police and knew of six violent acts at the premises itself within the prior six months. Crimes had occurred both at the premises and in the area, not merely in the surrounding neighborhood, as was the case in *Rozhik*, 617 N.Y.S.2d at 536. In *In re World Trade Center Bombing Litigation*, 776 N.Y.S.2d 713, 735 (Sup. Ct. 2004), the court held that whether a landlord's knowledge of prior criminal incidents is sufficient to make injuries to its tenants foreseeable depends on the location, nature, and extent of those previous criminal acts and their similarity, proximity, or other relationship to the crime in question. The court stated that a landlord does not need to have had a past experience with the exact criminal activity before liability can be imposed. Where "ambient crime" has infiltrated a landlord's premises, or where the landlord is otherwise on notice of a serious risk of such infiltration, the duty to protect the tenants arises. *Id.* Thus, in the present case, after receiving notice of violent crimes in the neighborhood and at the premises, a reasonably prudent person would have taken ordinary precautions to protect his or her tenants against a known risk of violent acts. JPM knew of violent criminal activity at its premises and in the area and yet failed to take any action to protect its tenants. In such a case, Reynolds's criminal conduct was foreseeable.

An identical crime need not have been committed at the premises to impose a duty on a reasonable person to take ordinary precautions to protect his or her tenants against the type of risk posed by criminal acts. Only the general risk of harm need be foreseen, not the specific harm. *Sharp v. W.H. Moore, Inc.*, 796 P.2d 506, 510 (Idaho 1990). The risk to be prevented is criminal activity—not exclusively sexual assault. In fact, the court in *Sharp* specifically noted that the "solid and growing national trend has been toward the rejection of the 'prior similar incidents' rule." *Id.*

4. Landlords Are Best Able to Protect Tenants from Harm

Many courts have noted that landlords are in the best position to take appropriate protective measures to protect tenants. *Kline v. Mass. Ave. Apt. Corp.*, 439 F.2d 477, 481 (D.C. Cir. 1970). In *Kline*, 439 F.3d at 482, the court noted that the most analogous relationship to that of modern apartment dwellers is that of innkeepers and guests. Other courts have also noted that similar to guests at inns, tenants in apartment buildings whose leases are often of short duration cannot be expected to make the expenditures necessary to secure a building's common areas or take other precautionary measures. *See, e.g., Tedder*, 728 S.W.2d at 347. Because landlords retain control over apartment common areas and grounds, they are in a superior position to take appropriate measures to secure the premises for the safety of the tenants. *Id.*

CONCLUSION

Although the mere relationship of landlord and tenant does not impose upon JPM the duty to protect Davidson against criminal acts by third parties, because the landlord knew of multiple violent crimes both in the area and at the premises, the attack on Davidson was a reasonably foreseeable probability. Thus, the landlord will likely be liable for the injuries suffered by Davidson because it failed to take steps to avoid a predictable risk.

A brief shall be concise, logically arranged with proper headings, and free of irrelevant, immaterial, or scandalous matter. The Court may disregard or strike a brief that does not comply with this paragraph.
Sup. Ct. R. 24.6

chapter 8

Legal Briefs

StyleLinks

http://supreme.lp.findlaw.com/supreme_court/briefs
Briefs filed with the U.S. Supreme Court since 1999 are available at this website.

www.ca8.uscourts.gov
Like many other courts, the Eighth Circuit Court of Appeals now provides its briefs on its website.

www.legaline.com/freebriefslinks.html
Attorney Robert J. Ambrogi provides a number of links to free briefs available on the Internet.

http://ualr.edu/cmbarger
Law Professor Coleen Barger provides a variety of resources and information on brief writing. Select "Appellate Resources."

A. Introduction

The initial documents submitted to courts in litigation cases, such as complaints and answers, are called *pleadings*. Pleadings are discussed in Chapter 9. This chapter discusses legal arguments made in support of or in response to motions in pending cases. When a party requests action from a court (for example, an order changing venue or dismissing a case), he or she makes a motion requesting the action.

Note that most motions include three core elements: the actual motion (a straightforward one- or two-page document formally requesting or moving the court for the desired action, such as moving the court to compel the defendant to answer interrogatories); a proposed order granting the motion (which will be signed by the judge if he or she grants the motion); and the legal argument in support of the motion (generally consisting of several pages with citations to legal authorities). This legal argument is generally called a *brief*, although it can be called a Memorandum of Law or Memorandum of Points and Authorities, perhaps to emphasize that each legal point made in the document must be supported by legal authority. Be careful not to confuse this type of memorandum with the internal office memoranda discussed in Chapter 7. Be careful not to confuse briefs submitted to courts with *case briefs*, which are summaries of the key elements in published cases, often prepared by students in preparation for law classes. A sample of a case brief is provided as Appendix G.

Briefs differ from letters and memoranda in their purpose and audience. Whereas letters and memoranda are intended primarily to inform and explain, briefs are intended to persuade judges. The writing techniques used for briefs are therefore different because each element of a brief should be drafted with its objective in mind: to persuade a court to rule in the client's favor. Trial briefs are submitted in pending cases, and appellate briefs are used to appeal an adverse decision (or submitted in support of a decision) made by the trial court. Moreover, the format for trial briefs is generally simpler than that for appellate briefs.

B. Tips for Writing Briefs

1. Be Persuasive

In some ways, you may find it easier to prepare a brief than an internal office memo. It is easier and more natural for most writers to advocate the client's position in a court brief than to maintain the objectivity required in an interoffice research memo. Aim at being persuasive throughout every portion of the brief. Even identifying the parties provides an opportunity to win over the audience. For example, when representing a corporation, personalize it by referring to the individuals involved (the directors and officers) rather than repeatedly calling it *the company*. Use the client's name (*Fran Nelson*) rather than *Defendant*. Similarly, the table of contents and headings provide an opportunity for you to persuade the court. Consider the following two headings.

Neutral Heading	Persuasive Heading
Punitive Damages	*Defendant's Reckless Conduct Entitles Plaintiff to Punitive Damages*

In many jurisdictions, headings often consist of a single sentence. They are numbered (using either Arabic or Roman numerals) and may appear in all capital letters centered on the page. Use parallel structure so that if a reader reads only these point headings in a brief, they provide a clearly written outline of the argument. Don't alternate between phrases and complete sentences. Maintain consistency in your headings.

Although you must be persuasive, you must be concise. The reader (whether a clerk or a judge) wants to know only two things: what relief you are requesting and why you deserve it. Use a thesis statement (see Figure 7-1) at the beginning of your brief to answer these questions.

2. Be Honest

Although you need not present the adversary's argument, you have an ethical duty to be honest and bring to the court's attention anything that would assist the court in reaching a decision. If you discover cases that do not support the client's position, address them in a straightforward fashion, and then show the reader why they do not apply. Argue that these adverse cases should be narrowly interpreted. Act on the assumption that your adversary will discover these cases and that if you introduce these problem areas yourself, you decrease the effect of the adversary's "smoking gun." Moreover, the integrity shown by an honest and direct discussion of these issues will carry over to the rest of your argument. Don't overstate or exaggerate your own case.

3. Know the Rules

Most courts issue rules relating to documents submitted to them. Some of these rules relate to the paper used, citation form, length of the document, and the elements required in a brief. Many courts now establish maximum page limits. For example, a newly revised federal rule has reduced the page allowance for principal briefs filed in the U.S. courts of appeal from fifty pages to thirty pages. Fed. R. App. P. 32. A failure to comply with the rules can be fatal. For example, in December 1997, the *National Law Journal* reported that after attorneys submitted a brief three times in the incorrect type size (using 10-point rather than 12-point font, as required by court rules), a court dismissed the case. Nearly all courts, including the U.S. Supreme Court, have posted their rules on their websites. Table T.1 of *The Bluebook* provides each state's judicial website. Additionally, you may always contact the court clerk to obtain a copy of the court's rules.

Ethics Alert: Follow the Rules

Always check the court's rules to ensure your brief complies with all requirements as to form, contents, and filing. In a recent case, an appeal brief was filed
six minutes late, and the court dismissed the appeal as untimely. *Alva v. Teen
Help*, 469 F.3d 946 (10th Cir. 2006). Thus, failure to comply with even seemingly
minor court rules and requirements may well be malpractice.

C. Trial Court Briefs

1. Introduction

Briefs submitted to trial courts may be written in support of a certain position or in
response or opposition to an argument. As in all legal writing, remember your
audience. The judge who will read the brief will be busy and will be frustrated with
a lengthy and repetitious document. Opposing counsel will scrutinize the brief
looking for errors and mischaracterizations of the law. Although it is futile to
believe you can persuade opposing counsel, aim at presenting a brief that at least
cannot be attacked by opposing counsel. A sample trial court brief is found in
Figure 8-2 at the end of this chapter.

2. Elements of a Trial Court Brief

The elements of a brief submitted to a trial court will vary from jurisdiction to
jurisdiction. The following elements are found in most briefs, but always review
your local court rules to determine if there is a required format.

a. Caption

Because the brief submitted to the court is a form of pleading, it must display the
caption of the case. The caption identifies the pertinent information about the case:
the court, the parties, the docket number, and the title of the document, such as
Defendant's Memorandum of Law in Support of Motion to Change Venue. Bluepages
B10.6.3 of *The Bluebook* and *ALWD* Rules 3 and 29 provide instructions for abbreviations and capitalization in titles of court documents.

b. Introductory Statement

The party submitting the brief typically begins with a short statement identifying
what the party is requesting, such as the following: *Defendant Vincent T. Parker
respectfully submits the following Memorandum of Law in support of his Motion to
Change Venue.*

c. Statement of Facts

To save the judge the time of reviewing all the pleadings submitted to the court to determine what the case is about, the brief should include a statement of facts. Although these facts must be accurate, strive to present them in a manner most favorable to the client. Use active voice and descriptive facts to emphasize facts supporting the client's position. Most facts are presented in chronological order, although you may discuss them by topic if you wish to emphasize certain facts. Present the facts in the third person and in the past tense unless the facts are still unfolding. Be careful not to jump the gun and argue your case. Thus, focus solely on the facts, not on legal theories or analysis. Don't overlook the importance of a well-written statement of facts. Because most judges have a thorough understanding of the law, they may begin forming impressions and drawing conclusions even as they read the facts.

d. Argument

The argument section is the heart of the brief. This section contains the analysis of the legal authorities that support the client's position. Use a thesis statement (see Figure 7-1) for each issue to provide an assertive encapsulation of your analysis and "set the stage" for the discussion to follow. As discussed in Chapter 7, many writers use the IRAC approach in writing. Other writers believe that IRAC is not well suited for persuasive writing because a neutral statement of the issue (the I in IRAC) is ineffective in a document that should be forceful in every regard. Thus, these experts prefer the CRAC approach with an assertive conclusion given first, followed by explanation of the legal rules governing the subject matter, application of the rules to the specific fact situation, and a summing up conclusion.

Divide your argument into sections, giving each section a persuasive heading and an Arabic or Roman numeral and centering the heading on the page. Use subheadings if needed, making sure all headings of the same type are presented consistently. Discuss authorities in the past tense as in *The court held that* . . . . When discussing statutes with several elements or a test used by the courts, discuss each element in the order provided in the statute or case. Watch the use of the phrase *this case;* a reference to *this case shows* may be interpreted as a reference to the client's particular case rather than a published authority. Be definite. Avoid expressions such as *it seems* or *it is likely*, which immediately convey the message that the author is not sure of the position taken. Do not use the first person. Thus, do not write *We argue*, or *We will show*. Instead use expressions such as *Defendant will show* or *Plaintiff has contended*. This keeps the focus on the parties, not on you as the writer. Discuss your strongest arguments first when the reader is most attentive. Try to bury weaker arguments about two-thirds of the way through the brief, and then end with a strong argument. As always, be sure to do more than summarize case holdings. Analyze cases and tell the reader how and why they apply to the client's particular fact situation. Finally, although the aim of your brief is to persuade, you need not denigrate the adversary's position. A logical and well-reasoned argument will command respect. A hostile and sarcastic diatribe will destroy your credibility.

e. Conclusion

The conclusion should be a very brief recap of the highlights of the argument. Use the conclusion as your final opportunity to deliver your message. Because it is a summary, no citations should be included. The last sentence of the brief should remind the reader of the relief requested, as in *For the foregoing reasons, Defendant Vincent T. Parker respectfully requests the Court grant his Motion for Change of Venue.*

f. Signature and Date

The brief is typically "closed" much like a letter, although the complimentary close is usually *Respectfully submitted,* and a date is included together with the attorney's bar number, signature, and identification of the firm.

g. Certificates of Service and Compliance

A certificate of service is placed at the conclusion of a pleading to verify that a copy of the document has been served on all parties. The method of service, such as hand delivery or first class mail, and the date of service must be specified. Many courts also require a certificate of compliance by the attorney or preparer of the document to verify that the document complies with all court rules, including those relating to word count limits.

h. Exhibits

A number of exhibits may be attached to the brief, such as transcripts of deposition testimony, declarations, answers to interrogatories, and so forth. Make sure that the titles and labeling of the actual exhibits are consistent with how they have been titled and labeled in the brief itself.

i. Order

Most courts require the parties to submit a proposed order with the brief so that if the judge agrees with a party, an order is ready for the judge's signature.

See Figure 8-2 at the end of this chapter for a sample trial court brief.

D. Appellate Briefs

1. Introduction

An appellate brief seeks reversal, affirmance, or some modification of a lower court's action. Although the trial court judge who rules on a motion may be familiar with the case and the facts presented in a trial brief and may, in fact, have been assigned to a case from its filing, appellate judges will have no such familiarity with cases before them. You will thus have to be as articulate and persuasive as possible to convince the appellate court to rule in your client's favor.

Appellate work is highly complex and is often carried out by law firms whose practices are devoted solely to appellate work. Because the focus of an appeal is so different from that of a trial (in that its focus is on determining whether a prejudicial error in law occurred at the trial rather than in determining whether given facts occurred), in many instances the appealing parties obtain new counsel exclusively for the purposes of preparing the appellate brief and conducting the oral argument. Because appellate work is so specialized and is a field in which few attorneys are engaged, a sample appeal brief is included as Appendix C rather than in this chapter.

2. Elements of Appellate Briefs

Many of the elements of an appellate brief are the same as the elements of a trial brief. Following are the elements typically found in an appellate brief, although their order may vary.

a. Cover Sheet

The cover sheet is a title page identifying the court hearing the appeal, the identities of the appellant and appellee (sometimes called the petitioner and the respondent), the docket number of the case, the lower court that handled the trial or prior appeal, the title of the document, and the attorneys representing the parties submitting the brief.

b. Identification of Parties

Unless all of the parties are identified on the cover sheet, a list of all parties to the lower court proceeding usually must be provided to allow justices to review it for conflicts of interest.

c. Table of Contents

A table of contents or index must be included to identify for the reader the page location of each element in the brief. Many software programs automatically generate a table of contents. The table of contents will include all headings and subheadings so phrase these as persuasively as possible.

d. Table of Authorities

An appellate brief must include a list of all authorities cited in the brief together with an indication of the page(s) in the brief on which the authority appears. As with the table of contents, many software programs automatically generate a table of authorities. Follow court rules as to citation form. Few courts have rules relating to tables of authorities, so follow these guidelines:

- Organize your authorities by category, so that all of your cases are listed together (alphabetically) under their own heading, all of the statutes are listed together (alphabetically for state statutes and by ascending title number for federal statutes) under their own heading, and all of the secondary authorities are listed together (alphabetically) under their own authority.
- Include the full citation (and any subsequent history) for all cases. Be consistent. Either present all case names in full or use abbreviations (such as *Acad.* for *Academy*) but don't mix and match the two styles.
- You need not include pinpoint cites or signals for the cases you have cited.
- Include a page reference for any cases cited in short form (as in *Id.* at 423).
- Review other briefs (for example, those filed with the U.S. Supreme Court, available at www.supremecourtus.gov) as models.

e. Jurisdictional Statement

The appellate brief should include a concise statement of the grounds upon which the court's jurisdiction rests, including a reference to the pertinent authority. The jurisdictional statement simply tells the appellate court which statute allows the appeal. A sample jurisdictional statement might read *This Court of Appeals for the Eighth Circuit has jurisdiction to hear this appeal pursuant to 15 U.S.C. § 1071(b) (2000).*

f. Constitutional and Statutory Provisions

If the case includes constitutional provisions, statutes, or regulations, they must be set forth in full together with their citations. If the provisions are especially lengthy, you may set forth their pertinent parts. Many courts allow the relevant constitutional and statutory provisions to be set forth in an appendix to the brief.

g. Question(s) Presented

Most courts require the parties to present the issues the court is being asked to address. In some briefs, such as those submitted to the U.S. Supreme Court, the question(s) presented is set forth immediately after the cover sheet, thus immediately signaling to the reader the focus of the argument to follow. These issues are presented in question format and are somewhat similar to the questions presented in an office memorandum but should be drafted in such a persuasive manner that the desired answer is obvious. For example, a petitioner's question may begin *Did the trial court err when it held* . . . whereas the respondent's brief may begin *Did the trial court properly hold* . . . .

h. Statement of the Case

The statement of the case or statement of facts includes only the facts that have been proven at trial. Thus, each factual statement is followed by a reference to the location in the lower court record or clerk's transcript where such fact was established. To some degree, the statement of the case will parallel the statement of facts for a brief submitted to a trial court. This section usually includes a brief overview of the case's procedural history, namely a review of what happened below and how the case arrived at this reviewing court. Be honest and straightforward. Establish credibility by being accurate and including all facts, even those unfavorable to the client's position. Remember the techniques of passive voice and placement to de-emphasize unfavorable facts. Present the statement of the case in narrative form, in chronological order, and in the past tense.

i. Summary of the Argument

A concise summary of the argument is often included. This is a preview of the argument to follow. This is the first section of the brief that allows advocacy and you should take advantage of this opportunity to persuade the reader to rule in favor of the client.

j. Argument

Like the argument in a trial court brief, the argument in an appellate brief is the heart of the document. This section analyzes the authorities and convinces the reviewing court to rule for the client. Divide the brief into separate sections with each section receiving its own point heading. The headings should correspond to the questions set forth earlier and should be parallel to each other. Use subheadings as needed. Read in sequence, the headings should provide an outline of the argument. If possible, discuss topics in the order discussed in the statement of facts. Use an assertive thesis statement (see Figure 7-1) for each issue in the argument section.

k. Conclusion

The conclusion of an appellate brief often does not summarize the argument section. This summary has already been given before the argument. Instead, the conclusion often merely specifies the relief sought, such as requesting the court to affirm or reverse the lower court's decision. Avoid formal citations in the conclusion.

l. Signature

The name, address, telephone number, and bar number of the attorney representing the party is set forth after the conclusion.

m. Certificates of Service and Compliance

The certificate of service demonstrates to the court that the brief has been provided to all parties and specifies the date and manner of service, such as hand delivery or first class mail. The certificate of compliance demonstrates to the court that the document complies with all court rules, including those relating to page and word count limits.

n. Appendix

Appellate briefs often include an appendix, which may consist of portions of the trial court transcript, jury instructions, or pleadings from the lower court action. Make it easy for the reader by using exhibit tabs, including a table of contents for the appended material, and highlighting relevant material. You cannot be sure a reader will thoroughly review materials in an appendix, so keep the focus of your argument in the body of the brief. Moreover, frequent references to extraneous material disrupt the flow of the argument. See Figure 8-1 for a chart comparing elements of trial and appellate briefs.

Figure 8-1   Elements of Trial and Appellate Court Briefs

Trial Court Briefs	Appellate Court Briefs
Caption	Cover Sheet
Introductory Statement	Identification of Parties
	Table of Contents
	Table of Authorities
	Jurisdictional Statement
	Constitutional and Statutory Provisions
	Questions Presented
Statement of Facts	Statement of the Case
	Summary of the Argument
Argument	Argument
Conclusion	Conclusion
Signature	Signature
Certificates of Service and Compliance	Certificates of Service and Compliance
Exhibits	Appendix
Order	

Tip Tips for Effective Brief Writing

- Know and follow the rules of the court to which the brief will be submitted.
- Do more than summarize cases. Show the reader how and why the authorities you rely on apply to the client's case.
- Write from the client's perspective. Do not use first person. Do not write *We argue*, and so forth. Use third person only, as in *The Appellant will show*.
- Avoid a rote method of writing. If each paragraph discusses one case and ends with a citation, the brief will have a rigid appearance and tone. Variety in analyzing cases will enhance readability.
- Avoid sarcasm, humor, or irony. These techniques are often misinterpreted in written documents because they largely depend on voice inflection and body language to convey meaning. Maintain a respectful tone toward the court and the other party.
- Avoid the overuse of quotations. A well-chosen quotation can give force to your writing; continual quoting dilutes the strength of the quotations. Avoid merely dropping quotations into the project. Explain their relevance.

(continued)

Tips for Effective Brief Writing

- Keep the focus on your argument. Fully develop the client's position before responding to the opposition.
- Do not distort or overstate your position. If any portion of the brief is not supported by valid authority, the entire brief is undermined.
- Focus on your best arguments. If some arguments are "long shots," do not include them. Including weak arguments causes readers to question the writer's credibility.
- Write clearly. In 2000, the Kentucky Supreme Court suspended a lawyer for sixty days for a "virtually incomprehensible" brief and dismissed his client's case.
- Avoid confusing labels such as *Cross-Respondent*. Use either the party's name (*Doyle*) or a functional description (*the employer*).
- Study and review other briefs. Briefs submitted to the U.S. Supreme Court may be accessed at www.supremecourtus.gov.

Footnotes or Not? Pros and Cons

Citations to legal authority can appear throughout the narrative text or in footnotes. There are two schools of thought on using footnotes in legal memos and court briefs.

Pros. Some experts advocate moving citations out of the body of text and into footnotes to unclutter the narrative. In fact, some judges in California are experimenting with writing citation-free opinions, placing all citations and extraneous comments in footnotes to create more readable and less distracting opinions.

Cons. Other experts believe that the placement of a footnote number at the end of a sentence jars curious readers who are then compelled to glance at the bottom of the page, abandoning important arguments in the body of the text. These experts suggest that if the point of a logical argument is to carry the reader seamlessly from the first sentence to the last, footnotes disrupt this objective. These experts point out that legal readers readily understand citation form and can easily skip over citations in the body of the text.

Rules for Footnotes

- Never use footnotes to circumvent court rules on page limits.
- Check your firm or office practice as well as court rules regarding the use of footnotes. Some courts require footnotes to be in the same size type as the body of a brief whereas others, such as the U.S. Supreme Court, require smaller type. Sup. Ct. R. 33.1(b) requires 10-point type.

(continued)

Footnotes or Not? Pros and Cons

- Don't assume all readers will read all footnotes. Thus, use footnotes to cite to legal authorities or to elaborate but never to set forth a main argument. Avoid these "talking" footnotes.
- Avoid footnotes that wrap from one page to the next (or beyond). Many readers will leave the narrative discussion, read the footnote, turn the page, and then resume reading where they are, rather than returning to the page on which the footnote began.
- Never use endnotes.

Having to read a footnote resembles having to go downstairs to answer the door while in the midst of making love.

Noel Coward

Figure 8-2   Sample Trial Court Brief

Following is an actual brief submitted to the United States District Court for the Southern District of California. Portions of the brief have been edited. The author wishes to apologize to the authors of the original brief for any revisions.

Seyamack Kouretchian (State Bar No. 171741)
Robert Berkowitz (State Bar No. 227888)
Rachel Lipsky (State Bar No. 239128)
COAST LAW GROUP LLP
169 Saxony Road, Suite 204
Encinitas, California 92024
Tel: (760) 942-8505
Fax: (760) 942-8515
Attorneys for Defendant,
Shawn Hogan.

UNITED STATES DISTRICT COURT
SOUTHERN DISTRICT OF CALIFORNIA

UNIVERSAL CITY STUDIOS PRODUCTIONS LLLP, a Delaware limited liability limited partnership, Plaintiff,	))))	Case No. 06 CV 0545 W WMc **DEFENDANT'S MOTION TO DISMISS FOR LACK OF SUBJECT MATTER**
vs.	))))	**JURISDICTION (Fed. R. Civ. P. 12(h)(3))**
SHAWN HOGAN, an individual Defendant.	)))	Judge: Hon. Thomas J. Whelan Date: November 27, 2006 Courtroom 7 10:00 a.m.

I.

SUMMARY OF ARGUMENT

The Plaintiff's Complaint for Copyright Infringement must be dismissed for lack of subject matter jurisdiction. Evidence recently obtained from the Plaintiff through discovery has revealed that the Copyright Certificate of Registration ("Copyright Registration") upon which the Plaintiff is relying is patently invalid. In addition, this evidence has revealed that the Plaintiff lacks standing to bring or maintain this action before this Court. Either of these circumstances—an invalid federal copyright or lack of standing—is sufficient, as a matter of law, to preclude this Court from asserting subject matter jurisdiction. For this reason, Defendant Shawn Hogan seeks an order dismissing the Plaintiff's Complaint.

II.

STATEMENT OF FACTS

On March 14, 2006, Plaintiff Universal City Studios Productions, LLLP filed suit against San Diego County resident, Defendant Shawn Hogan (hereinafter "Hogan"). In its Complaint, which consists of only one cause of action, the Plaintiff alleges that Hogan infringed the Plaintiff's Copyright Registration in the motion picture *Meet the Fockers* (hereinafter "Movie") by making a copy of it available over the Internet. Attached to the Plaintiff's Complaint is a copy of the Copyright Registration, which makes no reference whatsoever to the Plaintiff. Rather, the Copyright Registration identifies a third party, Universal City Studios, LLLP, (a Delaware limited liability limited partnership, which is neither a parent nor subsidiary of Plaintiff) as the copyright claimant and the author.

The Copyright Registration contains the following statements, all of which were certified under law to be correct:

1. that third party Universal City Studios, LLLP is a co-author of the Movie;
2. that third party Universal City Studios, LLLP submitted the copyright application;
3. that third party Universal City Studios, LLLP is the copyright claimant; and
4. that the individual signing the application is the authorized agent of third party Universal City Studios, LLLP.

The application was signed on January 20, 2005, by third party Universal City Studios, LLLP and received by the United States Copyright Office on January 25, 2005. Notably, the Plaintiff never alleges in its Complaint how it came to own the Copyright Registration, so Hogan was initially unable to contest the issue of subject matter jurisdiction and was thereby forced to file an answer.

In order to establish whether the Plaintiff actually had any rights in the Copyright Registration, on or about August 10, 2006, Defendant propounded and served upon the Plaintiff the Defendant's Request for Production of Documents and Things, pursuant to Fed. R. Civ. P. 34. In his Request No. 3 of the Defendant's Request for Production of Documents and Things, Hogan requested that Plaintiff produce "any and all documents that evidence or relate to a transfer of ownership of copyright registration no. PA-1-255-623."

On or about September 15, 2006, the Plaintiff responded to Hogan's said request as follows: "Universal will produce, or has produced, the following document evidencing the transfer of ownership of copyright registration no. PA-1-255-623: the operative assignment agreement related to the copyright."

Included with Plaintiff's response was a copy of the "operative assignment agreement" ("Assignment Agreement"). The Assignment Agreement indicated that third party Universal City Studios, LLLP had assigned all of its "right, title and interest in and to . . . " the Movie, "including . . . the copyright in and to [the Movie] . . . ." The Assignment Agreement further indicated that third party Universal City Studios, LLLP had divested itself of any and all rights in the Movie by assigning them to the Plaintiff on November 29, 2004.

Based upon the evidence recently uncovered, the following facts are now known:

1. On November 29, 2004, third party Universal City Studios, LLLP transferred all of its rights in the Movie to the Plaintiff;
2. At the time of the said assignment, there was no Copyright Registration;
3. Some two months after having assigned all "right, title and interest" in the Movie to the Plaintiff, third party Universal City Studios, LLLP applied for the Copyright Registration in its own name as an author and claimant;

4. At the time of the Copyright Registration, third party Universal City Studios, LLLP did not own any right, title, or interest in the Movie;
5. The Plaintiff has not identified any document other than the Assignment Agreement that it purports to evidence or relate to a transfer of ownership in or to the Movie or to the Copyright Registration; and
6. The Plaintiff's Complaint for Copyright Infringement against Hogan is specifically based upon the Copyright Registration.

In light of these facts, which expose the lack of subject matter jurisdiction by this Court, Hogan has filed this Motion to Dismiss.

III.

ARGUMENT

A. This Court Must Dismiss the Plaintiff's Complaint for Lack of Subject Matter Jurisdiction Because the Defendant's Purported Copyright Registration is Invalid and Unenforceable.

Whenever it appears by suggestion of the parties or otherwise that the court lacks jurisdiction of the subject matter, the court shall dismiss the action. Fed. R. Civ. P. 12(h)(3). An action for infringement may not be brought unless registration of the copyright claim has been made in accordance with the Copyright Act. 17 U.S.C. § 411 (2000). Thus, "[a] copyright registration is a jurisdictional prerequisite to an infringement action." *In re Napster, Inc. Copyright Litig.*, 2005 U.S. Dist. LEXIS 7236 (N.D. Cal. 2005) (citing 17 U.S.C. § 411); *see also* 2 Melville B. Nimmer & David Nimmer, *Nimmer on Copyright* § 7.16 (2002) (citing *Chicago Bd. of Educ. v. Substance, Inc.*, 354 F.3d 624, 631 (7th Cir. 2003), *cert. denied*, 543 U.S. 816 (2004)).

Only "the owner of copyright or of any exclusive right in the work may obtain registration of the copyright claim . . . ." 17 U.S.C. § 408 (2000). Once an author assigns its common-law copyright in a work, it thereby divests itself of all right to claim copyright in such work. *See* Nimmer, *supra*, § 5.01 (citing *Ripley v. Findlay Galleries, Inc.*, 155 F.2d 955 (7th Cir.), *cert. denied*, 329 U.S. 775 (1946)); *see also Grandma Moses Props., Inc. v. This Week Magazine*, 117 F. Supp. 348 (D.N.Y. 1953).

For this reason, a copyright registration obtained by a party other than the owner has no legal effect. *Warren v. Fox Family Worldwide, Inc.*, 328 F.3d 1136, 1143 (9th Cir. 2003) (citing 17 U.S.C. §§ 201(b), 501(b) (2000)) (holding that a copyright registration is invalid when obtained by the work's creator pursuant to a work-for-hire relationship), *Morgan, Inc. v. White Rock Distilleries, Inc.*, 230 F. Supp. 2d 104, 108 (D. Me. 2002). Thus, a claim based upon such a copyright registration must be dismissed for lack of subject matter jurisdiction. *Warren*, 328 F.3d at 1143.

It is a plaintiff who bears the burden of demonstrating that the court has subject matter jurisdiction to hear the action. *Warren v. Fox Family Worldwide, Inc.*, 171 F. Supp. 2d 1057, 1060 (C.D. Cal. 2001), *aff'd*, 328 F.3d 1136 (9th Cir. 2003). The general rule is that "[i]n any judicial proceedings the certificate of a registration . . . shall constitute *prima facie* evidence of the validity of the copyright *and of the facts stated in the certificate.*" 17 U.S.C. § 410 (2000) (emphasis added). However, the evidence recently disclosed by the Plaintiff to support its claim of ownership proves exactly the opposite conclusion—that the Copyright Registration has no legal effect.

The sequence of events as documented by the Plaintiff's evidence makes it clear that third party Universal City Studios, LLLP assigned *all* of its rights in the Movie two months *before* it applied for the Copyright Registration. Thus, at that time of registration, third party Universal City Studios, LLLP was not the owner of the copyright; nor was it the owner of any of the exclusive rights in the Movie. In other words, at the time of registration, third party Universal City Studios, LLLP had as much authority to apply for the Copyright Registration as did Hogan—absolutely none. For this reason, the Copyright Registration upon which the Plaintiff is relying is simply not enforceable.

Federal courts have unwaveringly enforced the statutory ownership requirement by giving no legal effect to copyright registrations obtained by anyone other than the actual owner of the copyright in the underlying work. Where, as here, the Copyright Registration upon which the pending action is based was obtained by somebody other than the actual owner in the copyright, the registration is plainly and fatally defective, invalid, and unenforceable. In fact, the Copyright Office would not have registered the subject copyright had it have known that third party Universal City Studios, LLLP was not the rightful copyright claimant at the time it submitted the application. *See* 37 C.F.R. § 201.7(c)(4)(vi) (2005), which states that a completed registration will be cancelled where "the 'claimant' named in the application does not have the right to claim copyright." The Plaintiff's attempt to nevertheless maintain this action before this Court is plainly improper and must, by order of this Court, cease because the Copyright Registration upon which the Plaintiff is relying is fatally defective, invalid, and unenforceable. For these reasons, Defendant Hogan requests that this Court grant this Motion to Dismiss the Plaintiff's Complaint for lack of subject matter jurisdiction.

B. This Court Must Dismiss the Plaintiff's Complaint Because the Plaintiff Does Not Have Standing to Bring or Maintain This Action.

The law is clear. "Standing is a jurisdictional requirement, and the court must dismiss an action for lack of subject matter jurisdiction if it determines that plaintiff lacks standing to assert a claim. *Warren*, 171 F. Supp. 2d at 1063. With regard to copyright infringement actions, the law is equally clear that only the legal or beneficial owner of an exclusive right under copyright has standing to assert a claim for infringement. "The legal or beneficial owner of an exclusive right under a copyright is entitled, subject to the requirements of section 411, to institute an action for any infringement of that particular right committed while he or she is the owner of it." 17 U.S.C. § 501(b). Section 411 provides that "no action for infringement of the copyright in any United States work shall be instituted until registration of the copyright claim has been made in accordance with this title."

If a plaintiff is not the author of the copyrighted work then he or she must establish an ownership interest through the chain of title in order to support a valid claim of copyright infringement. *Religious Tech. Ctr. v. Netcom On-Line Commun. Servs.*, 923 F. Supp. 1231, 1241 (N. D. Cal. 1995) (citing Nimmer, *supra*, § 12.11[C]); *see also Motta v. Samuel Weiser, Inc.*, 768 F.2d 481, 484 (1st Cir. 1985). If the plaintiff cannot establish this ownership interest, then he or she does not have standing to bring an action for copyright infringement. *Maljack Prods. v. Goodtimes Home Video Corp.*, 1994 U.S. Dist. LEXIS 5838 (C.D. Cal. Apr. 26, 1994); *see also Motta*, 768 F.2d at 484.

Once again, it is the evidence recently disclosed by the Plaintiff in support of its claim of copyright ownership that conclusively establishes that it lacks standing to bring or maintain the subject action. This is because this evidence shows that either the underlying Copyright Registration is invalid or that the Plaintiff does not have any right in the Movie that it can allege was infringed by Hogan. Whatever the case, the evidence is clear that the Plaintiff lacks standing to bring or maintain this action.

1. If the Assignment Agreement Is Valid, Then the Plaintiff Lacks Standing to Bring This Action Because the Copyright Registration Is Invalid.

The Copyright Act confers standing only upon those Plaintiffs who are asserting their rights under a valid copyright registration. By requiring compliance with 17 U.S.C. § 411, the Copyright Act expressly requires compliance with the entire title, including the requirement in 17 U.S.C. § 408 that the party applying for the copyright registration be the owner of the copyright. When the party that applied for the copyright registration is not the owner at the time of registration, then the registration has not been obtained in compliance with the Copyright Act, and the registration is invalid and unenforceable. The Plaintiff appears to claim that it has acquired rights in the Movie under the Assignment Agreement. However, the Assignment Agreement was executed two months *before* the Copyright Registration was applied for. If, therefore, the Assignment Agreement is effective to establish chain of title, then the document is also effective to prove that third party Universal City Studios, LLLP had divested itself of all rights, title, and interest in the Movie and, therefore, did not have any right to apply for and obtain the Copyright Registration.

The Plaintiff cannot have it both ways. Either third party Universal City Studios, LLLP assigned all "right, title and interest" in the Movie and then mistakenly or fraudulently obtained the Copyright Registration in its own name, or the Assignment Agreement is somehow invalid and third party Universal City Studios, LLLP properly applied for the Copyright Registration.

In bringing this action, the Plaintiff is relying upon an invalid Copyright Registration if it alleges that the Assignment Agreement is valid. Therefore, because the Plaintiff has failed to identify another valid copyright registration for the Movie, it lacks standing to bring or maintain this action for copyright infringement against Hogan. For this reason, this Court must dismiss this action for lack of subject matter jurisdiction.

2. If Plaintiff Alleges That the Copyright Registration Is Valid, Then the Plaintiff Lacks Standing to Bring This Action Because It Has Failed to Establish Chain of Title in the Movie.

The law requires that a plaintiff asserting an ownership interest in a copyrighted work document the chain of title by which it obtained its rights. The burden is on the Plaintiff to prove its ownership rights. If the Plaintiff alleges that the Copyright Registration is valid, then the Assignment Agreement is invalid because, according to the terms of the Copyright Registration, third party Universal City Studios, LLLP is the owner of the copyright in the Movie. If, therefore, the Assignment Agreement is invalid, then the Plaintiff has failed to set forth any evidence to document the chain of title through which it allegedly acquired rights in the Movie. Without any showing of how the Plaintiff acquired rights in the Movie, the Plaintiff lacks standing to bring this suit because it has failed to establish the ownership of any right which it can claim was infringed by Hogan. For this reason, this Court is respectfully urged to dismiss the Plaintiff's Complaint for lack of subject matter jurisdiction.

IV.

CONCLUSION

For the reasons set forth above, Hogan moves this Court for an order dismissing the Plaintiff's Complaint, without leave to amend, for lack of subject matter jurisdiction.

Dated: October 19, 2006   s/Seyamack Kouretchian
                                   Seyamack@CoastLawGroup.com
                                   Coast Law Group, LLP
                                   Seyamack Kouretchian
                                   Attorney for Defendant, Shawn Hogan

chapter 9

Pleadings and Transactional Documents

StyleLinks

http://topics.law.cornell.edu/wex/pleading
Cornell Law School's Legal Information Institute offers some basic information on pleadings and links to other sources.

www.courtinfo.ca.gov/forms
The California Judicial Council offers a variety of litigation forms, many of which may be filled out electronically.

www.kinseylaw.com
The website of the law offices of Eugene E. Kinsey of California provides numerous forms for complaints, answers, motions, and other pleadings.

A. Pleadings

1. Introduction

A pleading is a document submitted to a court in the course of litigation. In federal cases, the only pleadings are a complaint, an answer, an answer to a counterclaim, an answer to a cross-claim, a third-party complaint, and a third-party answer. Fed. R. Civ. P. 7(a). In some jurisdictions, the term *pleading* encompasses almost anything filed with the court in the course of a pending action.

Court rules today have eliminated older requirements that made pleading so complex and technical that a failure to follow rules could lead to a dismissal of the case. The new approach is called *notice pleading*, which generally means that a pleading must be sufficiently clear as to notify another party of the nature of one's claims or defenses.

2. Format of Pleadings

All jurisdictions have rules relating to the content and format for pleadings. Many state rules of civil procedure are patterned after the Federal Rules of Civil Procedure. For example, most state courts follow Fed. R. Civ. P. 8(d)(1) requiring allegations to be "simple, concise, and direct." Some courts have preprinted and fillable forms available on the Internet. For example, the Judicial Council of California provides a variety of pleading forms at its website at www. courtinfo.ca.gov/forms. Some of the more common rules imposed by courts for pleadings are as follows:

- **Caption.** All pleadings start with a caption that identifies the court, the docket number assigned to the case by the court, an identification of the parties to the case, and the title of the document, such as "Answer to Plaintiff's Complaint."
- **Introductory Matter.** Introductory paragraphs often identify the parties and state the basis for the court's jurisdiction (for example, there is often a reference to the particular statute that allows for the filing of the pleading).
- **Numbering.** Paragraphs are numbered consecutively.
- **Pleading in the Alternative.** Parties are allowed to plead in the alternative and inconsistently. For example, a complaint may allege that the same conduct is both a breach of contract and negligence.
- **Citations.** Pleadings routinely cite statutes but never cite cases.
- **Paragraph Content.** Most paragraphs include only a single allegation so that the other party can readily deny or admit the allegation. Most pleadings "tell a story" in that they set forth the party's claim or defense in a chronological fashion. For example, a complaint for breach of contract generally begins by alleging that a contract was entered into by the parties, then states that the contract was breached by the defendant, and then concludes by stating that the breach caused damage to the plaintiff.

- **Endings.** Most pleadings end with a *prayer*, which is the party's request for relief. Thus, a complaint usually requests money damages and an answer usually requests that the plaintiff's complaint be dismissed.
- **Incorporation by Reference.** Pleadings routinely incorporate other information by reference. Thus, paragraph 16 of a complaint might incorporate the allegations from paragraphs 1 through 5 so that the plaintiff does not have to repeat the information.
- **Responding to a Complaint.** Each allegation in a complaint must be responded to by the defendant. If the defendant does not expressly deny a fact or allege that he or she has no knowledge about the fact, it will be deemed admitted. Moreover, if a defendant does not specifically raise certain defenses in the answer, these defenses may be waived.
- **Amendments.** Don't count on being able to amend a sloppy pleading. Although leave to amend pleadings can be granted, in some instances, a failure to plead a matter may preclude proof of it at trial, and all courts eventually refuse to allow amendment of pleadings without good cause.
- **Certificate of Service.** All court pleadings after the complaint must be accompanied by a certificate of service, verifying that the pleading was provided to all parties, usually by mail or personal service. The complaint is accompanied by a summons issued by the court that will indicate how the defendant was served. The summons is then returned to the court with this information completed, usually by a professional process server.

3. Using Form Books

Form books provide suggested forms and models for various documents. There are some excellent form books for preparing pleadings. Most states have state-specific form books, and law firms that engage in litigation have numerous sample forms that can be used as guides. Make sure that you do not view forms as mere fill-in-the-blank documents. Use the form books or samples as helpful guides but modify or update them when needed. In addition, be careful when using a prior pleading as a form so you don't import errors and irrelevant allegations. Although preparing a pleading does not require the same level of creativity as an appellate brief, it does provide an opportunity to advocate for the client. Consider the following form books:

- *Federal Practice and Procedure* by Charles Alan Wright and Arthur R. Miller (usually called "Wright and Miller") is an excellent multivolume set relating to practice in federal courts that includes many forms.
- *American Jurisprudence Pleading and Practice Forms, Annotated.* This set consists of more than thirty volumes of forms and provides more than 40,000 forms relating to litigation, including forms for complaints, answers, discovery procedures, motions, and jury instructions.
- *Bender's Federal Practice Forms.* This twenty-volume set includes forms for use in federal practice.

See Figure 9-1 for a sample pleading.

Figure 9-1   Sample Complaint for Breach of Contract

Anna T. Carr
Carr & Nelson, LLP
1010 Second Avenue
Suite 1700
San Diego, CA 92110
State Bar No: 12898
(619) 276-1090
Attorney for Plaintiff

SUPERIOR COURT OF THE STATE OF CALIFORNIA

COUNTY OF SAN DIEGO

Liberty Associates, LLC	) **CASE NO: 08-1088**
	)
Plaintiff,	) **COMPLAINT FOR**
	) **BREACH OF**
	) **CONTRACT**
v.	)
	)
	)
Jackson Enterprises, Inc., and	)
	)
Does 1 through 10	)
	)
Defendants	

Plaintiff complains and for causes of action alleges as follows:

FIRST CAUSE OF ACTION

(For Breach of Contract Against Jackson Enterprises, Inc.)

1. Plaintiff Liberty Associates, LLC ("Plaintiff") is a Limited Liability
    Company organized and existing under the laws of the State of California
    with its principal offices in the City of San Diego, County of San Diego.

2. Defendant Jackson Enterprises, Inc. ("Defendant") is a corporation organized and existing under the laws of the State of California with its principal offices located at 1800 Pomerado Road, in the City of San Diego, County of San Diego.

3. Plaintiff is ignorant of the true names and capacities of Defendants sued as Does 1 through 10, inclusive, and therefore sues these Defendants by such fictitious names. Plaintiff will amend this Complaint to allege their true names and capacities when ascertained.

4. Plaintiff is informed and believes and thereon alleges that each of the Defendants was the agent and employee of each of the remaining Defendants and was at all times acting within the purpose and scope of such agency and employment.

5. On or about February 15, 2008, in the City of San Diego, County of San Diego, State of California, Plaintiff and Defendant entered into a written agreement, a copy of which is attached hereto as Exhibit "A" and made a part hereof. By the terms of the written agreement Defendant agreed to pay Plaintiff for certain construction services performed by Plaintiff for Defendant.

6. The consideration set forth in the agreement was fair and reasonable.

7. Plaintiff has performed all conditions, covenants, and promises required by it on its part to be performed in accord with the terms and conditions of the written agreement.

8. On or about September 1, 2008, the Defendant breached the agreement by failing and refusing to pay Plaintiff for the services provided by Plaintiff to Defendant.

9. By reason of Defendant's breach of the contract as alleged in this Complaint, the Plaintiff has suffered damages in the sum of Seventy-Five Thousand Dollars ($75,000).

10. By the terms of the written agreement, the Plaintiff is entitled to recover reasonable attorney fees incurred in the enforcement of the provisions of the agreement. By reason of the aforementioned breach of the Defendant, the Plaintiff has been forced to secure the services of the law firm Carr & Nelson LLP to prosecute this lawsuit.

WHEREFORE, Plaintiff requests judgment against Defendants, and each of them, as follows:

1. For compensatory damages in the sum of $75,000;

2. For interest on the sum of $75,000 from and after September 1, 2008 to date of judgment;

3. For reasonable attorney fees according to proof;

4. For costs of suit incurred; and

5. For such other and further relief as the court may deem proper.

Date: _____   _____

Anna T. Carr, Esq.

Carr & Nelson, LLP

Attorneys for Plaintiff

4. Legalese

Although this Handbook has discussed the importance of writing in plain English, you will find that the language used in pleadings tends to be more legalistic. For example, the prayer usually states "WHEREFORE, this Plaintiff respectfully prays that . . ." rather than "Therefore, the Plaintiff requests the following relief." The reliance on legalese is perhaps understandable given that many pleading forms have existed for hundreds of years. Moreover, many law firms use pleadings similar to the ones they used twenty years ago. Finally, although pleadings will be reviewed by clients and are often verified by clients (meaning that the client verifies by signature that he or she has read the pleading and that it is truthful and accurate), pleadings are primarily intended for a legal audience and thus there has been no aggressive movement to modernize them. For example, the sample complaint shown as Figure 9-1 uses far more terms of art and outmoded expressions than would be advisable in other legal writings, such as letters or memos. Experienced legal readers, however, are easily able to cut through these expressions to understand their meaning.

B. Transactional Documents

1. Introduction

The term *transactional documents* usually refers to documents used in various transactions, such as contracts, leases, employment agreements, and corporate minutes. Legal professionals seldom draft these documents "from scratch." Generally, they rely on forms or models that have proven useful in other instances.

In many cases, there is not a great deal of creativity in transactional documents, nor should there be. Later readers of a lease may examine it carefully trying to find a loophole so they can terminate the lease. The employee may later contend that he or she is not bound by a noncompetition provision in an employment agreement because the provision is unreasonable. Thus, because the document must protect the client in the future against interpretations that were unforeseen at the time the document was drafted, transactional documents tend to be overlong as they attempt to foresee and forestall every possible future problem raised by a hostile reader.

2. Drafting Considerations

There are a variety of considerations and objectives to keep in mind when preparing transactional documents.

- **Review applicable statutes.** In many instances, statutes control the content or form of documents. For example, most statutes require that a disclaimer of a warranty be printed "conspicuously." Similarly, an assignment of a registered trademark must be in writing and must include a statement that the goodwill relating to the mark is being assigned with it. 15 U.S.C. § 1060 (2000). Thus, some preliminary research may be needed to ensure that the document complies with all legal requirements. Although courts give great latitude to parties in structuring their transactions, and generally will not substitute their judgment for the judgment of the parties, applicable statutory provisions must be followed.

■ **Volunteer to draft the document.** The party who creates the initial draft of a document has certain advantages in selecting the structure and word choice. Some adverse parties will only perform a cursory review of a document presented to them to ensure it includes the basics of a transaction. Although there is no place for deceit or trickery, there is nothing wrong with trying to draft a document that protects the client to the greatest extent possible. On the other hand, it is a standard legal principle that any ambiguity in a contract is construed against the party who drafted it.

■ **Avoid making business decisions.** It is the legal professional's job to draft a document that memorializes the transaction and sets forth the parties' duties. Although attorneys can and should offer advice to clients, it is not appropriate for the drafter to insert himself or herself into the negotiations in such a way that the deal breaks apart.

■ **Avoid overreaching.** A good drafter will protect the client's interests but will not draft the agreement in such a lopsided way that the other party immediately rejects it and negotiations stall. Be fair and accurate. Consider using the tools on your word processor (namely, the "track changes" tool) to show the changes you have made to a document sent to you by another party, a technique called *redlining* because the changes usually show up in red on your computer screen. You can easily accept or reject changes.

■ **Use headings.** Because many agreements can be long, use descriptive headings for each section so the reader can readily find a needed provision. Similarly, consider using a table of contents for long documents. If the document will include several definitions, include a separate alphabetized definition section at the beginning of the document for all the defined terms.

3. Elements of Transactional Documents

Although the elements of transactional documents vary greatly, some common components are as follows:

a. Introductory Matter

Most documents begin with an introduction, identifying the name of the document, the parties who will sign it, and its effective date.

b. Recitals

Many documents include a recitals clause, indicating the purpose of the document. For example, a partnership agreement might provide *It is the intent of the parties to form a partnership under California law* . . . .

c. Consideration

Because all contracts require consideration, transactional documents usually include a statement similar to the following: *For valuable consideration, the receipt and sufficiency of which are hereby acknowledged, the parties agree as follows* . . . . This recital then prevents any party to the agreement from challenging the agreement on the basis that there was no consideration supporting it.

d. Operative Terms

The body of the document will include the terms of the parties' agreement, their duties, obligations, and the consequences of noncompliance.

e. Standard Provisions

Most agreements include a number of standard provisions, such as clauses stating the applicable law under which the agreement will be governed, whether the agreement is assignable, that the agreement can only be modified by another agreement in writing, how notice of default will be given, that references to the masculine *he* and *him* are meant to include the feminine, and so forth. These standard provisions are often called *boilerplate* because they routinely appear in most transactional documents.

f. Signatures

Agreements end with the parties' signatures.

4. Using Form Books

There are numerous well-known form books that provide suggested forms, language, and checklists for transactional documents. As with all form books, use the forms as a guide and feel free to modify the forms when needed. Most law firms and offices have numerous standard forms that have served clients well, and these are excellent starting places. Create your own form files of documents so you have samples on hand. Indicate who drafted the document so you can contact the drafter if you have questions. Be aware of the following limitations in using forms for drafting transactional documents:

- Using forms slavishly often results in importing unneeded material, including incorrect names and labels. Proofread carefully.
- Create defined terms to identify parties and issues and use these consistently throughout the document. Use your word processor's "find and replace" feature to ensure consistency.
- Avoid cross-referencing to so many provisions that a reader is hopelessly confused. For example, avoid statements such as *Tenant shall provide notice as provided in Paragraph 11(a)(ii); however, as provided in Paragraph 14(b)(iii), such notice must comply with all provisions of Paragraph 15 hereof.*

- Avoid legalese when you can. Like pleadings, forms tend to use more archaic language than some other legal writings. Trim away stuffy expressions when you can but realize that many law firms are wedded to their tried and true forms and are resistant to making changes. Some lawyers have seen so many agreements start with the word *Witnesseth* that they never question its use. Nevertheless, use expressions such as *lessee* rather than *party of the first part* and *as provided in paragraph 4* rather than *as provided hereinabove*. For example, consider the following two paragraphs:

Legalese

Lessee shall make and deposit as and for rent the sum of $650 per month, which payment shall be made on the first day of each and every month throughout the term of the lease. Payment shall be made to the Landlord at the address provided hereinabove in this Agreement.

Improved

Lessee must pay rent of $650 per month. Payment must be made to the Landlord on the first day of each month at the address provided in Paragraph 2.

- Make the document readable. Give your document a descriptive title such as *Employment Agreement* rather than *Agreement*. Use lists and consistent numbering to present the information logically. Make sure the information is presented in a parallel structure.
- Move bulky information into attachments. Use attachments or exhibits to identify long lists of items (for example, a list of items purchased or a list of partners) rather than including such information in the body of the document.

Ethics Alert: Preserving Client Confidentiality

An emerging issue relating to client confidentiality is the duty to "scrub" documents so as to eliminate metadata, which is information relating to the creation, management, and tracking of an electronically created document. For example, if you use a law office form lease that was originally created for client Smith for new client Jones, metadata would reveal that the lease was originally created for client Smith and would reveal its critical terms and provisions. Metadata mining also allows readers to view changes and deletions made through the course of a document's drafting, the sequence of those changes, delays in sending e-mails, and other confidential information. Failure to "scrub" metadata out of confidential client documents can lead to a waiver of attorney-client privilege or work product privilege. Ethics opinions about metadata mining are still evolving, with some jurisdictions holding that recipients of documents cannot mine for metadata because it invades another attorney's client confidences and other jurisdictions holding that senders have a duty to scrub metadata, and if they fail to do so, the recipient is free to mine for it. Most law firms are now using sophisticated software that scrubs or strips metadata out of confidential documents.

Following are some well-known form books used in drafting transactional documents:

- *American Jurisprudence Legal Forms, 2d.* This sets consists of more than twenty-five alphabetically arranged volumes of more than 20,000 forms and provides forms for contracts, wills, and leases as well as for hundreds of other topics.
- *West's Legal Forms 3d.* This set of books, consisting of more than thirty volumes, contains a variety of forms for general law practice, including bankruptcy forms, forms for the purchase and sale of real estate, and forms relating to business organizations such as partnerships and corporations.
- *Current Legal Forms with Tax Analysis* by Jacob Rabkin and Mark H. Johnson is a thirty-four-volume set of forms for law practice, with an emphasis on business forms. The forms are excellent and include a number of checklists and practice guides and tips for drafting transactional documents.

See Figure 9-2 for a sample partnership agreement.

Figure 9-2 General Partnership Agreement

THIS AGREEMENT is entered into on _____, 20___, among Ann Myers ("Myers"), an individual residing at _____, Gregory Klein ("Klein"), an individual residing at _____ _____, and Philip Hendrix ("Hendrix"), an individual residing at _____.

Myers, Klein, and Hendrix are sometimes referred to individually as "Partner" and collectively as "Partners."

RECITALS

WHEREAS, the Partners desire to form a partnership for the purpose of _____ and have decided that it is in their best commercial interests to do so.

NOW, THEREFORE, for good and valuable consideration, the receipt and sufficiency of which are hereby acknowledged, the Partners agree as follows:

1. *Formation and Purpose of Partnership.* The Partners hereby form a general partnership (the "Partnership") under the laws of the State of _____ for the purpose of _____ _____ and the carrying on of any and all activities necessary and incident thereto.
2. *Partnership Name and Address.* The name of the Partnership is "MKH Enterprises" and its principal place of business shall be located at

_____, in the City of
_____, State of _____,
and at such other places as may be mutually agreed upon by the Partners
in writing.

3. *Term.* The Partnership shall commence on _____,
    20___ and shall continue until dissolved by mutual agreement of the
    Partners or as provided in Paragraph 13 below.

4. *Capital Contributions.*
    (a) *Initial Capital Contributions.* Each Partner shall contribute the
    following amounts in cash ("Initial Capital Contribution") on or before
    _____, 20___ or this Agreement shall be void.

Name	Amount
Myers	$ _____
Klein	$ _____
Hendrix	$ _____

    (b) *Additional Capital Contributions.* At such times as the Partners
    agree that additional capital is necessary to operate the business of the
    Partnership, the Partners shall contribute additional capital in accordance
    with their respective Partnership Interests (as defined in Paragraph 5) at
    the relevant time and in accordance with the agreed amount of the addi-
    tional capital contribution and the method of payment thereof deter-
    mined by the Partners. If any Partner fails to make an additional capital
    contribution required to be made under this Agreement within the time
    period prescribed, such Partner shall be deemed to be a "Defaulting
    Partner" and a non-defaulting Partner shall be entitled to make the con-
    tribution on behalf of the Defaulting Partner and such contribution shall
    be a personal debt due and owing to the non-defaulting Partner from the
    Defaulting Partner(s) with interest at the rate of _____ percent (__%)
    per annum until paid. No money or assets shall be distributed by the
    Partnership to a Defaulting Partner until the Defaulting Partner shall
    have paid in full the amount owed to the non-defaulting Partner(s),
    together with interest. The term "capital contribution" shall mean a
    Partner's Initial Capital Contribution together with any additional capital
    contribution.

    (c) *Return of Capital Contribution.* No interest shall be paid on any
    Partner's capital contribution. No Partner has a right to receive a return
    of all or any part of his or her capital contribution except as expressly
    provided in this Agreement or in the event of liquidation or dissolution of
    the Partnership, and then only to the extent of the net assets of the
    Partnership available for distribution.

5. *Interest of Partners in Partnership.* The Partners shall own the following interest in the Partnership ("Partnership Interest" or "Partnership Interests"):

Name	Interest in Partnership
Myers	_____%
Klein	_____%
Hendrix	_____%

Any change in the Partnership Interest of any Partner shall be reflected in writing and signed by all Partners.

6. *Profits and Losses.* Partners shall share in the profits and losses of the Partnership in accordance with their respective Partnership Interests.

7. *Voting.* The Partners shall be vested with voting rights in the Partnership equal to their respective Partnership Interests. Except as otherwise agreed by the partners in writing or except as otherwise provided in this Agreement, actions of the Partnership shall require majority action of the outstanding Partnership Interests.

8. *Management.* In the general operation of the Partnership business, all the Partners must be consulted and their advice must be obtained as much as is practicable. However, for the purpose of ensuring continuity in the conduct of the Partnership business, the general management of the Partnership business shall vest solely in Myers who shall be the Managing Partner. Myers is entitled to enter into agreements on behalf of the Partnership for the conduct of partnership operations in the ordinary course of business. Persons dealing with the Partnership are entitled to rely on the power and authority of Myers.

Notwithstanding the foregoing, nothing in this Agreement is intended to grant Myers the authority to make all decisions regarding the business of the Partnership. The authority vested in Myers pertains only to the right to bind the Partnership, without the consent or approval of any other Partner, for contracts or obligations in the ordinary course of business that are necessary, appropriate, or incidental to the Partnership's business.

Myers shall not undertake any of the following business activities without the majority vote of the Partners:
(a) borrow money in excess of _____Dollars ($____);
(b) purchase or sell any real estate;
(c) enter into any agreement that would require the Partnership to make any payment of more than _____Dollars ($____) per year;
(d) compromise any claim or institute any litigation or other proceeding on behalf of the Partnership; or
(e) sell all or substantially all of the Partnership's assets.

9. *Duties of Partners.* Each of the Partners shall give his or her undivided time and attention to the Partnership business and shall use his or her best efforts to promote the interests of the Partnership. Partners shall have fiduciary duties to each other and to the Partnership.

10. *Books of Account.* Books of account of the transactions of the Partnership shall be kept at the principal place of business of the Partnership and shall be available at all reasonable times for inspection by any Partner. Financial statements shall be prepared on a quarterly basis and shall include a statement of cash flow. The financial statements shall be prepared by independent certified public accountants selected by the Partners. The tax and accounting year of the Partnership shall be the calendar year. Any Partner, at his or her sole expense, may cause the books of the Partnership to be audited at any time. No later than thirty (30) days after the close of the fiscal year, an annual accounting shall be prepared by the Partnership's independent certified public accountants.

11. *Bank Accounts.* The funds of the partnership shall be kept in such bank accounts or in such manner designated by the Partners. Checks drawn on Partnership funds in any account shall be signed by Myers or such person or persons as the Partnership shall designate from time to time.

12. *Withdrawals, Distributions, and Expenses.*

(a) *Withdrawals.* Each Partner shall be permitted to withdraw from the funds of the Partnership _____ Dollars ($_____) per _____ for the Partner's living expenses. The sums so drawn shall be charged to the Partner and at the annual accounting shall be charged against that Partner's share of the profits. If the Partner's share of the profits is insufficient to equal the sum drawn, the Partner must pay the amount of the deficiency within ten (10) days after notice from the Partnership and said deficiency shall draw interest at the rate of ____ percent (__%) per year until paid.

(b) *Distributions.* So far as is practicable, the net cash flow, if any, of the Partnership (after allocation of an amount agreed upon by the Partners for working capital obligations and contingencies) shall be distributed among the Partners in accordance with their respective Partnership Interests at least annually or on a more frequent basis as decided by the Partners.

(c) *Expenses.* Partners who have incurred expenses on behalf of the Partnership in the ordinary course of Partnership business shall be reimbursed therefor upon submission to the Partnership of appropriate evidence of such expenses, as determined in the sole discretion of the Partners.

13. *Dissolution.* The Partnership shall be dissolved upon the agreement of all Partners or the sale or other disposition of all or substantially all of its assets. Upon dissolution of the Partnership, the Partners shall proceed with reasonable promptness to liquidate the assets of the Partnership. Thereafter, the assets of the Partnership shall be used and distributed in the following order: first, to pay or provide for the payment of all Partnership liabilities to any person (other than Partners) and liquidating expenses; second, to pay or provide for the payment of all liabilities to any Partner; and third, to distribute to the Partners, in accordance with their respective Partnership Interests, the remaining assets of the Partnership.

14. *Change of Partners.* Any change of Partners shall be done only in the manner set forth in this Paragraph and any attempt to transfer otherwise shall be void.

(a) *Withdrawal of Partner.* Any Partner may withdraw from the Partnership by giving to each of the other Partners and the Partnership at least thirty (30) days' prior written notice of the Partner's intent to withdraw. On withdrawal of a Partner, that Partner's Partnership Interest shall be determined by appraisal of the value of the Partnership, and the withdrawing Partner shall be repaid his or her capital contribution within thirty (30) days of the appraisal of the Partnership's value. After deduction for any draw or indebtedness, the withdrawing Partner shall receive cash payments in _____ (__) equal installments, commencing immediately after the end of the fiscal year for the Partner's Interest in the Partnership's profits. The withdrawal of a Partner under this Paragraph 14(a) shall have no effect upon the continuance of the Partnership or its business.

(b) *Bankruptcy, Death, or Permanent Disability.* The bankruptcy, death, or permanent disability of a Partner shall not result in the dissolution of the Partnership, unless required by law. The death of a Partner, the filing of any petition by or against any Partner under the United States Bankruptcy Act, or the permanent disability of a Partner due to sickness or injury shall immediately terminate all right, title, and interest of that Partner in the Partnership. The deceased, bankrupt, or permanently disabled Partner's share of the Partnership shall be established based on the Partner's date of death or permanent disability or the date of filing of any petition under the United States Bankruptcy Act, and, after deduction for any draw or any indebtedness of the Partner, the Partner's estate, trustee in bankruptcy, or the permanently disabled Partner shall be paid a cash payment representing the Partner's capital contribution to the Partnership, the Partner's share of the net profits or losses for the current fiscal year to the date of death or permanent disability or of such filing of such petition, and the Partner's share of the current Partnership business as of the date of death or permanent disability or the date of filing of such petition.

(c) *New Partners.* New partners may be added to the Partnership by invitation from the then-existing Partners or by purchase of a withdrawing, deceased, bankrupt, or permanently disabled Partner's Interest. An invitation to a new partner may be extended on a vote of existing Partners representing _____ percent (__ %) of the Partnership Interests. When a Partner's interest is to be sold to a third party by a Partner leaving the Partnership, a vote on the acceptability of the proposed new partner shall be made by a vote of existing Partners representing _____ percent (_____%) of the outstanding Partnership Interests. A new partner must execute an amendment to this Agreement agreeing to the terms of this Agreement. In the event a proposed new partner is not found acceptable as provided in this Agreement, the Partnership must purchase the departing Partner's interest at the price and upon the terms offered by the third party and the Partnership may resell the interest to a candidate acceptable to the Partners.

15. *Miscellaneous Provisions.*

(a) *Valuation.* Any valuation or appraisal of the Partnership or any Partner's interest in the Partnership shall be conducted by an independent appraiser selected by Partners representing a majority of the outstanding Partnership Interests.

(b) *Notices.* All notices required by law or this Agreement shall be in writing and may be delivered to the Partners personally or may be deposited in the United States mail, postage prepaid, addressed to the Partners at their addresses identified in this Agreement.

(c) *Disputes.* Any dispute arising under the terms of this Agreement that cannot be resolved amicably by the parties shall be submitted to binding arbitration in accordance with the rules of the American Arbitration Association.

(d) *Amendments to Agreement.* No modification of this Agreement shall be valid, nor shall any waiver of any term or provision unless such modification or waiver is in writing and signed by all of the Partners.

(e) *Time of Performance.* Whenever performance by a Partner or the Partnership is required under this Agreement, time shall be of the essence.

(f) *Counterparts.* This Agreement may be executed in one or more counterparts, but all such counterparts shall constitute one and the same Agreement.

(g) *Severability.* In the event any provision of this Agreement is invalid or unenforceable, then such provision shall be deemed severable from this Agreement.

(h) *Successors and Assigns.* Subject to the provisions hereof, this Agreement shall inure to the benefit of and be binding upon the heirs, personal representatives, successors, and assigns of the parties.

(i) *Entire Agreement.* This Agreement contains the entire understanding of the parties hereto with respect to the subject matter hereof and there are no other agreements or understandings, whether written or oral, with respect to the subject matter hereof.

(j) *Applicable Law.* This Agreement shall be governed under the laws of the State of _____.

IN WITNESS WHEREOF, the Partners have executed this Agreement at _____, _____, as of the date and year given in this Agreement.

_____
Ann Myers

_____
Gregory Klein

_____
Philip Hendrix

chapter 10

Legal Conventions and Legal Writing Blunders

StyleLinks

http://ualr.edu/cmbarger
Professor Barger of the William H. Bowen School of Law, University of Arkansas, offers information on legal writing as well as numerous writing resources.

http://members.tripod.com/legal_write
This site, called "LegalWrite v. Wrong" offers several tips and strategies on legal writing as well as links to other sources.

www.lclark.edu/dept/legalwrt/resources.html
Lewis & Clark Law School's Legal Writing Department offers links to several excellent legal writing sites.

A. Legal Conventions

There are a few customs or practices commonly seen in legal writing that are not commonly encountered in other forms of writing. For example, the language in certain documents such as wills, contracts, and deeds remains traditional and somewhat legalistic despite efforts to write in plain English. Recognize that in some instances, you will not be successful in fighting such customs and practices. Some other customs or conventions commonly seen in legal writing include the following.

1. Defined Terms

Because many terms or names are long and may have to be repeated throughout a legal document, legal writers tend to identify fully a term or name when it is first used and then label it by indicating in parentheses the shorthand way they will refer to it later. For example, consider the following shorthand label for *Plaintiff's Supplemental Responses to Defendant's Third Set of Interrogatories ("Supplemental Responses")*. If two parties will be labeled, consider the following form: *Patricia Allen and Maria Lopez (collectively, "Plaintiffs")*. The reference in the parentheses is now called a *defined term*, and the writer must use it consistently in every later reference. Some writers use quotation marks around the defined term the first time it is used; others do not. It is not necessary to use the word *hereinafter*. Thus, avoid a reference such as the following: *Plaintiff Sterling Appliance and Repair, Inc. (hereinafter referred to as "Sterling")*. Although defined terms are useful in many documents, they may not be needed. For example, if a complaint only identifies one plaintiff, establishing a label or defined term for the party may be uneeded. When using defined terms, make sure the term appears after being defined (there's no point in identifying Josephson Manufacturing Associates Inc. as *Josephson* if the party will not be referred to again). Also, be careful when using initials so that you don't confuse your reader with language such as the following: *JMAI later refused to deliver the goods to CACB and instead returned them COD to PRBL*.

2. Repetitive Terms

The consistent use of defined terms will result in some repetition in your writing. Resist the urge to achieve variety in your writing by selecting new words for established terms. It is better to be thought of as boring than confusing.

3. Labels

Note that the actor and the person acted upon are usually referred to by the signals *-or* and *-ee*, as in *offeror-offeree* and *franchisor-franchisee*, although many nonlegal dictionaries would spell the terms *offerer* and *franchiser*.

4. *Including But Not Limited to* Phrases

When introducing a list, the word *including* is probably sufficient because it signals that the list is not exhaustive; however, in nearly all instances, to be safe, most legal writers will write *including but not limited to* in contracts and other documents, as in the following: *The employee must perform all assigned duties, including but not limited to* . . . . Such language is intended to prevent the employee from claiming that he or she was required only to perform the listed duties and no others. The word *namely* and phrase *consisting of* signal a complete list. Thus, a statement that *The employee must perform the following duties, namely* . . . would require the employee to perform only the identified duties and no others. Consequently, to allow "wiggle room," most lists are introduced by the phrase *including but not limited to.*

5. Money Amounts

To reduce errors it is customary in legal writing to spell out a money amount and then identify the figures in parentheses, as in *Defendant will pay the sum of Forty Thousand Dollars ($40,000).* In 1999, the Financial Times reported that a comma in the wrong place in a sales price figure cost Lockheed Martin $70 million. The comma (used in Europe to mark decimal points rather than periods) was misplaced by one decimal point. Combining both the figure with the words may have saved the company this loss.

6. Numbers

Legal writers usually spell out all numbers and then identify the number in parentheses, as in *There will be twelve (12) directors' meetings this year.*

7. Initial Phrases

Many legal writers capitalize the first word or two in many documents or sections. Thus, many contracts begin with the words THIS AGREEMENT, and many corporate resolutions begin with the words RESOLVED THAT. Similarly, many pleadings, such as complaints, are introduced by the archaic phrase COMES NOW THE PLAINTIFF.

8. The *Whether* Clause

Many issue statements begin with the word *whether*, as in *Whether a trademark may be abandoned by three consecutive years of nonuse.* Such a phrase is an incomplete sentence but is acceptable to most attorneys.

9. d/b/a References

The abbreviation *d/b/a* is short for *doing business as* and indicates that one or more persons are doing business under a business name rather than their personal names. Thus, a plaintiff might sue *Dan Greenwood, d/b/a Creative Caterers of Charleston*. Do not include *d/b/a* in formal case citations.

10. Law Firm Names

Punctuation and presentation of law firm names varies widely. Some firms use commas and others do not. A current trend is to reduce the four or five names in a firm to two, as in *Jones Day*. Follow the firm practice as shown by its letterhead or on its website.

11. Ordinals

In legal citation, use *2d, 3d,* and *102d Cong.* rather than *2nd, 3rd,* and *102nd Cong.* All other ordinals, such as *1st, 5th,* and so forth, follow the generally accepted presentations. Present these ordinals "on line" as in *5th,* rather than in superscript form (as in *5ᵗʰ*). Outside of the legal context, use the generally accepted presentations, as in *The theater is on 42nd Street.*

12. Pagination

It is common to omit any number on the first page of a legal writing. In a brief, the argument often begins as page number one (1). Introductory pages, which include the Table of Contents and Table of Authorities, are often numbered with romanettes (small roman numerals, as in *i, ii, and iii*).

B. Common Legal Writing Blunders

There are several blunders commonly committed by beginning legal writers. Some are oddly phrased constructions; others are defects in reasoning and analysis. Thus, pay careful attention to the following topics:

1. Labels and Numbering

Never label or number an item *A* or *I* unless a *B* or *II* will follow.

2. Defined Terms

Once you define a term or use a label, it must be used consistently. Thus, once you tell a reader that the defendant Kyle Walters will be referred to as *Walters,* you must continue this reference, and not later refer to the defendant as *Mr. Walters.*

Figure 10-1   Plagiarism

Plagiarism is taking another's ideas, thoughts, or expressions and representing them as your own. The word *plagiarism* is derived from the Latin for *literary thief* or *kidnapper*. Plagiarism is a serious ethics violation. It is perfectly acceptable, however, to paraphrase another's material. Paraphrasing is taking the ideas or expressions of another and putting them in your own words. Nevertheless, even paraphrased material must be attributed to the original author. Follow these guidelines in legal writing, as in all writing:

- When you quote from any authority, use quotation marks and give the full citation and the pinpoint, namely, the page on which the specific material appears.
- When you paraphrase an authority, give the full citation and the pinpoint.
- When an entire paragraph includes paraphrased material and the sentences in the paragraph are closely connected, it is acceptable to give the citation at the end of the paragraph, rather than giving citations at the end of each sentence. Similarly, it is permissible to give a citation to a legal authority, such as a case, and give the facts from that case in several sentences without repeating the citation at the end of each sentence.
- Do not assume that material in the public domain (for example, statutes and cases) can be used without attribution. When you rely on such materials, give the full citation and the pinpoint.
- Using material from the Internet is not only an ethics violation, it may also be a copyright violation. Just as it is easy for a writer to find material on the Internet and "cut and paste" the material into a writing, it is easy for the reader to locate the original source on the Internet and realize that you have plagiarized.
- Understand that in law firms and office settings, professionals routinely share their writings, memos, and briefs with each other. This sharing of materials is considered practical and cost-effective for clients. Such use with the permission of another is not plagiarism.
- When in doubt, err on the side of caution and give a citation.

3. Supporting Authorities

Do not conclude that a test or element of an argument is satisfied without supporting authority. Every assertion you make or conclusion you provide must be supported by some legal authority. See Figure 10-1 for information about citing to authorities and plagiarism.

4.   Conclusory Language

Avoid conclusory language. Simply writing *The defendant's conduct was reckless* is not persuasive. You must tell the reader why the defendant's conduct was reckless; give specific facts and reasons that support this conclusion.

5.   Including Facts

Be sure to include facts from the cases you rely on so the reader can easily see why the authorities you cite apply to your case. Thus, a statement such as *The present case is governed by Powell because of its similarity* . . . without any discussion of the facts of *Powell* will leave the reader in the dark as to why *Powell* is controlling.

6.   Other Legal Authorities

Let experts help. In many instances, A.L.R. annotations, law reviews, and treatises provide depth and texture to a discussion. Don't think that a document can cite only to cases and statutes.

7.   Tone in Court Documents

Although it is important to be persuasive in court documents, arrogantly telling a court what it must do is inappropriate. Thus, write *The Plaintiff respectfully urges this Court to grant this Motion* . . . rather than *This Court must grant this Motion* . . . . Also, be sure your tone in court documents is not too informal or conversational. Thus, write *The Court further stated* . . . rather than *The Court goes on to state* . . . .

8.   Title Headings in Statutes

When discussing a statute, it is generally not necessary to give the title of the statute. For example, avoid the following construction: *Under 17 U.S.C. § 201 (2000), Ownership of Copyright, the authors of a joint work are co-owners of copyright in the work.* Omit the title *Ownership of Copyright.* It is distracting. On the other hand, it is perfectly acceptable to refer to a specific act by its name, as in *The Lanham Act prohibits counterfeit use of trademarks.*

9.   Complete Discussion

If your argument asserts, for example, that three elements of a certain test must be satisfied, you must discuss all three elements (in the order you listed them), and each section must be supported with legal authorities. When discussing the three elements, either discuss each one separately or discuss them all together. For example, it is awkward and unparallel if you combine elements one and two and then discuss element three in its own section. Similarly, your argument is incomplete if you analyze only some of the elements of the test or merely recite the elements of the test and then jump to the conclusion that the test is satisfied. If for some reason you do not need to address one element or one portion of a test, say so, rather than leaving the reader wondering where the discussion is.

10. Concurring and Dissenting Opinions

Do not rely too heavily on a concurring or dissenting opinion. Recognize that these opinions are persuasive at best. Start your argument and analysis with the majority opinion. Bolster it with sparing use of concurring or dissenting opinions, if you like, but don't lead with these. Similarly, plurality opinions (those in which no single rationale enjoys the agreeement of five justices) are of limited precedential value. If you rely on a dissenting, concurring, or plurality opinion, you must indicate such in a separate parenthetical in your citation. *Bluebook* R. 10.6.1, at 91; *ALWD* R. 12.11(a), at 93.

11. The Complete Package

Include all the information the reader will need. Don't make the reader search through other pleadings or files to make sense of your document.

12. Use of Headnotes

Never quote from headnotes in a case. Headnotes are summaries of what the publisher of the case believed the court said. Rely on the majority opinion itself. The headnotes are meant to be guides or an index to the information in the case. Relying on a headnote in a case would be the equivalent of relying on a table of contents in a book. When you read a case, find the author of the opinion. The author's name is a signal that every word thereafter was written by the court. Similarly, be careful that you are relying on the majority opinion and not on a dissenting or concurring opinion. It is easy to drift into a dissenting or concurring opinion, especially when reading cases on Lexis or Westlaw, where the screen doesn't display page breaks as cleanly as they are shown in books.

13. Addressing Readers

Do not address the reader of a document by name. Thus, in a letter, do not write *Mr. Lee, you should therefore* . . . . It is sufficient to write *You should therefore* . . . . The only legal document in which a reader is directly addressed is correspondence. Briefs do not address the reader, the judge, by indicating *Your ruling of June 10* . . . . Similarly, memos do not address readers directly.

14. Authors of Court Opinions

Do not continually mention the author of a case. It is sufficient to write *The Court held . . . .* It is not necessary to write *Justice Thomas noted that . . . .* The author of an opinion is often immaterial. It is a court, acting as a collective unit, that states the law, not a particular justice. Similarly, when discussing the *Harris v. Jackson* case, for example, avoid references to the *Harris Court*, which many writers dislike. Write *The Court in Harris held that . . . .* In fact, the U.S. Supreme Court's guidelines for counsel arguing before the Court state, "Do not refer to an opinion of the Court by saying: 'In Justice Ginsburg's opinion.'" You should say: "In the Court's opinion, written by Justice Ginsburg." U.S. Supreme Court Guide for Counsel 10 (2007), *available at* http://www.supremecourtus.gov/oral_arguments/guideforcounsel.pdf. You may, however, refer to a court by the name of its presiding judge or chief justice, as in *the Roberts Court*.

15. New Topics

Don't introduce any new issues or topics in a conclusion that have not been previously analyzed in the document. A conclusion summarizes material previously presented; it does not introduce new topics.

16. Citations

Use case citations to tell a reader what a court held in a published case. For example, assume the client's name is Klein. It would be inappropriate to write *Klein's conduct is reasonable. Young v. Carr, 435 U.S. 36 (1998).* Such a statement implies that the Supreme Court case *Young v. Carr* analyzes Klein's conduct. Additionally, all citations must be correct according to *Bluebook, ALWD,* or local rules.

17. Over-Quoting

Don't give so many quotations from legal authorities or so many citations to the authorities that it appears that your project was assembled from a hodgepodge of authorities rather than being the result of your own analysis. Don't just drop quotations into a project without explaining their relevance to your analysis.

18. Mini-Conclusions

Analyze throughout a memorandum or brief. Do not discuss all the legal authorities in one section and then give your conclusions as to how and why they apply in another section. Make your presentation seamless, and for each point you make, give the law, apply it, and provide a mini-conclusion. Only then should you move on to the next point.

19. Headings

Always give sufficient headings that the reader can readily determine the topic that will be next addressed. Review each heading to make sure each is parallel and that each advances your argument. Although it is common for writers to use all uppercase letters for major point headings, some experts suggest that the easiest way for something to be ignored is to place it in a heading in all uppercase letters. Consider whether your heading will be more visible if you use underscoring or bolding.

20. Use of First Person

Do not use the first person (*I, we*) in any document other than correspondence. In briefs, do not write *We will show that* but rather *The Plaintiff will show that*. In most instances you are writing on behalf of the client; thus, third person is appropriate.

21. Use of Party Names

When discussing the litigants in a case, identify them by their legal status rather than by their names. Thus, write *The Plaintiff argued* rather than *Ms. Davis argued*. On the other hand, if their legal status is confusing (for example, they are cross-complainants or cross-respondents) or if several parties share the same legal status, consider identifying them by their roles, such as *buyer, landlord,* or *employee*. When referring to a party in a case precedent, it is typical to refer to that party as *the plaintiff* or *the defendant* (with the definite article *the*). In contrast, when you refer to a party in the matter that is the subject of your document, it is typical to refer to that party as follows: *Plaintiff has alleged* or *Defendant has offered*, without the definite article *the* and with an initial capital letter. *Bluebook* B10.6.2; *ALWD* R. 3.3.

> **Correct Example:**   In *Dixon v. United States*, 548 U.S. 1, 3 (2006), the defendant alleged she acted under duress at the time of her illegal purchase of a firearm. In the present case, however, Defendant has alleged . . . .

22. Tense

Use correct tense. Use the past tense when describing the facts, procedural background, and holding of a case. Use present tense when discussing what the law is, whether you discuss a statute, case, or regulation. Thus, for example, write *The Lanham Act provides that* . . . . Do not shift tenses unless there is an actual change in time.

23. Writing *This Case*

Watch the use of the expression *this case*. When you are analyzing case law in a memo or court document, references to *this case* are confusing because readers are unsure whether you are referring to the published precedent or the client's case.

24. Abbreviations

Avoid using abbreviations in text. Thus, do not write *The defendant lived in Los Angeles, CA until Nov. 2008*. Spell out *California* and *November*.

25. Collective Nouns

Always refer to corporations, groups, and other similar entities as *it* or *its* rather than *they* or *their*. Thus, write *The corporation held its meeting* or *The committee released its report*. If you wish to refer to the members of these entities, write *The members of the board of directors held their meeting*.

26. Cross-References

If your document includes numerous instances of *as explained below* and *as discussed previously*, this is a strong signal that your writing is poorly organized. These references require readers to either jump ahead or back in your document, disrupting your narrative and confusing your reader. Use your word processor's "find" feature to locate such phrases and then work to keep all related issues and discussion points together in the same section rather than scattered throughout your project.

27. The Biggest Blunder—Violating Court Rules

Remember that courts have the power to enforce strict compliance with their rules. Courts routinely dismiss cases or refuse to accept documents that do not comply with their rules, including those regarding length, cover colors, and timeliness. Remember *Alva v. Teen Help*, 469 F.3d 946 (10th Cir. 2006), in which the court dismissed an appeal that was filed six minutes too late.

sectionfour

Postwriting Steps and Document Design

■ After writing, the real work begins: proofreading and editing. These are among the most difficult tasks in writing. This section of the Handbook provides you with some techniques for effective proofreading and for revising your writing. Additionally, although no amount of "tricks" can make up for a poorly written document, there are several strategies you can adopt to make your project more visually appealing and thus more readable. This section describes methods of displaying your writings so that they present a polished and professional appearance.

chapter 11

Postwriting Steps

StyleLinks

http://owl.english.edu/owl/resource/561/01
Purdue University's Online Writing Lab provides an excellent review of the steps in editing and proofreading.

www.unc.edu/depts/wcweb/handouts/proofread.html
The Writing Center of the University of North Carolina offers a thorough overview of the proofreading process.

www.gpoaccess.gov/stylemanual.index.html
Chapter One of the Government Printing Office *Style Manual* provides a list and explanation of the standard proofreaders' marks.

http://www.merriam-webster.com/mw/table/proofrea.htm
Merriam-Webster's site displays illustrations of proofreaders' marks.

A. Introduction

One of the most difficult writing tasks begins only when most writers think they have finished a project. Steps taken in the postwriting stage provide a final opportunity to ensure a document is correct in all respects. Don't underestimate the difficulty of postwriting. All major publishers require that writings be edited by professional editors and proofreaders for the very reason that writers are notoriously unlikely to catch their own errors.

You cannot review (literally, "re-see") for all errors and flaws in a project at the same time. Thus, divide your review into two parts. During stage one, review for content and meaning. During stage two, review for technical errors, such as spelling and punctuation. The task of cite-checking, namely, checking the format and validity of your citations, is a separate task and should not be combined with any revising or polishing of your document. Before you do anything, however, take three critically important steps:

- **Get some distance from the project.** Try to allow at least a few hours (and, if possible, overnight or longer) to pass between the completion of your first draft and your initial review. It is extremely difficult to review effectively a project with which you are too familiar. If you can come to the review "cold," you will be better able to detect flaws (just as the project's ultimate reader will be able to locate errors). A harsh reality of today's busy law office environments, however, is that legal professionals do not always have the luxury of putting aside a project for a few days and then returning to it to proofread it. Even a short break, however, may help refresh you and allow you to approach the project with a more critical eye.
- **Work on a hard copy.** Never engage in a full review while the document is on the screen of your computer. It is too difficult to see the flow of the project when you can only see part of a page at a time. Moreover, you need to see the document the way it will appear to the reader.
- **Enlarge your project.** For better reviewing, copy your document on 11" × 17" paper or enlarge it to 120 percent of its size. This gives you room to make notes and reduces the eyestrain caused by on-screen revision. Moreover, changing the look of the document may trick you into thinking you are looking at an unfamiliar project and thus help you catch errors.

Remember to expect the unexpected. Allow time for human error or machine malfunction. Don't work so close to the deadline that a stalled photocopier causes you to miss a deadline. Understand that someone else's project may bump yours. People will get sick. Leave some margin for error.

B. Proofreading Stage One: Reviewing for Content and Meaning

Your initial review should focus on whether you have accurately conveyed all the information needed (and no more than what is needed). Focus on content. Consider the following strategies:

- Review the project from the perspective of the reader and ask if the reader will understand the writing.
- Review your thesis statement. Does it fully encapsulate the argument or discussion to follow?
- Keep the purpose of the writing in mind. If the project is a brief, its purpose is to persuade. If the project is a memorandum, its purpose is to inform. Check to see if the writing meets these goals. Review to ensure the tone is appropriate for the reader and whether the project is either too formal or too breezy.
- Review to ensure the writing flows smoothly and that its organization assists the reader's comprehension. Move paragraphs and sections to other locations if you believe they would be better placed elsewhere.
- Stay focused on your task. Ask someone to hold your calls and find a quiet space where you can concentrate on your project.
- Make sure the first page of each draft includes a date and a time. Often, several versions of a project will accumulate, and some drafts will vary only slightly from each other. Identifying each version with the date and time will help you keep them straight.
- Read the project aloud. This will help you locate awkward phrasing, repetitive sections, and missing transitions.
- Read only the headings and topic sentences to ensure they advance your message and that taken alone they provide a complete mini-view of the content of the document.
- Ensure your headings, numberings, and presentations of lists are consistent and that their structure is parallel, especially if you have worked on the project with others.
- Focus on one or two problem areas at a time, such as overlong sentences or legalese. Work on correcting these, and then move on to other weak spots. Remember some easy tips to focus on problem areas: You can detect passive voice by looking at a noun introduced with the word *by* (as in *The complaint was filed by the plaintiff*); you can detect nominalizations by looking for words ending in *-ent*, *-ant*, and *-ion*; and you can detect wordiness by looking for prepositional phrases such as *during the time that* and changing them to one-word replacements, such as *during* or *when*. To obtain visual cues about your problem areas, use a colored marker to highlight every nominalization or use of passive voice. Do patterns emerge?
- Consider using a revision or writing checklist to remind you to check for certain errors. A writing checklist is found on the inside back cover of this Handbook.

C. Proofreading Stage Two: Reviewing for Technical Errors

1. The Effect of Technical Errors

The best argument in the world can be quickly sabotaged by what most writers think of as minor errors, namely, errors in grammar, punctuation, and spelling. These types of technical or surface errors in legal documents have a disproportionately negative effect on a reader. Thus, no review is complete without a final run-through to make sure that there are no technical or mechanical errors that will detract from the message of your writing.

2. Using a Style Sheet

Most professional editors develop a style sheet that they rely on when editing. The style sheet is their blueprint for the correct spelling of names, how they intend to present headings, how issues will be numbered, and so forth. During the process of review, they then have a quick guide they can consult to ensure accuracy and consistency. Develop your own style sheet and include a list of planned exhibits so you can readily ensure consistency in their names and numbering. Similarly, many writers use a project checklist to remind themselves to check various items during the proofreading stage. See Figure 11-1 for a sample project checklist you can use to ensure all projects are in final form.

3. The Limitations of Spell-Checkers

As always, do not over-rely on your computer's spell-checker. Spelling checkers are wonderful tools, but they have their limitations because they cannot tell you to use *form* rather than *from* because both words are properly spelled. There is no substitute for human proofreading, as shown by the fact that a review of some recently published court decisions disclosed 23 cases referring to "Santa Clause" and 817 cases referring to the "trail court."

4. Techniques to Slow Down

Because a standard reading of your project will naturally focus on content and you will read groups of words and phrases rather than isolated words, you must force yourself to slow down and focus on each word.

Try these techniques:

- Slide a ruler or piece of paper under each line as you read the document. This will prevent you from jumping ahead to the next sentence or idea and force you to focus on each word. Pointing at each word with a pencil also helps you focus on individual words.
- Read the project backward, from the last page to the first page and from right to left. Although this technique is excellent for finding spelling errors

Figure 11-1   Project Checklist

Moving target _____   Type of project _____

Nearing final form _____   Client _____

Final form _____   File/Billing No. _____

Due date _____   Supervisor _____

Spell Checked   _____

Proofread   _____

Cite-Checked   _____   *Bluebook/ALWD/*Other _____

Shepardized/KeyCited   _____

Quotations Checked   _____

Defined Terms Consistent   _____

Consistency in Headings   _____

Numbering Is Accurate   _____

Consistency in Exhibits   _____

No Widows or Orphans   _____

All Exhibits Attached   _____

Court Rules Checked   _____

Create Table of Authorities _____

Create Table of Contents   _____

Special Filing/Mailing Notes _____

Other   _____

and typos, it will not help you locate a missed word or ensure that you used *complaint* rather than *compliant*.

- Read the document aloud by yourself or read with a partner who has a copy of the document. Reading aloud allows a double check because you not only see what is being read but also hear it. Additionally, if your partner stumbles over certain sections, you will know these need more work.
- Read sections of the document out of order to make sure you stay focused on the mechanics of spelling, grammar, and punctuation, and do not begin concentrating on content.
- Read something else for a while as a quick break and then switch back to your project.
- Dictate complicated materials (such as patent claims or descriptions of real property) into a tape recorder. Then play back the recording, listening and proofreading against your text.

5. Asking for Help

You can ask someone to proof the project for you. Having someone else review the document can be extremely helpful because the newcomer will have no familiarity with the project. He or she will then review the writing with a fresh approach and no preconceived ideas or expectations. Note, however, that each reviewer of a document will tend to add rather than to delete language. If you want the reader to review only for technical errors, say so, or you may receive a project with substantial corrections and suggestions. If you have asked for help, give the reviewer the courtesy of being open to his or her comments or suggestions without becoming defensive.

6. Using Templates and Forms

Using a sample document prepared for an earlier transaction or case increases the risk of importing incorrect terms into later documents. Thus, a document prepared for a tenant needs to be scrupulously checked when it is later used for a subtenant. Use the "find and replace" feature in your word processor to locate terms and names and ensure they are uniformly presented.

7. Using Technology to Help with Proofreading

A number of software programs can help with proofreading. Thomson West's new program Deal Proof is specially tailored to help with the proofreading of complex documents. With the click of a button you can make sure that terms are defined only once, that each defined term is used in the document, that numeration is correct, and that phrases are used consistently.

Case Illustration: Competent Representation Extends to Proofreading

In *Devore v. City of Philadelphia*, No. Civ. A. 00-3598, 2004 WL 41405, at *3 (E.D. Pa. Feb. 20, 2004), the court slashed an attorney's rate from $300 per hour to $150 per hour because of his careless writing and numerous typos. Thus, the duty to represent a client competently is broad enough to encompass even seemingly minor matters such as proofreading, editing, and cite-checking.

D. Proofreading for Others

> No passion in the world is equal to the passion to alter someone else's draft.
>
> H.G. Wells

If you are asked to review someone else's work, obtain clear instructions so you know if you should review for content or review only for mechanics, such as typos and spelling errors. Reviewing for mechanical errors in someone else's writing is generally quite easy. If you are not familiar with the content, the errors will jump out at you (just as they will for the ultimate reader, such as the client or judge).

If you are asked to review for content, consider the following:

- Be realistic. Recognize that each writer has a unique style. Just because an idea is not expressed in the exact way you would express it does not mean it is inaccurate or vague.
- Limit your corrections to meaningful changes. It is unproductive to change *glad* to *happy* or *but* to *however*. Your credibility as an effective reviewer will be jeopardized if you make such meaningless changes.
- Be specific. Comments such as "weak" or "expand" placed beside a paragraph are nearly useless. Specifically explain why the section is weak and give a suggestion for improving it.
- Be diplomatic. Harsh comments such as "What are you thinking?" are inappropriate. Try phrasing suggestions diplomatically, such as "Have you considered . . . ?" or "Let's discuss some alternatives." These approaches focus on the two of you as colleagues in the writing process rather than on the writer's perceived inadequacies. Focus on the reader and suggest "Will the reader know what this means?" rather than writing "This is unclear."

E. Proofreaders' Marks

Although there is some variety in the marks writers use to show errors, most legal writers employ the standard marks, called proofreaders' marks, used by professional editors. Many attorneys learned these marks while in law school, so their use among legal professionals is common.

Most dictionaries (including online dictionaries) will provide descriptions and illustrations of proofreaders' marks. These marks are designed to show support staff where and how to make corrections in your project. Be sure all of your working drafts are double-spaced and have generous margins so you will have sufficient room to note corrections. The most commonly used proofreaders' marks are shown in Figure 11-2.

Figure 11-2 Commonly Used Proofreaders' Marks

Mark	Explanation	Example
≡	Capital letters	president bush
/	Lowercase letters	the eleventh Juror
∿	Boldface	April 16, 2008
⌒	Close up space	in as much
¶	Begin new paragraph	¶ The plaintiff
ℓ	Delete	The hearing was was
Stet	Let original text stand	Many courts have concluded
∧	Insert	The plaintiff and his attorney argued
#	Add space	to the court.The defendant then
∿	Transpose	complaint
⊏	Move left	⊏ any jury
⊐	Move right	⊐ any jury
⋏	Insert comma	the plaintiff Josh Brownell stated
⋎	Insert apostrophe	its a sad day
⊙	Insert period	to the court The jury also requested
○	Spell out	Newport, RI

F. The Final Run-Through

Just before your writing is sent to the reader, check these four items:

- **Widows and Orphans.** A *widow* or an *orphan*, respectively, is a heading or isolated line occurring at the top of a page or an isolated line or heading occurring at the bottom of a page. Omit this awkward placement. Many software programs now protect against widows and orphans. Always keep at least two lines together.
- **Numbering.** Quickly scan the project to make sure the page numbering is correct. If the document has a table of contents, review it to make sure all page references are correct. If footnotes are used, check their numbering for accuracy. Make sure the numbering of headings and subheadings is accurate.
- **Dates, Names, and Amounts.** Do one final check to make sure dates, names, and money amounts are correct.
- **Exhibits.** Make sure all exhibits or attachments to the project are included and are properly marked and that their titles and labeling are consistent with the way they are presented in the document itself.

▶ Tip: Approach cite-checking as a task distinct from revising. First, check the format of the citations to ensure they are in *Bluebook* or *ALWD* (or local) form. Then check your primary authorities (either by Sheparding or KeyCiting) to ensure the law you rely on is still valid.

Tips ➡ For Successful Reviews

- Energy levels are usually higher in the morning, so try to schedule your review as the first thing you do in the day.
- Devote extra attention to the parts of the project that were prepared last. More errors occur when you are tired.
- Watch for substitutions of letters in small words, such as *now* for *not*.
- Pay extra attention to your known problem areas. For example, if you tend to misspell the word *judgment*, watch for this. Use your word processor's "find" feature to locate your typical errors.
- Consider preparing a "lessons learned" memo to yourself, noting the techniques that worked well and those that did not so that your next project can benefit from what you learned.
- Always ask yourself the most important question for any writing project: *Will my reader understand my writing?*

Challenge   ?   Proofreading

Correct the errors:

Too discourage corporations form simply holding onto profits and not distributing them the Internal Revenue service has devised certain penaties that gives corporations a strong incentive to distribute profits to shareholders rather than haording them. Corporations that acummulate earnings beyond the reasonable needs of the buisiness to avoid having shareholders pay income tazes on earnings that should have been distributed to the sahreholders are subject to an accumulated income tax tax in the amount of fifteen (51) percent of the accumulated taxable amount in excess of Two Hundred and Fifty Thousand Dollars ($150,000) altho certain credits were allowed.

chapter 12

Document Design

StyleLinks

www.sec.gov/pdf/handbook.pdf
See Chapter 7 of the SEC's *A Plain English Handbook* for information on
document design, use of graphics, font size, and so forth.

**http://writing.colostate.edu/guides/documents/desktop_
publishing/list3.cfm**
Colorado State University offers information on preparing figures, illustrations,
tables, and other layout and design elements.

http://www.ca7.uscourts.gov/Rules/Painting_with_Print.pdf
The excellent article *Painting with Print*, which discusses incorporating concepts
of layout design into legal writings, is available at the website of the Seventh
Circuit Court of Appeals.

A. Principles of Document Design

1. Introduction

Even if your project is well written, clear, and readable, it should be presented in such a manner that it creates a favorable impression on the reader. One of the reasons that many appellate courts insist that a brief submitted must be professionally printed rather than merely typed is that printed briefs are easier to read and present a uniform appearance. A good document reflects careful design choices. On the other hand, no amount of design techniques can overcome a poorly written document. Thus, use document design to enhance your writing, not obscure it.

The term *document design* refers to the conventions that determine the way that a written project looks, including quality of paper, typeface, formatting, and headings and other visuals. Visually appealing documents are easier to understand.

2. Paper

Use the highest quality paper possible. Some courts require that the paper used for documents be of a certain quality. For example, the U.S. Supreme Court requires all 8½″ × 11″ documents to be produced on unglazed opaque white paper. Sup. Ct. R. 33.2(a).

Select a paper of sufficient weight so that page two of a document doesn't show through to page one. Although some law firms and offices use cream or ivory-colored paper, most use white. White is the more traditional color, and many readers find it easier to read because black type provides a greater contrast on white paper than on cream paper.

3. Typeface

There are several decisions to make about typeface, including whether the typeface should be serif or sans serif, monospaced or proportionally spaced, and what size of typeface should be selected.

a. Typeface or Font Style

Typeface selection can dramatically affect the readability of your document. Typefaces (called *fonts* on word processors) come in two styles: serif and sans serif. A serif typeface has small lines or wings at the top or bottom of each letter. This Handbook is printed in serif typeface. Most newspapers and magazines use a serif type because the small connecting lines draw the reader's eye from letter to letter and word to word, making the text easier to read. Sans serif typefaces (*sans* means *without* in French) do not have the connecting lines or added strokes. Almost all experts agree that a serif typeface should be used for text. Sans serif is acceptable for headings or emphasis. Consider the following:

This is Times New Roman, a serif font, in 12-point size.

This is Century Schoolbook, a serif font, in 12-point size.

This is Courier New, a serif font, in 12-point size.

This is Arial, a sans serif font, in 12-point size.

This is Univers, a sans serif font, in 12-point size.

Do not use a decorative style of font, such as Comic Sans, or one that uses script or cursive, in legal writing.

b. Mixing Typefaces

Generally, do not mix more than two typefaces in a document. In fact, most experts recommend using one typeface throughout a document, selecting its Roman, italic, and bold styles as needed. Too many variations will make your writing look like an advertisement rather than a serious work. Moreover, readers assume that headings in the same size and font signal information of the same importance. Switching fonts confuses readers and obscures the significance of the headings.

c. Roman Typeface

Writing may be presented in ordinary Roman letters (as most of this Handbook is), *italics*, or **boldface**. Use ordinary Roman type for most of your writing. Italics or underscoring are generally used only for emphasis (except for their in citation form, are discussed in Appendix A). Use boldface only for headings or special purposes, such as emphasizing a deadline date in a letter to a client.

d. Proportional or Monospace Typeface

Some typefaces, such as Courier, are monospaced, meaning that every letter takes up the same amount of space, whether it is a capital M or a lower case i. Times New Roman and Garamond are proportionally spaced, meaning that a capital M takes up more space than a lowercase i. Courier type uses about 30 percent more space than Times New Roman. Generally, proportionally spaced typefaces are easier to read. Consider the following:

This sentence, in Times New Roman font, is proportionally spaced.

This sentence, in Courier New font, is mono-spaced.

e. Size of Typeface

Type size is measured in "points," such as 10-point type or 12-point type, with a larger number showing larger print. Review the fonts shown earlier and note that although all are presented in 12-point size, they are not all equal in size. Some courts require documents to be printed in a certain size type. Similarly, some statutes require certain information, such as language disclaiming a warranty, to be of a specified type size. Unless there are rules you must follow, select 12-point because it is the most readable size. Larger type sizes in text appear artificial and convey a sense of shouting, although they are effective for headings, if used consistently. United States Supreme Court rules require that the text of documents be typeset in a "Century" family (for example, Century Schoolbook) in 12-point type. Sup. Ct. R. 33.1(b).

On occasion a client may insist that certain information be included in a contract, invoice, or other form. To fit all the information or terms in the document, you may need to use a much smaller type size, such as 6-point or 8-point. Alternatively, most photocopy machines can reduce the size of an image. These reductions, however, impair readability and convey the message *this is fine print.*

B. Formatting and Layout

Designers give careful consideration to the way text looks on a page, including white space, justification, paragraph length, and so forth.

1. White Space and Margins

Pages filled with a solid block of text cause eyestrain and frustration. Using adequate white space (space where no words appear) will make the project more readable and cause headings and quotations to be more easily noticed. Using white space shows readers which items in a project are related; greater distance between sections indicates separation, and proximity indicates correlation. Although the technique of leaving ample white space on a page, including adequate or generous margins, may seem like an artificial device, readings studies have shown that it results in a more readable project. Margins should be at least one inch on all sides and should be larger than one inch if the project will be bound along the top or left side or if the reader will be making notes in the margins.

2. Justification

Research has shown that the easiest text to read is text that is left justified (meaning the text is aligned, or flush, at the left margin) and ragged right (meaning the text at the right margin has a ragged edge, such as a typewriter would produce). A *fully justified* text is one in which both the right and left edges are flush, or even, with all words starting and ending at the exact same location in each line. This text is fully justified. Although full justification presents a clean and crisp-looking document, it may be more suited for transactional documents, such as contracts, than for legal correspondence and briefs. The disadvantage of full justification is that the spacing between words may be either cramped or stretched out to ensure the text is even, inhibiting the flow of reading and causing "rivers" of white space to cascade downward vertically through the text. Although word processors are improving, only a professional typesetter can reduce the uneven spacing that occurs with full justification. The current trend is to use left justified and right ragged edges in legal correspondence and court documents.

3. Spacing

Line spacing refers to the amount of space between each line in a document. Correspondence is single-spaced with double-spacing between paragraphs. Single-spacing is easy to read and allows the reader to comprehend at a glance the structure of a document. Headings and indented quotations are then more noticeable. Many courts require documents submitted to them to be double-spaced. Double-spacing is helpful when editing and proofing a document because it allows room for edits to be made on the page.

As to word spacing, leave one space between words and one space after most punctuation marks, such as commas. The current trend is to use one space after a period rather than two, as was common when typewriters were used, although many writers still use two spaces after a period. In most documents, paragraphs are indented five spaces.

Most word processing programs protect against odd line breaks by ensuring that words are not hyphenated at the end of a line, that a line will not begin with a period or comma, and so forth.

4. Document Length

Many courts impose limitations on document length. For example, the federal rules provide that a principal brief cannot exceed 30 pages or 1,300 lines of text or 14,000 words (with headings and footnotes counting toward line and word counts). Fed. R. App. P. 32(a)(7).

If your project exceeds a maximum length requirement, you can revise the project and omit needless words, use smaller margins, drop textual material into footnotes (which are often in smaller type), or use smaller point type size. Check court rules to make sure you comply with any requirements as to margins and type size. For example, the United States Supreme Court rules flatly require margins of at least three-fourths of an inch, impose word count limits, and insist on 12-point type for text and 10-point type for footnotes. Sup. Ct. R. 33.1. Another disadvantage of squeezing material into a document is that it creates a more cramped appearance, and few, if any, readers will be fooled by artificial techniques adopted to meet length requirements. Some word processing programs, including some WordPerfect versions, include a feature called "Make It Fit," which will shrink margins and reduce font size and line spacing to ensure that a document fits on one page (or a prescribed number of pages). The danger of using such techniques, however, is that you may well violate court rules on formatting and margins.

One common cause of excessive document length is having too many editors. Nearly every reader of a document will make changes, and the changes are nearly always additions rather than deletions. Ask for help from a colleague, but understand that if too many readers review the project, it will grow in length.

To enhance readability, keep paragraphs less than one-half page in length. Although paragraph length is dictated by content, the use of more frequent, shorter paragraphs improves reader comprehension.

5. Headings

Headings not only provide the reader with a signal as to what will follow, but also create visual drama on a page. The number of headings you use will be determined by the content of the document. Most legal writers use more than one technique for headings. Headings in the same location, typeface, or font style signal information of the same importance. Headings and subheadings should be consistently numbered, as shown in Figure 12-1. Do not use a *1* or an *A* unless a *2* or a *B* will

---

Figure 12-1 Headings

- Main headings are often centered, presented in all capital letters, and single-spaced. Each is usually given a Roman numeral. Some writers use boldface print to make headings stand out.
- Subheadings that occur within a main heading should be flush left and use capital letters only for the first letter in each major word. Do not capitalize articles and short conjunctions and prepositions (those of four or fewer letters). *Bluebook* R.8. Each subheading should be labeled with a capital letter and should be underlined or boldfaced for emphasis.
- Separate all headings and subheadings from the text by double-spacing above and below.
- Following is a common structure for headings and subheadings:

  I.

      A.

      B.

          1.

          2.

              a.

              b.

              c.

  II.

      A.

      B.

  III.

follow. Proofread only your headings to make sure their structure is parallel and that you haven't skipped over or repeated a letter or number.

a. Placement

Headings and subheadings may be centered, placed flush left, or indented. Main section headings, such as "STATEMENT OF FACTS," are typically presented in all capital letters, centered, and single-spaced. Subheadings are usually set flush left. Again, maintain parallelism in the headings. If one subheading is flush left and boldfaced, all other subheadings of the same level should be flush left and boldfaced.

b. Phrasing

Headings should be concise and descriptive. They can be single words (such as *Argument*), phrases (such as *Jury Selection*), or sentences (*Failure to Provide Adequate Notice of Shareholders' Meetings Violates California Law.*). Whatever the selection, headings at the same level must be stated in parallel terms and must appear in the same format. For example, all subheadings could be phrases or complete sentences. If the heading or subheading is a complete sentence, follow it with a period. Make sure there are no page breaks immediately following any heading; move the heading to the next page, if needed.

In persuasive documents, such as briefs submitted to courts, use persuasive headings rather than neutral ones. Thus, write *Quoting Excerpts of Copyrighted Material in News Reports Is a Permissible Fair Use* rather than *The Fair Use Doctrine.*

c. Emphasis

Each heading can be emphasized by centering or by using all capital letters, underscoring, italics, or boldface type. Use capital letters sparingly because they are more difficult to read than lowercase letters, and some experts believe they are easy to ignore. Again, each level of heading should be consistent with other equivalent levels. This approach will help readers recognize how you approach important information.

d. Lists

The guidelines applicable to headings apply equally to lists. The elements of a list must be parallel, and the formatting should be consistent. Don't use bullets in some lists and dashes in others.

6. Visuals

Visuals, such as tables, graphs, charts, or figures, are not as commonly used in legal writing as in other types of writing although they may be used to illustrate financial and statistical results. When used sparingly, they can make a point far more effectively than words can. Note that color is seldom used in legal documents. If you use such visuals, follow these guidelines:

- Keep the design simple;
- Place each visual as close as possible to the text section discussing the information;
- Show time moving forward if the visual shows information that occurs over a period of time; and
- Use your "eye" and sense of judgment to determine if the visual is helpful or merely a form of eye candy.

appendix A

Citation Form

A. Introduction

A critical part of the writing process in many documents is citing to legal authorities. Every legal assertion made in a document must be supported by legal authority. These supporting authorities appear as citations in your document. Citations must appear in a standard and consistent format so that any reader will be able to retrieve the legal authority you cited and verify that you have accurately represented the status of the law. Thus, legal writers communicate using the same "language" or citation form. Errors in citation form will cause the reader to lose respect for the author of a document and conclude that if an author cannot be depended on to cite correctly, the author likely cannot be depended on to conduct thorough analysis.

Case Illustration: Court Complaints About Citation Form

Recently, courts have been complaining that too many briefs are riddled with citation errors. *See, e.g., Edison Mission Energy, Inc. v. FERC*, 394 F.3d 964, 969 n.1 (noting that failure to indicate relevant pages in citations in briefs is sanctionable under the Federal Rules of Appellate Procedure); *Hurlbert v. Gordon*, 824 P.2d 1238, 1245-46 (Wash. Ct. App. 1992) (stating that counsel's errors in briefing and poor citation form made it impossible for the court to find information in the record, hampering the work of the court, and justifying the imposition of monetary sanctions against counsel).

Professor Peter W. Martin of Cornell University Law School offers excellent explanations of citation form with examples of citations in both *Bluebook* and *ALWD* format at *www.law.cornell.edu/citation*.

B. Citation Systems

There are two primary guides to citation form in the United States.

- *Bluebook.* The oldest and best-known system of citation is found in *The Bluebook: A Uniform System of Citation* (Columbia Law Review Ass'n et al. eds., 18th ed. 2005) (*The Bluebook*). *The Bluebook* is complex, and the rules are often poorly worded with few examples. Nevertheless, because most judges and practicing professionals were taught to use *The Bluebook* for citation form, it is the most commonly used citation manual.
- *ALWD.* ALWD & Darby Dickerson, *ALWD Citation Manual* (3d ed., Aspen Publishers 2006). In 2000, the Association of Legal Writing Directors and Professor Darby Dickerson produced an alternative to *The Bluebook.* Called *ALWD* (pronounced "all wood"), the citation system was intended to provide an easy-to-learn and user-friendly alternative to *The Bluebook.* In many instances, the *ALWD* format is identical to *Bluebook* format. For example, the format for lower court cases, most statutes, constitutions, journals and periodicals, and encyclopedias is identical. Rules for spacing are identical, and most short forms are identical. There are, however, differences in many abbreviations, and the presentation and numerous examples in *ALWD* make it far easier to use than *The Bluebook.*

Although there are other guides to citation form, the most notable of which is the *University of Chicago Manual of Legal Citation,* usually referred to as the *Maroonbook,* and used primarily in the Chicago metropolitan area, *The Bluebook* is probably the best-known system at this time, although *ALWD* continues to attract a great deal of interest because of its sensible rules and approach. Follow your school, firm, or office practice. Note, however, that if local citation rules exist for a court or jurisdiction, they must be followed and will supersede any citation system.

C. Law Reviews

According to *Bluebook* Rule 2.2, the main text of law review pieces contains no citations; instead, citations appear in footnotes. The presentation of citations in law review footnotes differs greatly from the style of citations used by practitioners. Thus, *The Bluebook* is primarily directed to showing how to cite in law review footnotes and presents information for practitioners in a separate section called the Bluepages. Although there are many differences between the two methods, the most noticeable are the following:

- Law review footnotes usually use large and small capitals (as shown in the word PATENT) for many citation forms whereas practitioners never use large and small capitals and always use ordinary Roman typeface (as shown in the word *Patent*).

- Full case names are not italicized in law review footnotes unless they are grammatically part of the sentence whereas they are always underscored or italicized by practitioners.

ALWD does not differentiate between citation form for law review footnotes and for practitioners; it endorses ordinary Roman type and does not use any form of LARGE AND SMALL CAPITALS.

D. Using This Appendix

This appendix is intended to provide a quick reference only to citation form and thus the focus is on the most commonly encountered types of citations and their examples rather than on explanations of the underlying rules for citation form. Consult *The Bluebook* and *ALWD* for explanation of the rules. The examples in this section are fictitious.

E. Quick Reference for Citations (*Bluebook* and *ALWD* Forms)

Note that references to the Bluepages in *The Bluebook* are shown as "B."

Type of Citation and *Bluebook* and *ALWD* Rule	*Bluebook* Law Review Footnote Form	Bluebook Practitioner Form (Note that underscoring may be substituted for italics in any example.)	ALWD Form (Note that underscoring may be substituted for italics in any example.)
State Cases (if court rules require parallel citations) at (*Bluebook* B5, Rule 10, and Table T.1; *ALWD* Rule 12.4)	Allen v. Carr, 201 N.C. 118, 429 S.E.2d 16 (1984) Harris v. Lee, 101 N.C. App. 12, 409 S.E.2d 90 (1982)	*Allen v. Carr,* 201 N.C. 118, 429 S.E.2d 16 (1984) *Harris v. Lee,* 101 N.C. App. 12, 409 S.E.2d 90 (1982)	*Allen v. Carr,* 201 N.C. 118, 429 S.E.2d 16 (1984) *Harris v. Lee,* 101 N.C. App. 12, 409 S.E.2d 90 (1982)
State Cases (in all other instances) (*Bluebook* B5, Rule 10, and Table T.1; *ALWD* Rule 12.4)	Allen v. Carr, 429 S.E.2d 118 (N.C. 1984) Harris v. Lee, 409 S.E.2d 90 (N.C. Ct. App. 1982)	*Allen v. Carr,* 429 S.E.2d 16 (N.C. 1984) *Harris v. Lee,* 409 S.E.2d 90 (N.C. Ct. App. 1982)	*Allen v. Carr,* 429 S.E.2d 16 (N.C. 1984) *Harris v. Lee,* 409 S.E.2d 90 (N.C. App. 1982)

Type of Citation and *Bluebook* and *ALWD* Rule	*Bluebook* Law Review Footnote Form	*Bluebook* Practitioner Form (Note that underscoring may be substituted for italics in any example.)	*ALWD* Form (Note that underscoring may be substituted for italics in any example.)
U.S. Supreme Court Cases (*Bluebook* B5, Rule 10, and Table T.1; *ALWD* Rule 12.4)	Daley v. Fisk, 520 U.S. 103 (1998)	*Daley v. Fisk,* 520 U.S. 103 (1998)	*Daley v. Fisk,* 520 U.S. 103 (1998) (*ALWD* permits parallel citations)
U.S. Courts of Appeal Cases (*Bluebook* B5, Rule 10, and Table T.1; *ALWD* Rule 12.6)	Lawrence v. Mather, 103 F.3d 114 (8th Cir. 1999)	*Lawrence v. Mather,* 103 F.3d 114 (8th Cir. 1999)	*Lawrence v. Mather,* 103 F.3d 114 (8th Cir. 1999)
U.S. District Court Cases (*Bluebook* B5, Rule 10, and Table T.1; *ALWD* Rule 12.6)	Blakely v. Yost, 742 F. Supp. 2d 942 (C.D. Cal. 2000)	*Blakely v. Yost,* 742 F. Supp. 2d 942 (C.D. Cal. 2000)	*Blakely v. Yost,* 742 F. Supp. 2d 942 (C.D. Cal. 2000)
U.S. Constitution (*Bluebook* B7, Rule 11; *ALWD* Rule 13)	U.S. CONST. amend. IV	U.S. Const. amend. IV	U.S. Const. amend. IV
State Constitution (*Bluebook* B7, Rule 11; *ALWD* Rule 13)	CAL. CONST. art. XX, § 4	Cal. Const. art. XX, § 4	Cal. Const. art. XX, § 4
Federal Statutes (*Bluebook* B6, Rule 12, and Table T.1; *ALWD* Rule 14)	17 U.S.C. § 101 (2000) 17 U.S.C.A. § 101 (West 1998) 17 U.S.C.S. § 101 (LexisNexis 1996)	17 U.S.C. § 101 (2000) 17 U.S.C.A. § 101 (West 1998) 17 U.S.C.S. § 101 (LexisNexis 1996)	17 U.S.C. § 101 (2000) 17 U.S.C.A. § 101 (West 1998) 17 U.S.C.S. § 101 (Lexis 1996)

Type of Citation and *Bluebook* and *ALWD* Rule	*Bluebook* Law Review Footnote Form	*Bluebook* Practitioner Form (Note that underscoring may be substituted for italics in any example.)	*ALWD* Form (Note that underscoring may be substituted for italics in any example.)
State Statutes (*Bluebook* B6, Rule 12, and Table T.1; *ALWD* Rule 14 and App. 1)	Ariz. Rev. Stat. Ann. § 104 (1992) Cal. Evid. Code § 52 (West 1998)	Ariz. Rev. Stat. Ann. § 104 (1992) Cal. Evid. Code § 52 (West 1998)	Ariz. Rev. Stat. Ann. § 104 (West 1992) Cal. Evid. Code Ann. § 52 (West 1998)
Federal Rules (*Bluebook* B6, and Rule 12.8.3; *ALWD* Rule 17.1)	Fed. R. Civ. P. 12(b)(6)	Fed. R. Civ. P. 12(b)(6)	Fed. R. Civ. P. 12(b)(6)
Federal Regulations (*Bluebook* B6 and Rule 14.2; *ALWD* Rule 19.1)	Cheese Import Regulations, 42 C.F.R. § 131 (1999); or 29 C.F.R. § 605.89 (2000)	Cheese Import Regulations, 42 C.F.R. § 131 (1999); or 29 C.F.R. § 605.89 (2000) (include title if helpful)	42 C.F.R. § 131 (1999); or 29 C.F.R. § 605.89 (2000) (include title if helpful)
Federal Register (*Bluebook* Rule 14.2; *ALWD* Rule 19.3)	Standard Industrial Codes, 64 Fed. Reg. 278 (Dec. 6, 1997)	Standard Industrial Codes, 64 Fed. Reg. 278 (Dec. 6, 1997)	64 Fed. Reg. 278 (Dec. 6, 1997) (title is optional)
Administrative Decisions (*Bluebook* Rule 14.3; *ALWD* Rule 19.5)	Network Solutions, Inc., 18 F.C.C.2d 909 (2000) Stevens Textile Co., 403 N.L.R.B. 120 (1985)	*Network Solutions, Inc.*, 18 F.C.C.2d 909 (2000) *Stevens Textile Co.*, 403 N.L.R.B. 120 (1985)	*Network Solutions, Inc.*, 18 F.C.C.2d 909 (F. Commun. Commn. 2000) *Stevens Textile Co.*, 403 N.L.R.B. 120 (Natl. Lab. Rel. Bd. 1985)
Looseleaf Services (*Bluebook* Rule 19 and Table T.15; *ALWD* Rule 28.1)	*In re* Walmart Stores, Inc., 5 Bus. Franchise Guide (CCH) ¶ 42,201 (D.N.J. Aug. 12, 1995)	*In re Walmart Stores, Inc.*, 5 Bus. Franchise Guide (CCH) ¶ 42,201 (D.N.J. Aug. 12, 1995)	*In re Walmart Stores, Inc.*, 5 Bus. Fran. Guide (CCH) ¶ 42,201 (D.N.J. Aug. 12, 1995)

Type of Citation and *Bluebook* and *ALWD* Rule	*Bluebook* Law Review Footnote Form	*Bluebook* Practitioner Form (Note that underscoring may be substituted for italics in any example.)	*ALWD* Form (Note that underscoring may be substituted for italics in any example.)
Attorneys General Opinions (*Bluebook* Rule 14.4; *ALWD* Rule 19.7, 20.7)	65 Op. Cal. Att'y Gen. 104 (1994); 49 Op. Att'y Gen. 918 (1988)	65 Op. Cal. Att'y Gen. 104 (1994); 49 Op. Att'y Gen. 918 (1988)	65 Cal. Op. Atty. Gen. 104 (1994); 49 Op. Atty. Gen. 918 (1988)
Books (*Bluebook* B8 and Rule 15; *ALWD* Rule 22.1)	2 J. Thomas McCarthy, McCarthy on Trademarks and Unfair Competition § 4:13 (4th ed. 1998)	2 J. Thomas McCarthy, *McCarthy on Trademarks and Unfair Competition* § 4:13 (4th ed. 1998)	J. Thomas McCarthy, *McCarthy on Trademarks and Unfair Competition* vol. 2, § 4:13 (4th ed., West 1998)
	7 Samuel Williston, Treatise on the Law of Contracts § 901 (Walter H. Jaeger ed., 3d ed. 1964)	7 Samuel Williston, *Treatise on the Law of Contracts* § 901 (Walter H. Jaeger ed., 3d ed. 1964)	Samuel Williston, *Treatise on the Law of Contracts* vol. 7, § 901 (Walter H. Jaeger ed., 3d ed., West 1964)
Periodical Materials and Law Reviews (*Bluebook* B8 and Rule 16 and Table T.13; *ALWD* Rule 23.1)	David J. Hayes, Jr., *Due Process*, 41 Emory L.J. 164 (1997)	David B. Hayes, Jr., *Due Process,* 41 Emory L.J. 164 (1997)	David B. Hayes, Jr., *Due Process,* 41 Emory L.J. 164 (1997)
	Janet R. Sanders, *Corporate Takeovers,* 12 J. Bus. L. 18 (2001)	Janet R. Sanders, *Corporate Takeovers,* 12 J. Bus. L. 18 (2001)	Janet R. Sanders, *Corporate Takeovers,* 12 J. Bus. L. 18 (2001)
Dictionaries (*Bluebook* Rule 15.8; *ALWD* Rule 25.1)	Black's Law Dictionary 791 (8th ed. 2004)	*Black's Law Dictionary* 791 (8th ed. 2004)	*Black's Law Dictionary* 791 (Bryan A. Garner ed., 8th ed., West 2004)

Type of Citation and *Bluebook* and *ALWD* Rule	*Bluebook* Law Review Footnote Form	*Bluebook* Practitioner Form (Note that underscoring may be substituted for italics in any example.)	*ALWD* Form (Note that underscoring may be substituted for italics in any example.)
Legal Encyclopedias (*Bluebook* B8 and Rule 15.8; *ALWD* Rule 26.1)	76 AM. JUR. 2D *Trademarks* § 13 (1986) 95 C.J.S. *Trial* § 32 (1988) 14 CAL. JUR. 3D *Contracts* §§ 14-18 (1994)	76 Am. Jur. 2d *Trademarks* § 13 (1986) 95 C.J.S. *Trial* § 32 (1988) 14 CAL. JUR. 3d *Contracts* §§ 14-18 (1994)	*76 Am. Jur. 2d Trademarks* § 13 (1986) 95 C.J.S. *Trial* § 32 (1988) *14 CAL. JUR. 3d Contracts* §§ 14-18 (1994)
Restatements (*Bluebook* B6 and Rule 12.8.5; *ALWD* Rule 27.1)	RESTATEMENT (SECOND) OF TORTS § 13 (1986)	Restatement (Second) of Torts § 13 (1986)	*Restatement (Second) of Torts* § 13 (1986)
A.L.R. Annotations (*Bluebook* Rule 16.6.6; *ALWD* Rule 24.1)	James W. Gray, Annotation, *Nuisance Theory,* 56 A.L.R.4th 145 (1990)	James W. Gray, Annotation, *Nuisance Theory,* 56 A.L.R.4th 145 (1990)	James W. Gray, *Nuisance Theory,* 56 A.L.R.4th 145 (1990)
Electronic Databases (*Bluebook* B5 and Rule 18; *ALWD* Rule 12.12)	Bowes v. Capital Group, No. 94-1765, 1995 U.S. App. LEXIS 1202, at *2 (4th Cir. Oct. 8, 1995) Green v. Taylor, No. 97-CAS-120, 1998 WL 44102, at *1 (D.N.J. Feb. 10, 1998)	*Bowes v. Capital Group,* No. 94-1765, 1995 U.S. App. LEXIS 1202, at *2 (4th Cir. Oct. 8, 1995) *Green v. Taylor,* No. 97-CAS-120, 1998 WL 44102, at *1 (D.N.J. Feb. 10, 1998)	*Bowes v. Capital Group,* 1995 U.S. App. LEXIS 1202 at *2 (4th Cir. Oct. 8, 1995) *Green v. Taylor,* 1998 WL 44102 at *1 (D.N.J. Feb. 10, 1998)
Internet Source (article available solely on Internet) (*Bluebook* Rule 18; *ALWD* Rule 40.1)	Brenda Sandburg, *PTO's Destination: Silicon Valley* (1999), http://www.lawnewsnet.com/stories	Brenda Sandburg, *PTO's Destination: Silicon Valley* (1999), http://www.lawnewsnet.com/stories	Brenda Sandburg, *PTO's Destination: Silicon Valley,* http://www.lawnewsnet.com/stories (last accessed June 28, 2008)

F. Special *Bluebook* and *ALWD* Citation Issues

1. General Comments

- Practitioners never use LARGE AND SMALL CAPITALS in citations. They always use ordinary Roman type. LARGE AND SMALL CAPITALS are used only for law review footnotes in *The Bluebook* system. *ALWD* does not recognize LARGE AND SMALL CAPITALS as appropriate for any citation.
- Practitioners may underscore or italicize case names, book titles, names of articles in journals, and so forth. Select one method and be consistent. Use this same method for signals (such as *see* and *id.*).
- In citations, use the abbreviations "2d," "3d," and "102d Cong." rather than "2nd," "3rd," and "102nd Cong." All other ordinals (4th, 5th, and so forth) are the same as in general use. Do not use a superscript. Thus, use "8th" rather than "8th."

2. Abbreviations in Case Names: *Bluebook* and *ALWD*

- Under *Bluebook* Rule 10.2.1(c), when a citation appears in a textual sentence (meaning that the citation is needed to make sense of the sentence), you may abbreviate only well-known acronyms (such as FBI and CIA) and the following abbreviations in case names: "&," "Ass'n," "Bros.," "Co.," "Corp.," "Inc.," "Ltd.," and "No." (Rule 10.2). *ALWD* Rule 12.2(e) follows the same general approach but uses the abbreviation "Assn."
- When a citation appears as a stand-alone citation, for example, after a declaratory sentence, you must abbreviate any of the nearly 170 words identified in Table T.6 of *The Bluebook*, such as "Hosp." or "Cas." even if the word is the first word in a party's name. Many of *The Bluebook* and *ALWD* abbreviations differ from each other. ALWD Rule 12.2(e) states that you may abbreviate words in its Appendix 3 when the case name appears in a stand-alone citation.

Correct Example for Law Review Footnotes

Trademarks may be abandoned by nonuse. Bates Constr. & Div. Auth. v. S. Maint. Comm., 499 U.S. 16 (1999).

Correct Example for Practitioners (for Bluebook and ALWD)

Trademarks may be abandoned by nonuse. *Bates Constr. & Div. Auth. v. S. Maint. Comm.*, 499 U.S. 16 (1999).

3. Spacing (*Bluebook* Rule 6.1(a), *ALWD* Rule 2.2)

- Close up adjacent single capital letters. Treat an ordinal (2d, 3d, 4th, and so forth) as a single capital letter.

Correct Examples: U.S.
F.3d
N.W.2d

■ Place spaces before and after multiple letter abbreviations.

Correct Examples: F. Supp. 2d
Fed. R. Crim. P.
Cal. 4th

■ Be careful with the abbreviations for the names of periodicals. Their spacing is odd. Mimic the spacing shown in *Bluebook* Table T.13 and *ALWD* Appendix 5.

Bluebook Correct Example
for Law Review Footnotes: 46 B.C. L. Rev. 190

Bluebook Correct Example
for Practitioners: 46 B.C. L. Rev. 190

ALWD Correct Example
for Any Purpose: 46 B.C. L. Rev. 190

■ Always place a space after a section or paragraph symbol, as in 35 U.S.C. §102 (2000). To pluralize sections, use two symbols, as in §§ 102–104.

4. Punctuation

■ If the citation supports or contradicts a previous declaratory sentence, follow it with a period.
■ If the citation is used as a clause within a complete sentence, follow it with a comma.
■ If the citation is used in a "string" of other citations, separate the citations from each other with semicolons and follow the order required in *Bluebook* Rule 1.4 and *ALWD* Rule 45. The ordering system for *The Bluebook* and *ALWD* differ, especially with regard to the order of lower federal court cases.

5. Pinpoints

Give a pinpoint citation (a reference to the page on which specific material appears) for all citations (*Bluebook* Rule 3.2; *ALWD* Rule 5.2). See the following examples and *The Bluebook* and *ALWD* for rules relating to the citation of multiple pages.

Bluebook *Correct Example for Law Review Footnote*

Hardy v. Bailey, 520 U.S. 118, 124 (1992)
Jackson v. Emerson Inc., 109 Wis. 2d 99, 104, 691 N.W.2d 145, 150-51 (1994)
Steven Mills, *Bankruptcy Law,* 31 STAN. L. REV. 308, 314-15 (1998)

Bluebook *and* ALWD *Correct Examples for Practitioners*

Hardy v. Bailey, 520 U.S. 118, 124 (1992)
Jackson v. Emerson Inc., 109 Wis. 2d 99, 104, 691 N.W.2d 145, 150-51
   (1994)
Jackson v. Emerson Inc., 691 N.W.2d 145, 150-51 (Wis. 1994)
Steven Mills, *Bankruptcy Law,* 31 Stan. L. Rev. 308, 314-15 (1998)

Note that whereas *The Bluebook* requires one to drop repetitious digits for page spans, the *ALWD* approach is optional so that all digits may be retained if desired, as in 314-315.

6. Quotations (*Bluebook* Rule 5; ALWD Rules 47-49)

The approach to presenting quotations is nearly identical in *The Bluebook* and in *ALWD*.

- Quotations of forty-nine words or fewer are enclosed in double quotation marks (" ") and placed in the narrative portion of your text. Always put periods and commas inside your quotation marks. Quotations within quotations are shown by single quotation marks (' ').
- Quotations of fifty words or more are indented left and right, justified, and appear without quotation marks (quotation marks within this block should appear as they do in the original). Place the citation at the left margin on the line immediately following the quotation and not within the block.
- Use an ellipsis (. . .) to show an omission in the middle of a quoted sentence. Do not start a sentence with an ellipsis (*Bluebook* Rule 5.3; *ALWD* Rule 49.3(b)); instead, use brackets, as in "[N]oncompetition agreements must be reasonable." If the omitted matter includes the end of a sentence, add another period to the ellipsis (. . . .).
- Use brackets ([ ]) to show a minor alteration in a quotation, such as a change from uppercase to lowercase. Use the signal "[sic]" to show a misteak [sic] in the original material.

Note that *ALWD* provides that if a quotation is more than fifty words *or* exceeds four lines of typed text, it should be presented as a block quotation. *The Bluebook* approach does not refer to lines of text but provides only that if the quotation is more than fifty words, it should be presented as a block quotation.

7. Short Forms

Short forms may be used for most citations once the citation has been given in full in the document. The treatment of short forms is much the same in *The Bluebook* and in *ALWD*.

- Use *id.* to send the reader to the most immediately preceding authority, no matter what the preceding authority is. *Id.* may be capitalized or not, depending on its location in a sentence.

- Use the form "*id.* at __" to send the reader to a different page within the preceding citation.

Bluebook *Correct Example for Law Review Footnotes*

First reference: Thomas v. Murphy Bros., 520 U.S. 118, 124 (1995)
Second reference: *Id.* at 128-29.

- Do not use the word "at" before a section symbol or paragraph symbol (*Bluebook* Rule 3.3). *ALWD* permits the use of "at" before the symbols (*ALWD* Rule 14.6).

Correct Example (Bluebook)

First reference: 42 U.S.C. § 101 (2000)
Second reference: *Id.* § 114

Bluebook. Use one of the following forms to send a reader to a preceding case that is not immediately preceding:

Correct Examples for Practitioners

First reference: *Geary Bros. v. Levy Ass'n*, 521 U.S. 16, 19 (2001)
Later references: *Geary*, 521 U.S. at 23; or
                    521 U.S. at 23;
                    In *Geary*, the Court also held . . . (See Rule 10.9(c)),
                    which allows a reference to a case by one of the parties'
                    names without any further citation if the case has been
                    cited in full in the same general discussion.)

ALWD. Use the following forms to send a reader to a preceding case that is not immediately preceding:

First reference: *Ryan v. O'Neill*, 521 U.S. 118 (1999)
Later references: *Ryan*, 521 U.S. at 124; or
                    521 U.S. at 124;
                    In *Geary*, the Court also held . . . (*ALWD* Rule 12.21(c)(2))

■ Use the signal *supra* (meaning *above*) to send a reader to a previous secondary authority that is not the immediately preceding authority. The signal *supra* cannot be used to send a reader to a case, statute, constitutional provision, or regulation. *Supra* always appears with the name of an author or the title of a work (*Bluebook* Rule 4.2 and Bluepages B8.2; *ALWD* Rule 11.4). Thus, *supra* is used primarily to send readers to a previously cited book or law review article.

Bluebook *Correct Example for Law Review Footnotes*

First reference: Susan Gray, DUE PROCESS § 12 (1999)
Later reference: Gray, *supra* note 4, § 14

Bluebook *and* ALWD *Correct Example for Practitioners*

McCarthy, *supra*, at 177.

■ The first reference to a statute must give the full citation. Later references may use any short form that is understandable to the reader.
■ Although *The Bluebook* and *ALWD* clearly require a year and a reference to the publisher (unless the set is official) for citations for statutes, almost all practitioners omit the parenthetical.

Correct *Bluebook* and ALWD Example: 15 U.S.C. § 1051 (2000)

Example in Common Use: 15 U.S.C. § 1051

G. Differences Between *The Bluebook* and *ALWD*

Although the basic methods of citation are much the same in *The Bluebook* and *ALWD*, there are some notable differences, including the following:

■ **Parallel Citations for U.S. Supreme Court Cases.** *The Bluebook* (Bluepages B5.1.3 and Table T.1) does not permit parallel citations for U.S. Supreme Court cases. *ALWD* does (*ALWD* Rule 12.4(c)).
■ **Case Names.** The abbreviations used in case names are different in the two citation systems. See *Bluebook* Table T.6 and *ALWD* Appendix 3. Additionally, if the United States is a party, *Bluebook* Rule 10.2.2 requires reference to *United States*. *ALWD* cites as *U.S.* (*ALWD* Rule 12.2(g)).
■ **Treatises and Dictionaries.** The publisher of a treatise or dictionary is not included in the parenthetical with the date under *The Bluebook* approach (Rule 15) but it is under the *ALWD* approach. Also, the placement of a volume number for a set of books varies.
■ **A.L.R. Annotation.** The word *Annotation* is part of the citation under *The Bluebook* approach (Rule 16.6.6) but is omitted when citing using *ALWD* (Rule 24).

- **Miscellaneous.** There are many differences in abbreviations between *The Bluebook* and *ALWD*. For example, *The Bluebook* abbreviates the word *Publishing as Publ'g* and *ALWD* abbreviates it as *Publg.*
- When giving page pinpoints, *ALWD* allows one to retain all digits (example: 914–916). *The Bluebook* requires one to drop repetitious digits (example: 914–16).
- There are several differences in how signals are presented. For example, *ALWD* does not italicize the signal et seq. *The Bluebook* does.
- Capitalization of headings in court documents differs slightly. *Bluebook* Rule 8 states that prepositions of four or fewer letters should not be capitalized (unless they begin the title or follow a colon). *ALWD* Rule 3 states that no prepositions should be capitalized (unless they begin a title or follow a colon).

Bluebook Example: Punitive Damages Are Recoverable Under the Act

ALWD Example: Punitive Damages Are Recoverable under the Act

Challenge ❓ Citation Form

Using either *The Bluebook* (using the format required for practitioners) or *ALWD*, correct the following citations. You need not include punctuation after the citations.

- Phillips Company versus Henderson, 102 Federal Supplement, Second Series, page 33, decided by the Southern District of New York in 2006.
- United States of America versus Timothy Taylor, 155 Federal Reporter, Third Series, page 230, decided in 2004 by the Eighth Circuit.
- Harold Anthony vs. Bailey Brothers, a 2005 case decided by the Supreme Court of Minnesota in volume 859 of the relevant reporter, second series, at page 560, with a quotation appearing on pages 565 through 568.
- Masterson versus Ellen Caldwell, a United States Supreme Court case decided in 2005, at volume 540, page 118.
- Section 2244 of Title 18 of the United States Code.
- California Probate Code Section 1140.
- Section 114 of volume 6 of a book written by Cynthia Dawson, entitled "Calculating Spousal Support," published in its third edition in 2006.
- A law review article authored by Gregory T. Anderson, entitled "Complying with Sarbanes–Oxley Requirements," and published in 2007 in volume 32 of the South Carolina Law Review, beginning on page 340.

appendix B

English as a Second Language

StyleLinks

http://owl.english.purdue.edu/owl/resource/678/01
Purdue University's Online Writing Lab offers resource pages, handouts, information on spelling and grammar, and quizzes for ESL learners.

www.english-at-home.com
This site provides games, quizzes, tests, and other tools for ESL learners.

www.eslcafe.com/students
This excellent website provides numerous links to ESL resources as well as handouts on grammar and usage and quizzes.

http://law.case.edu/faculty/friedman/raw/ESL%20Resources.htm
RawData's website offers numerous links to excellent ESL resources.

http://ualr.edu/cmbarger/WritersResources.HTM#ESL
Professor Coleen Barger offers links to ESL websites.

http://babelfish.yahoo.com/
Yahoo's Babelfish site offers translations to and from various languages.

A. Introduction

If English is your second language, you have probably already noticed a number of oddities and contradictions in English and in legal writing. Some are purely linguistic differences and others are cultural differences. This appendix provides a very brief overview of some common trouble spots for legal writers learning English as a second language ("ESL").

B. Grammar

A number of grammar issues cause confusion for nonnative speakers of English, including word order, placement of adjectives and adverbs, the use of prepositions, verb tense, and determining the correct article to use before a noun.

1. Standard Word Order

In English, unlike many languages, word order is important in sentences and significantly affects meaning. Generally, the standard sentence structure in English is subject-verb-object, as in *John mailed the document,* whereas in many other languages, the verb is placed first. Follow the standard English sentence structure in most instances because English readers are often confused by deviation from this expected pattern.

Moreover, a simple change in word order may change a direct statement to a question. Consider the following:

Statement: *The brief was filed today.*

Question: *Was the brief filed today?*

Each sentence contains the same words; however, a slight change in word order results in a completely different meaning.

2. Adjectives

In English, adjectives usually appear before the nouns they modify or describe. Consider the following example: *Elena is preparing for a difficult trial.* The adjective is *difficult* (because it describes something about the trial), the noun is *trial,* and the adjective is placed before the noun.

Some adjectives, however, appear after linking verbs. A *linking verb* is a verb, often of the senses, that does not show action, such as *seem, feel,* and the forms of the verb *to be,* such as *is* and *was*.

Correct Examples: *The attorney <u>seemed familiar</u>.*
The music <u>sounds haunting</u>.
The ice cream <u>tastes cold</u>.

3. Adverbs

Adverbs (words that modify or describe verbs) may appear either before or after the verb they describe but they should be placed as close to the verb as possible.

Poor	Better
The judge stated that there would be no continuance of the trial <u>angrily</u>.	The judge <u>angrily</u> stated that there would be no continuance of the trial. *or* The judge stated <u>angrily</u> that there would be no continuance of the trial.

4. Prepositions

Prepositions (*at, by, for, from, in, of, to, with,* and so forth) link nouns to other words and show relationships in sentences. Some prepositions show time relationships (*after, before, during, since*); some show place relationships (*at, below, in, on, to*); and others show manner relationships (*for, of, with*). Prepositions come before nouns and pronouns. Although Romance languages (such as Spanish, French, and Italian) also use prepositions, using prepositions in English is difficult because of their many idiomatic uses. An *idiom* is a phrase or expression whose meaning cannot be understood from the ordinary meanings of the words, as in the use in English of the phrase *give in* meaning *to yield* or *to surrender.*

Following are some prepositional expressions commonly used in legal writing:

according to	*innocent of*
appeal to	*liable for*
comparable to or *comparable with*	*on the contrary*
consistent with	*opposed to*
dependent on or *dependent upon*	*refer to*
different from	*regardless of*
familiar to or *familiar with*	*relevant to*
guilty of	*reliance on* or *reliance upon*
in contrast	*responsible for*
in light of	*similar to*

See Chapter 4 for a list of common idioms in legal writing.

5. Pronouns

In English, any noun may be replaced by a pronoun. Thus, *the attorneys* can be replaced by *they* or *them, the plaintiff* can be replaced by *he, she,* or *it,* and *the corporation* can be replaced by *it.*

6. Tense

Tense refers to *when* action takes place. Generally, English verbs have six basic tenses. Verbs change form to indicate whether an action takes place in the past, present, or future.

Tense	Form	Use	Examples
Present	Singular	Shows action happening now	I am happy. She argues the case today.
Past	Often ends in -ed	Shows action that happened in the past	I was happy. She argued the case last month.
Future	Often used with will	Tells about action that will happen	I will be happy. She will argue the case next week.
Present Perfect	Has or have used with main verb	Tells about a past action that continues or is complete at the time of the statement	She has been happy. She has argued the case every day thus far.
Past Perfect	Had used with main verb	Tells about past action that was completed before another past action or speculates about something that did not happen	The witness had practiced his testimony before the trial. If she had argued with me, I would have responded.
Future Perfect	Will have used with main verb	Tells about action that will take place before another future action	The trial will have ended by Tuesday. By the time the month is over, she will have argued the case five times.

The *progressive* tenses indicate continuing or progressive action. They consist of a form of *to be* together with an *-ing* form, as in *The attorney is concluding* or *The judge will be listening* for hearsay evidence.

English uses simpler tense forms than many languages and often nonnative speakers will use progressive and perfect tenses rather than the simpler present, past, and future tenses that are most common in legal writing.

Remember to discuss the following in the past tense:

- Acts that occurred in the past, as in *The accident occurred on May 18, 2008.*
- The procedural history of a case you are discussing, as in *The court below dismissed the plaintiff's complaint and the plaintiff appealed.*
- The holding of a case you are discussing, as in *The court held that failure to hold an annual shareholders' meeting was a violation of law.*

Use the present tense when you are discussing a current statute or a rule of law, as in *The rule in this state is that punitive damages are recoverable upon a showing of reckless and willful misconduct.* Avoid shifts in tense.

Helping or Auxiliary Verbs

Helping or auxiliary verbs accompany main verbs. Some common helping verbs include *could, do, may, might, shall, should, will, would,* and any form of the verb *to be.* ESL learners frequently have trouble distinguishing the meanings of the following helping verbs:

- **Can** shows ability or possibility, as in *She can file for damages because of the breach of contract* or *She can fail this class if she does not study.*
- **Could** shows past ability or possibility, as in *She could play the piano before she was injured.*
- **May** shows permission or possibility, as in *She may file the claim so long as the statute of limitations has not expired* or *You may be liable for copyright infringement.*
- **Might** shows possibility, as in *Your motion might be denied by the court.*
- **Must** indicates obligation or requirement, as in *You must file the brief today.*
- **Shall** indicates obligation (although it is a slightly more legalistic word than *must*) and is often used in statutes, as in *An injured party shall provide notice to . . . .*
- **Should** shows advisability, as in *You should pay the rent early this month.*
- **Should have** indicates advice that was not taken or expectations not met, as in *You should have notified the insurance company as soon as you were injured.*
- **Will** shows future action, as in *We will select the jury next week.*
- **Would** indicates intention or a request, as in *We told Maria that we would prepare her lease for her review.*

7. Nouns

There are two primary difficulties for ESL learners with regard to noun use: forming plurals of certain nouns and using the correct article or determiner before a noun. The use of articles (*a, an, the*) can be particularly difficult for nonnative speakers because many languages do not use articles.

a. Plurals of Noncount Nouns

Most nouns form plurals by adding *s* to the singular form as in *plaintiff-plaintiffs*. But some nouns, usually called *noncount* nouns (because they name something that cannot be counted in English, such as *wealth, democracy, intelligence,* or *evidence*), do not form plurals. Thus, you cannot write *the evidences of the plaintiff* no matter how many separate exhibits, documents, and other pieces of evidence a plaintiff introduces at trial.

b. Use of Articles: *A, An,* and *The*

Native speakers of English can often rely on their "ear" or intuition for determining the article that should be placed before a noun. Nonnative speakers often have more difficulty with articles because many languages do not use articles.

English has three articles: *a, an,* and *the*. Use *a* before words that begin with a consonant sound (such as *a brief, a court*) and *an* before words that begin with a vowel sound (such as *an attorney, an opening argument, an hour, an honest mistake*). Remember to focus on the sound a word makes and not its initial letter. Thus, write *a union* because the letter *u* sounds like a *y* consonant and *a one-legged man* because the letter *o* sounds like a *w* consonant.

When you write about a topic, use *a* or *an* with a noun when the reader has not yet been introduced to the topic or the noun you mention. Once you have introduced and described the noun, you can then introduce it with *the*. For this reason, *a* and *an* are called *indefinite articles* and *the* is called a *definite article*.

Correct Example

Sarah was asked to prepare <u>a memorandum</u> on nuisance law. After Sarah prepared <u>the memorandum</u>, she placed a copy in her files.

You can also use *the* when referring to an institution or entity that will be known to the reader, as in *File the brief with <u>the court</u>*.

Some other rules about using articles are as follows:

- Plural nouns require a definite article; they are never preceded by an indefinite article. Thus, you would write *I filed <u>the briefs</u> today* and not *I filed <u>a briefs</u> today*.
- The articles *a* or *an* generally do not precede a noncount noun. Thus, you would not write *A confidence is an appealing trait*.
- Some noncount nouns may not require any articles at all. Thus, *Biology is my field of study*, not *<u>The biology</u> is my field of study* or *<u>A biology</u> is my field of study*.
- Articles generally do not precede a proper noun. Thus, write *President Bush delivered the speech*, not *The President Bush delivered the speech* (there are some exceptions to this rule, as in *the United States, the Bushes, the New York Yankees*).

c. Demonstrative Pronouns

In addition to the articles *a*, *an*, and *the*, other words that are placed before nouns can be confusing. Nonnative speakers often have difficulty selecting the right demonstrative pronouns (*this*, *that*, *these*, *those*) to place before a noun. Consider these rules:

- Use *this* and *these* for items that are near, as in *this pen on my desk* and *these exhibits that we reviewed.*
- Use *that* and *those* for items that are far, as in *that courthouse* or *those Justices on the Court.*
- Use *this* and *that* for singular nouns, whether they are count nouns or noncount nouns, as in *this client* and *that knowledge.*
- Use *these* and *those* before plural count nouns, as in *these documents* and *those footnotes.*

Some Troublesome Words

- **Few** can mean either *not many* or it can mean *some.*

  Correct Examples: *Few lawsuits go to trial* (meaning *not many lawsuits go to trial*).

  A few shareholders attended the meeting (meaning *some, but not many, shareholders attended the meeting*).

- **Little** can mean *not many* or it can mean *not enough.*

  Correct Examples: *There is little time left to appeal* (meaning *there is not much time to appeal*).

  He gave me a little help with cite-checking (meaning *he gave me some, but not much, help with cite-checking*).

- **Much** cannot be used with a plural count noun. Thus write *Many shareholders attended*, not *Much shareholders attended.*
- **Many** cannot be used with a noncount noun. Thus, write *Much evidence was admitted*, not *Many evidence was admitted.*

C. Spelling and Vocabulary

Spelling in English is often illogical and is not always phonetic. Thus, the letter group *ough* is pronounced differently in each of the following words: *cough, tough,* and *though,* and there are more than twenty ways to spell the "oo" sound (as in *too, two, to, blue,* and *stew*). Similarly, the words *defendant* and *dependent* sound much the same yet are spelled differently. You will need a good dictionary if you are a nonnative speaker (as do most native speakers). *Merriam-Webster's Collegiate Dictionary,* now in its eleventh edition, is an excellent dictionary. *Merriam-Webster's* website, www.merriam-webster.com, offers a free, online dictionary, word games, and a word of the day. Review Chapter 3 of this Handbook for rules and tips on spelling. Nevertheless, you will simply have to memorize the spelling of certain words.

If you learned English outside of the United States, you will have to learn the American spellings of some words. Many dictionaries will use *Brit.* to indicate that a spelling is a British one.

British Spelling	American Spelling
judgement	judgment
colour, labour, behaviour	color, labor, behavior
grey	gray
centre, metre, theatre	center, meter, theater
analyse, criticise, organise	analyze, criticize, organize
specialise	specialize
catalogue, dialogue	catalog, dialog
counselling, signalling	counseling, signaling
banque, cheque	bank, check
defence, licence	defense, license

Build your vocabulary with daily tear-off calendars that offer a "word of the day" lesson. Ask for help. Ask friends and colleagues to help you if you mispronounce a word or have difficulty finding the right word.

D. Some Cultural Comments About Legal Writing

The American legal system is often called an *adversarial system,* meaning that its defining feature is that two sides are pitted against each other. Similarly, lawyers are often called *advocates* because they are meant to argue fiercely for a client's position. Thus, some legal writing is frankly partisan and may often take an approach that readers in America would view as direct and entirely appropriate but that some ESL readers would view as blunt and rude.

Consider the following general comments about American legal writing.

1. Adopting the Right Style

In America, the favored legal writing style is plain English, which emphasizes simple, direct, everyday language. In many cultures, a more elaborate writing style is not only common but is expected. Such a manner of writing would reflect well on the writer's intelligence and thoughtfulness. In American legal writing, a premium is placed on being direct and adopting a straightforward readable style. It is the writer's responsibility to ensure that the reader understands the writing.

2. Being Concise

Because a reader's time is valuable, legal writers tend to "get to the point" rather quickly in a document. Long-winded openings and introductions are frowned upon. Thus, in a letter, generally no more than one sentence is devoted to an introduction (for example, *As you requested, I obtained a copy of the employment agreement . . .*). The legal writer will then proceed to address the issue.

Because many legal topics are complex, legal writing that makes a difficult subject easy to understand is valued. Moreover, because readers are often impatient, legal writers tend to move immediately into their central argument. Finally, the recent trend of courts to impose page and word count limitations has forced legal writers to become direct. Thus, avoid lengthy introductions or general explanations of an area of law and move directly to the substance of the document. For example, if a brief addresses whether silent prayer in public schools is prohibited under the First Amendment to the U.S. Constitution, a long overview of the history of the First Amendment, the intent of the drafters of the Constitution, and quotations from the Framers of the Constitution is unneeded. The judge reading the brief will be familiar with the law and will skip over such a digression anyway. In some cultures, exploration of this side topic might be considered a useful introduction or an illustration that the writer is highly knowledgeable about this area of the law. In America, such a long-winded introduction might be considered either an ineffective digression or perhaps padding and might make a reader think that there is no substance to the argument.

3. Being Too Direct

Although legal writing in America prizes directness, in some instances, one can be too direct, leaving an impression of rudeness. Consider softening requests or instructions with *please*. Thus, rather than write *You must come to our office to sign your will*, write *Please call me to make an appointment so you can come in and sign your will*. Almost all readers bristle when they see the words *you must*; replace with *you should*, if applicable.

4. Giving Advice

In some situations, such as office memoranda, assigning attorneys want and expect recommendations as to strategy and tactics. They want more than a summary of cases; they want and need a candid discussion as to how these cases apply to the client and, if the cases are unfavorable, how such obstacles can be overcome. Similarly, legal professionals are expected to give their opinions as to the value of a case, how discovery should progress, and whether a witness seems credible. In some cultures, giving advice to a senior attorney would be considered brash and impertinent. Thus, you may need to discard any innate reluctance to give your opinion, particularly when it is part of your assignment.

5. Including Analysis

Because the American legal system is based on the concept of following precedents, every assertion made in a legal document must be supported by adequate authority. Even a commonplace truism such as *One who breaches a contract is liable for damages caused by the breach* must be supported by a citation. Thus, readers will expect the writer to prove each and every point and expertly guide the reader through each step in the analysis. Although case law can be interpreted in a light most favorable to the client, it is unethical to mischaracterize a legal authority. Furthermore, you must include citations to all authorities relied on. If you rely on a legal authority, give the citation. If you quote from an authority, give the citation. Finally, although responding forcefully to an adversary is expected, make sure that your response is aimed at the adversary's argument, not at the adversary personally.

6. Asking for Help

Ask your colleagues to review your writing for the tone and style of the document. Be aware of the differences in cultures and understand that the style of writing you may have learned may need to be revised for a different legal audience. For example, if your language does not use the articles *a, an,* or *the,* review for their correct use. Read legal newspapers, memos written by your colleagues, court opinions, and briefs filed in court to get the flavor and feel for American legal writing.

Challenge ?

Make corrections to the following passage.

> Our client wish to file an complaint in federal court. A case may be brought in federal court if jurisdiction only is based on either a federal question or diversity of the parties. A federal question exist if the case involves a federal statute or an constitutional provision. For diversity to exist, each of the plaintiff and the defendant must be from different states and the case is alleging more than $75,000 in damage. Our client has been alleging that she is subjected to a hostile work environment at the job and has been sexually harassed therefore. Sexual harassment has been forbidden at federal law. Our client must institute a lawsuit in the federal court therefore.

Sample Appellate Court Brief

[Note: This brief is located at the following website and is reproduced exactly as filed with the U.S. Supreme Court: http://supreme.lp.findlaw.com/supreme_court/briefs/02-964/02-964.mer.pet.rep.pdf]

No. 02-964

In the Supreme Court
of the United States

GEORGE H. BALDWIN,

Petitioner,

v.

MICHAEL REESE,

Respondent.

On Writ of Certiorari to the
United States Court of Appeals for the Ninth Circuit

PETITIONER'S REPLY BRIEF

HARDY MYERS
Attorney General of Oregon
PETER SHEPHERD
Deputy Attorney General
*MARY H. WILLIAMS
Solicitor General
JANET A. KLAPSTEIN
ROBERT B. ROCKLIN
Assistant Attorneys General
400 Justice Building
Salem, Oregon 97301-4096
Phone: (503) 378-4402
Counsel for Petitioner

*Counsel of Record

TABLE OF CONTENTS

Page

I. The phrase "ineffective assistance of counsel" is not a legal term of art that necessarily identifies a federal claim for the Oregon appellate courts; therefore, Reese did not alert the state courts that he was raising a federal claim. 1

II. Even if a state court applies the same legal analysis to similar claims raised under the state and federal constitutions, a state prisoner still must make it clear to the state court that he is raising a federal claim. 4

III. Oregon courts—like most appellate courts—address only the claims that litigants present to them. Nothing in Oregon law required the state appellate courts to address an issue that Reese did not raise clearly as a claim of error. 7

IV. The State has not abandoned its concern that the factual basis for Reese's inadequate assistance of counsel claim has changed throughout the various proceedings. 9

V. Some additional points warrant a brief response. 11

CONCLUSION 14

i

[This page intentionally left blank.]

TABLE OF AUTHORITIES

Page

Cases Cited

Hempel v. Palmateer,
   187 Or. App. 70, 66 P.3d 513 (2003)............................... 3, 6

Krummacher v. Gierloff,
   290 Or. 867, 627 P.2d 458 (1981) 2

Lichau v. Baldwin,
   166 Or. App. 411, 999 P.2d 1207 (2000)........................... 3

Lichau v. Baldwin,
   333 Or. 350, 39 P.3d 851 (2002) 6

Lounsbury v. Thompson,
   ___ F.3d ___ (9th Cir. 2003) (WL 21993253)................... 12

Peterson v. Lampert,
   319 F.3d 1153 (9th Cir. 2003) 6

Sanders v. Ryder,
   ___ F.3d ___ (9th Cir. 2003) (2003 WL 22053440)............ 2

State v. Castrejon,
   317 Or. 202, 856 P.2d 616 (1993) 12

State v. Moore,
   334 Or. 328, 49 P.3d 785 (2002) 5

State v. Smith,
   301 Or 681, 725 P.2d 894 (1986) 5

State v. Tanner,
   304 Or. 312, 745 P.2d 757 (1987) 5

Storm v. McClung,
   334 Or. 210, 47 P.3d 476 (2002) 5

Stranahan v. Fred Meyer, Inc.,
   331 Or. 38, 11 P.3d 228 (2000) 5

iii

Stupek v. Wyle Laboratories Corp.,
   327 Or. 433, 963 P.2d 678 (1998) 12

Wells v. Maass,
   28 F.3d 1005 (9th Cir. 1994) 11

Constitutional and Statutory Provisions

Or. Const. art. I, § 10 5

Or. Rev. Stat. § 138.660... 8

Other Authorities

Or. R. App. P. 9.17(2)(b)(i) 12

Or. R. App. P. 9.20(2)... 11

REPLY BRIEF FOR PETITIONER

Reese argues, as he must, that he fairly presented to Oregon's highest court a federal constitutional claim of ineffective assistance of appellate counsel, even though he cited no authority as the legal basis of his claim. Reese seizes on the State's acknowledgment that, in certain narrow circumstances, a state prisoner necessarily identifies a federal issue even without citing federal authority.[1] Expanding from this, Reese argues that a state prisoner can alert a State's highest court to the federal nature of his claim if (1) he phrases his claim in terms associated only with federal rather than state constitutional claims; or (2) the state courts apply the same legal analysis in deciding the claim under either the state or federal constitution; or (3) state law requires the state appellate court to address issues not actually presented by the petitioner. The State disagrees that a state prisoner would satisfy the fair presentation requirement by complying with Reese's second proposed option. Although Reese's first and third options *might* satisfy the fair presentation requirement in certain circumstances, those circumstances are not present in this case.

I. The phrase "ineffective assistance of counsel" is not a legal term of art that necessarily identifies a federal claim for the Oregon appellate courts; therefore, Reese did not alert the state courts that he was raising a federal claim.

Reese argues that he alerted the Oregon appellate courts to the federal nature of his claim by using the phrase "ineffective assistance of counsel." Brief of Respondent at 27–29. As the

---

[1] The example the State gave was that a "due process claim" in Oregon courts would necessarily be a federal claim because the Oregon Constitution does not contain a due process clause.

2

State noted in its opening brief, Oregon courts often refer to "inadequate assistance of counsel" instead of "ineffective assistance of counsel" because the Oregon Supreme Court has stated that, under state constitutional principles, "the term 'adequate' assistance of counsel may be more accurate than 'effective' assistance of counsel." Brief of Petitioner at 4 n. 5 (*quoting Krummacher v. Gierloff*, 290 Or. 867, 872 n. 3, 627 P.2d 458, 462 n. 3 (1981)). Reese asserts that he fairly presented the federal nature of his claim to the state appellate courts because he "referred to his claim almost exclusively as a claim of 'ineffective,' not 'inadequate,' assistance."[2] Brief of Respondent at 29.

Although the Oregon Supreme Court may have expressed a preference for the phrase "inadequate assistance of counsel" under the state constitution, it has not transformed that phrase into a legal term of art nor does it treat the phrase "ineffective assistance of counsel" as denoting a claim arising only under the federal constitution. Rather, practitioners and judges alike

---

[2] The Ninth Circuit recently took Reese's argument one step further. Although only the Oregon Supreme Court has expressed a preference for the use of the phrase "inadequate assistance of counsel" when referring to claims under the Oregon Constitution, the Ninth Circuit held that a state prisoner had fairly presented a federal claim to the *Washington* state courts because he "consistently and exclusively" mentioned ineffective assistance of counsel. *Sanders v. Ryder*, ___ F.3d ___, ___ (9th Cir. 2003) (2003 WL 22053440). Thus, the Ninth Circuit apparently believes "ineffective assistance of counsel" is a term of art designating a federal claim, not only for Oregon courts, but for all courts in that circuit. *Sanders* demonstrates the problems that inevitably arise each time courts are permitted to move away from a hard-and-fast rule that state prisoners must cite the federal constitutional provision or a leading federal case to establish that they fairly presented a federal claim to the state courts.

3

often use the phrases interchangeably. For example, in *Lichau v. Baldwin*, 166 Or. App. 411, 415, 999 P.2d 1207, 1210 (2000), the Oregon Court of Appeals wrote:

> Petitioner filed a petition for post-conviction relief alleging multiple grounds of trial court error, prosecutorial misconduct, and *inadequate* assistance of counsel. In support of the *ineffective* assistance of counsel claim, petitioner alleged that trial counsel failed to conduct an adequate investigation of his alibi defense.

(Emphasis added); *see also Hempel v. Palmateer*, 187 Or. App. 70, 75, 66 P.3d 513, 515 (2003) ("Petitioner's federal inadequate assistance claim fails for the same reasons that his state claim fails.").

Reese himself used the terms interchangeably before the state appellate courts.[3] Thus there simply is no support for Reese's argument that the Oregon appellate courts must have treated Reese's reference to "ineffective assistance of counsel" as necessarily raising a federal claim.

But even more troubling than Reese's unsupported description of Oregon law is the broader implication his rule would have for all federal habeas litigation. To hold that the exhaustion requirement is satisfied by referring to a claim "almost exclusively" in language that *may* constitute a term of art will increase litigation in federal habeas corpus proceedings on this issue and on other federal claims that have state-

---

[3] Even before this Court, Reese does not treat the phrase "ineffective assistance of counsel" as a term of art reserved for the federal constitution. For example, see Brief of Respondent at 29; in the heading on that page, Reese uses the term "ineffective" when referring to both the state and federal constitutions.

4

court analogs. Whether a given word or phrase is a term of art for the state courts and whether a state prisoner who used that word or phrase almost—but not quite—exclusively fairly presented a federal claim to the state courts makes a guessing game of the federal habeas corpus proceedings. As the State pointed out in its opening brief, the potential for wasting resources litigating procedural default issues is a legitimate concern for this Court in explaining the requirements of exhaustion of state remedies through fair presentation of claims in the state courts. Rejecting Reese's novel "term of art" principle is one way to ensure a more efficient use of those limited resources.

II. Even if a state court applies the same legal analysis to similar claims raised under the state and federal constitutions, a state prisoner still must make it clear to the state court that he is raising a federal claim.

Reese argues that, because the state courts would have applied the same test for a claim of ineffective assistance of appellate counsel under either the Oregon or United States Constitutions, he should be deemed to have provided the state appellate courts with sufficient opportunity to consider a claim under the federal constitution. Brief of Respondent at 29–35. Effectively, Reese wants to benefit from his own failure to refer explicitly to either constitution.

There are at least four problems with Reese's argument. First, even when state courts analyze an issue under the state constitution in the same way they analyze a related issue under the federal constitution, it is critical first to identify for the state court the source of the claim because that source defines the authority of the state court. This is especially true for the state's highest appellate court, which is free to modify its analysis under the state constitution, but is bound by this Court's decisions concerning the federal constitution.

5

Thus, for example, even if the Oregon Supreme Court currently applies the same analytical process and standards for resolving state and federal claims of ineffective (or inadequate) assistance of appellate counsel, that may not always be the case. The Oregon Supreme Court frequently has diverged in its interpretation of the state constitution from this Court's interpretation of similar provisions under the federal constitution. *See, e.g., State v. Moore*, 334 Or. 328, 331, 49 P.3d 785, 787 (2002) (rejecting state's suggestion that the court reexamine and discard the "unavailability" requirement under Article I, section 11, of the Oregon constitution in light of changes in this Court's analysis of Confrontation Clause claims); *State v. Tanner*, 304 Or. 312, 315–316, 745 P.2d 757, 758–759 (1987) (rejecting federal analysis of exclusionary rule based on deterrence rationale; under the state constitution the exclusionary rule is predicated on an individual's privacy rights); *State v. Smith*, 301 Or. 681, 725 P.2d 894 (1986) (right against compelled self-incrimination differs under state and federal constitutions). In fact, the Oregon Supreme Court recently has emphasized its willingness to reexamine any prior state constitutional decision when presented with a principled argument demonstrating that the challenged decision was inconsistent with the court's template for constitutional construction. *Stranahan v. Fred Meyer, Inc.*, 331 Or. 38, 53–54, 11 P.3d 228, 237 (2000) (inviting parties to suggest new analyses); *Storm v. McClung*, 334 Or. 210, 222–223, 47 P.3d 476, 482 (2002) (reconsidering prior interpretation of Article I, section 10, of the Oregon constitution).

Although the Oregon appellate courts currently may follow the same analysis in addressing ineffective assistance of counsel claims brought under either the state or federal constitutions, they do not, as Reese suggests, simply merge the state claim into the federal claim. Nor do they treat the state claims as controlled by federal case law. Instead, when claims are raised under both constitutions, the state courts

6

raised under both constitutions, the state courts treat each claim separately and they analyze the state constitutional claims under the state constitution and the case law addressing the state constitution. *See, e.g., Lichau v. Baldwin*, 333 Or. 350, 358–359, 39 P.3d 851, 856 (2002) (following court's methodology of addressing claims under the state constitution before addressing similar claims under the federal constitution; the court expressly declined to reach the federal claim after first addressing the state claim); *Hempel v. Palmateer*, *supra*, 187 Or. App. at 73–75, 66 P.3d at 514–15 (2003) (same for claim of inadequate assistance of appellate counsel).

A second problem with Reese's argument is that it improperly shifts the focus away from what the state prisoner must do to alert the state courts to a federal claim and, instead, focuses on what the state courts may do even when the state prisoner fails to alert them to a federal claim. As the State discussed at some length in its opening brief, the Ninth Circuit similarly transformed the fair presentation requirement from an obligation of the state prisoner to an obligation of the state courts. The Ninth Circuit's transformation finds no support in the Court's case law; neither does the transformation Reese now urges. If all that matters for fair presentation is what the state courts did (or could have done) in analyzing a claim, a state prisoner could exhaust a federal claim in state court by relying exclusively on the state constitution as the only basis for relief. Even the Ninth Circuit has refused to expand the fair presentation requirement that far. *Peterson v. Lampert*, 319 F.3d 1153, 1159 (9th Cir. 2003) (en banc).

The third problem for Reese is that his first two options for meeting the fair presentation requirement are inconsistent. If, as he asserts, the state courts use the federal analysis whether appellate counsel's performance is challenged under the state or federal constitution or both, it is unlikely that the

7

state courts would use a distinct term ("inadequate") to refer to assistance of counsel claims under the state constitution. The only reason for the Oregon Supreme Court to suggest a preference for a different term under the state constitution is because the state appellate courts treat the state and federal claims as distinct and independent claims.

Moreover, if the Court accepts Reese's argument that the state courts use the same test for both state and federal claims, the Court must reject Reese's primary argument that, simply by reading the post-conviction trial court's memorandum opinion, the state appellate courts would necessarily have known that Reese's appeal involved a federal claim. The post-conviction trial court's citation to a federal case would not necessarily mean that the court decided a federal question. The court could just as easily have been resolving only the state constitutional issue or both the state and federal issues and the citation to a federal case could never alert the state appellate courts that Reese was pursuing only his federal constitutional claim on appeal.

III. Oregon courts—like most appellate courts—address only the claims that litigants present to them. Nothing in Oregon law required the state appellate courts to address an issue that Reese did not raise clearly as a claim of error.

Reese argues that certain procedural aspects of Oregon law governing post-conviction trial court decisions and summary affirmance in the Oregon Court of Appeals necessarily mean that the state appellate courts were alerted to the federal source of Reese's claim. Brief of Respondent at 35–39. The State touched on this argument in its opening brief. Brief of Petitioner at 29–30 n. 13. A few additional comments are warranted in response to Reese's argument. First, the summary affirmance statute does not alter the general requirement that appellants properly must present issues they want the appel-

8

late court to consider. Although Or. Rev. Stat. § 138.660 permits the Oregon Court of Appeals to summarily affirm, it focuses on whether any "substantial question of law is *presented by the appeal*." (Emphasis added). The Oregon Court of Appeals does not consider the merits of an issue never presented properly in the appeal. Nor does the fact that the decision to summarily affirm is described as "a decision upon the merits of the appeal," Or. Rev. Stat. § 138.660, change the basic appellate requirements for raising claims. Instead, in enacting that provision, the legislature merely confirmed that the losing party could petition for review by the Oregon Supreme Court on the merits of the appeal instead of simply on the decision to summarily affirm. The statute does not transform the intermediate appellate court's decision into one that encompasses issues that no party ever properly raised.

Nor is it necessary, as Reese asserts, for the Oregon Supreme Court to examine the merits of the post-conviction trial court judgment in order to address the petition for review. To the contrary, that court may deny a petition for review when it identifies, simply by examining the petition for review itself, no colorable issues for the court to address. A petition seeking review of an order of summary affirmance is no different in this regard than a petition from an unwritten decision of the Oregon Court of Appeals. Certainly, Reese offers nothing to support his assertion that the Oregon Supreme Court must have looked through the Oregon Court of Appeals' decision and back to the memorandum opinion of the post-conviction trial court when it denied his petition for review.

The only support Reese offers for this argument is based on his apparent misunderstanding of the requirements for preserving error. Brief of Respondent at 39–40. Preservation requirements are distinct from the party's obligation to properly frame an issue for appellate court review. State appellate courts have consistently refused to address inadequately pre-

9

sented claims on appeal, even when those claims were adequately preserved in the trial court. *See* Brief of Petitioner at 28–31.

IV. The State has not abandoned its concern that the factual basis for Reese's inadequate assistance of counsel claim has changed throughout the various proceedings.

Throughout his brief, Reese presumes that he raised or attempted to raise only a single ineffective-appellate-counsel claim in the state post-conviction and federal habeas corpus proceedings.[4] When the factual allegations shift during the proceedings from multiple factual complaints to undefined allegations to newly raised factual issues, an ineffective-appellate-counsel claim cannot be treated as a single claim.

In the amended petition Reese's counsel filed with the post-conviction trial court, he claimed his appellate counsel on the direct appeal was ineffective for: (1) failing to withdraw as Reese's attorney due to conflict of interest; (2) failing to notify Reese of change of counsel for his case; (3) failing to

---

[4] *See, e.g.,* Brief for Respondent at 4 ("Counsel filed a first amended formal PCR petition raising the claim of ineffective assistance of appellate counsel * * *."); 5 (Reese's PCR brief in the Oregon Court of Appeals "did not explicitly cite to federal authority for the ineffective assistance of appellate counsel claim * * *."); 7 (discussing the Magistrate Judge's ruling that Reese "had fairly presented his claim of ineffective assistance of appellate counsel."); 12 (Reese "raised his federal constitutional claim of ineffective assistance of appellate counsel in a petition for post-conviction relief" and "fairly presented the substance of his ineffective assistance claim" in the State appellate courts); 14 (Reese "raised every claim he had made in the Oregon Court of Appeals before the Oregon Supreme Court, including the claim of ineffective assistance of appellate counsel.").

10

raise unspecified issues that had been preserved for appeal; (4) failing to file a timely notice of appeal; and (5) failing to obtain trial transcripts in a timely manner. J.A. 17. The post-conviction trial court's ruling ("Appellate counsel need not present every colorable issue.") apparently addressed only the third claim. J.A. 23.

In the post-conviction appeal to the Oregon Court of Appeals, Reese pursued the fourth claim (attorney failed to file a timely petition for review in the Oregon Supreme Court), and the third claim (attorney failed to raise issues), still without specifying the issues that Reese thought counsel should have raised ("Barton did fail to raise issues on appeal."). J.A. 32. In his petition for review of the post-conviction decision in the Oregon Supreme Court, Reese simply alleged "inadequate assistance of appellate counsel." J.A. 47–48.

In his federal habeas corpus petition, Reese alleged four ineffective-appellate-counsel claims for failing to raise any issues, failing to raise two still-unidentified legal issues, failing to withdraw, and failing to exhaust state remedies by refusing to file a petition for review in the Oregon Supreme Court. *See* Supp. App. to Pet. for Cert. 5. The claim Reese most vigorously pursued—and the centerpiece of this case in the district court—was that his appellate counsel was ineffective for filing a *Balfour* brief and for not identifying any meritorious issues to raise in the direct appeal. Thus, for the first time in the process, the case became focused on a claim that appellate counsel provided ineffective assistance by complying with the *Balfour* process. *See* Supp. App. to Pet. for Cert. 13–18.

To demonstrate that he exhausted his available state-court remedies, Reese must show that he raised—at each level of the state courts—the specific claim he now wants to pursue in federal habeas corpus: that his appellate counsel on direct appeal was ineffective under the federal constitution because he

11

filed a *Balfour* brief. It is not enough for a state prisoner to argue in the state courts that his appellate counsel was ineffective for failing to file a petition for review and then to argue in federal habeas corpus that his counsel was ineffective for failing to raise a particular issue. Although the State has focused on Reese's failure to identify a federal source for his specific claim, the state has not, as Reese argues, abandoned all objections to the inadequate presentation of the factual basis of his inadequate assistance of appellate counsel claim. See Brief of Respondent at 42–43. To determine whether Reese properly alerted the state appellate courts to the federal nature of his claim, the Court must first focus on the precise boundaries of that claim.

V. Some additional points warrant a brief response.

First, Reese inaccurately describes the Oregon Supreme Court's review of issues not raised in a petition for review. Brief of Respondent at 40 and n. 25. Although the Ninth Circuit has stated that the Oregon Supreme Court "retains the power to address claims which are not raised in the petition for review," *Wells v. Maass*, 28 F.3d 1005, 1010 (9th Cir. 1994), the state court, in fact, applies that practice to cases in which it has allowed review and the court deems it necessary to address an issue in order to reach the issues properly presented to the court. *See* Oregon Rule of Appellate Procedure 9.20(2);[5] *Stupek v. Wyle Laboratories Corp.*, 327 Or. 433,

---

[5] Oregon Rule of Appellate Procedure 9.20(2) provides:

> If the Supreme Court allows a petition for review, the court may limit the questions on review. If review is not so limited, the questions before the Supreme Court include all questions properly before the Court of Appeals that the petition or the response claims were erroneously decided by that court. The Supreme Court's opinion need not ad-

12

437, 963 P.2d 678, 680 (1998) (under Oregon Rule of Appellate Procedure 9.20(2), court may consider issue not presented on review, that was properly raised on appeal and preserved below, but court "ordinarily will not do so unless the issue requires resolution"); *State v. Castrejon*, 317 Or. 202, 211–212, 856 P.2d 616, 622 (1993) (explaining scope of court's discretion under the rule); *see also* Oregon Rule of Appellate Procedure 9.17(2)(b)(i) (prohibiting a party from addressing issues not raised in the petition for review itself or changing the substance of the questions presented in a petition for review).[6]

Second, Reese asserts that, in a subsequent case, the Ninth Circuit has narrowed the holding in this case. Brief of Respondent at 41–42. To the extent that it matters to the Court's consideration, the Ninth Circuit continues to reach inconsistent results in this area by speculating on what the state appellate courts might have done when presented with an incomplete or inadequate claim of error. *See Lounsbury v. Thompson*, ___ F.3d ___, ___ (9th Cir. 2003) (WL 21993253) (a state

---

dress each such question. The court may consider other issues that were before the Court of Appeals.

[6] Oregon Rule of Appellate Procedure 9.17(2)(b)(i) provides:

(b) The brief on the merits of the petitioner on review shall contain:

(i) Concise statements of the legal question or questions presented on review and of the rule of law that petitioner proposes be established. The questions should not be argumentative or repetitious. The phrasing of the questions need not be identical with any statement of questions presented in the petition for review, but the brief may not raise additional questions or change the substance of the questions already presented.

13

prisoner fairly presents to the state court a substantive claim that he was incompetent to proceed to trial when he limits his state court appeal to solely a procedural competency challenge because the state appellate court would probably have examined the substantive claim to determine whether the alleged procedural defect was harmful).

Finally, Reese argues that the Court should not attempt to clarify the rule for proper exhaustion even though Reese agrees the issue is complex and there is disagreement between and within the federal appellate courts. Reese asserts that clarifying the requirements will only add to the complexity. Brief of Respondent at 46–50. Contrary to Reese's assertion, the State emphasizes that it is not asking the Court to announce a new rule for fair presentation of claims in state courts. Instead, the State urges the Court to clarify in plain terms what it has said before: it is the obligation of state prisoners to fairly present their federal claims in state court by giving the state court a fair opportunity to consider and resolve those federal claims. The State is confident that, instead of adding to the complexity and confusion, the Court can simplify the requirements for "fair presentation" consistent with the purpose underlying that requirement. In doing so, the Court will benefit state prisoners by minimizing the traps for the unwary. And it will reduce the costs incurred by the States and the federal courts in repeatedly litigating the question of procedural default.

14

CONCLUSION

For the foregoing reasons, as well as the reasons set forth in the Petition for Certiorari and in the Brief of Petitioner, the Court should reverse the judgment of the Ninth Circuit Court of Appeals.

Respectfully submitted,

HARDY MYERS
    Attorney General of Oregon
PETER SHEPHERD
    Deputy Attorney General
MARY H. WILLIAMS
    Solicitor General
JANET A. KLAPSTEIN
ROBERT B. ROCKLIN
    Assistant Attorneys General
    Counsel for Petitioner

September 18, 2003

appendix D

Answer Keys to Challenges

Readers: Note that for some challenges, other answers may be acceptable. Correct or suggested answers are shown in italics. In some instances, alternative answers are provided.

Section One: The Mechanics of Writing: Grammar, Punctuation, and Spelling

Chapter 1

Challenge: Sentences

Rewrite the following to correct them.

- He was not prepared for trial. If you want my opinion.

  If you want my opinion, he was not prepared for trial.

- He summarized the transcript. Because his supervisor requested it.

  He summarized the deposition because his supervisor requested it.

- Blake drafted the brief. Which was longer than the court rules allowed.

  Blake drafted the brief, which was longer than the court rules allowed.

  Blake drafted the brief. It was longer than the court rules allowed.

- The attorney drafted the complaint, he included both causes of action.

  The attorney drafted the complaint and included both causes of action.

  The attorney drafted the complaint, which included both causes of action.

- Ask the clerk to file the answer, it must be filed by Friday.

  Ask the clerk to file the answer. It must be filed by Friday.

  Ask the clerk to file the answer; it must be filed by Friday.

Challenge: Subject-Verb Agreement

Select the correct word.

- Neither Paul nor Pamela <u>is</u>/are attending the conference.
- The witness, together with the experts, have/<u>has</u> testified.
- The last thing the firm needs <u>is</u>/are attorneys without practical experience.
- The staff have/<u>has</u> prepared their/<u>its</u> report.
- Most of the money <u>is</u>/are available for settlement.
- The expert and the attorneys has/<u>have</u> left.
- Either the jurors or the bailiffs has/<u>have</u> requested a break.
- Either the document or the attachment <u>was</u>/were altered.
- Neither the tenant nor the landlords <u>have</u>/has filed a complaint.
- Management <u>has</u>/have decided to submit the proposal.
- Don't pick a juror just because <u>he or she is</u>/they're available.
- The set of rules that govern/<u>governs</u> federal litigation is the Federal Rules of Civil Procedure.

Challenge: Modifiers

Rewrite the following.

- Unclear and too long, the judge has ordered us to rewrite the brief.

  Because the brief was unclear and too long, the judge has ordered us to rewrite it.

  The judge has ordered us to rewrite the unclear and lengthy brief.

- Moving the exhibits, her back was hurt.

  As she was moving the exhibits, she hurt her back.

- Having arrived late, a reprimand was issued by the judge.

  Because he (or I or she) arrived late, the judge issued a reprimand.

- Reviewing the deposition, the error was obvious.

  As he [or I or she] reviewed the deposition, the error was obvious.

- The judge agreed to admit the evidence with misgivings.

  With misgivings, the judge agreed to admit the evidence.

- Reviewing the exhibit, the errors were apparent.

  My review of the exhibit disclosed its apparent errors.

While reviewing the exhibit, I noticed its apparent errors.

While I reviewed the exhibits, I noticed its apparent errors.

As he (or she) reviewed the exhibits, he (or she) noticed its apparent errors.

- I anticipate help in proofing the brief from everyone.

  I anticipate help from everyone in proofing the brief.

- New attorneys who attend depositions often gain confidence.

  New attorneys who often attend depositions gain confidence.

  New attorneys who attend depositions can often gain confidence.

- Fix the following newspaper headline: "Detective's Hunch Led Him to Attack Suspect."

  Detective's Hunch Led Him to the Attack Suspect

  Detective's Hunch Helped Locate Attack Suspect

Challenge: Pronoun Use

Rewrite or select the correct pronoun.

- Her/<u>she</u> and James have docketed the trial date.
- It was me/<u>I</u> who prepared the lease.
- The contract was drafted by Megan and I/<u>me</u>/myself.
- Between you and I/<u>me</u>, Harry's conduct was inappropriate.
- Frank and him/<u>he</u> have left for the meeting.
- Patricia has instructed the expert and <u>her</u>/she not to respond to the question.
- The brief that/which was long was submitted after the deadline.

  The brief that was too long was submitted after the deadline.

  The brief, which was too long, was submitted after the deadline.

- The judge admonished the attorney, and he looked unhappy.

  The judge admonished the attorney, and the judge looked unhappy.

  The judge admonished the attorney, and the attorney looked unhappy.

- After someone has argued a case, they/<u>he or she</u> are/<u>is</u> often relieved.
- A law student must study diligently if *he or she*/they want/<u>wants</u> to pass the bar exam.
- He is the attorney <u>who</u>/whom negotiated the settlement.
- She will depose the engineers, who/<u>whom</u> she will meet on Tuesday.
- Who/<u>whom</u> did the board appoint as their/<u>its</u> treasurer?

Challenge: Gender-Linked and Special Pronouns

Correct the following:

- Each juror must affirm the verdict he reached.

  Each juror must affirm the verdict he or she reached.

  Jurors must affirm the verdicts they reach.

  Each juror must affirm any verdict.

  Jurors must affirm the verdicts reached.

- A counselor should maintain the confidentiality of her patients.

  A counselor should maintain the confidentiality of his or her patients.

  Counselors should maintain the confidentiality of their patients.

  A counselor should maintain patient confidentiality.

Select the correct word.

- He told me he was pleased by you/<u>your</u> drafting of the contract.
- An alibi may prevent <u>his</u>/him being accused of the crime.
- The decision by the appeals court was a setback for <u>us</u>/we appellants.
- *David likes trial preparation more than he likes me.* (or *David likes trial preparation more than I do.*)

Challenge: Conjunction Junction

- The attorney made a persuasive argument, but the motion was denied.
- Neither the brief nor the motion <u>was</u>/were proofread.
- Either the attorneys or the client <u>has</u>/have discussed settlement of the case.
- The defense counsel argued the case. In addition, she did so succinctly.
       (or The defense counsel argued the case and she did so succinctly.)
- She was not only well prepared <u>but also</u> was professional in her demeanor.
- Either the bailiff or the court clerks has/<u>have</u> read the docket.

Chapter 2

Challenge: Punctuation

Punctuate the following sentences correctly, correct the punctuation errors, or indicate if the sentence is correct.

- The witness, not her attorney, failed to attend the hearing.
- The trial occurred in May 2008.
- The witness was a tall, distinguished gentleman.
- November 8, 1980, is her birthday.

- In spring I will begin school. (Because the introductory phrase is short, the comma is optional. Note that the sentence could also be written *I will begin school in the spring.*)
- Concluding the opinion, Judge Bates wrote, "The defendant abandoned the trademark."
- Concluding the opinion, Judge Bates wrote that the defendant abandoned the trademark.
- Having strong research and writing skills is essential for legal professionals.
- The exhibits include pleadings, reports, and surveys.
- The report, which was prepared by the engineer, was lengthy.
- The judge reviewed the document, and he found several inconsistencies in it.
- The judge reviewed the document and found several inconsistencies in it.

  This sentence is correct (because the coordinating conjunction "and" does not connect two independent clauses but rather connects an independent clause and a clause that cannot stand on its own).

- The witness, however, was contradicted by Dr. Ellis, the expert.

Challenge: Apostrophes

Punctuate the following.

- Judy <u>Davis's</u> acting award is a prized possession.
- The appellate <u>court's</u> record disclosed errors.
- The Iowa <u>corporation's</u> audit was printed yesterday.
- The Iowa and Ohio <u>corporations'</u> audits were printed yesterday.
- Mr. <u>Higgins's</u> will has been prepared.
- Ms. <u>Anthony's</u> will has been prepared.
- The agenda included a discussion of <u>women's</u> rights.
- He was given one <u>month's</u> salary as severance.
- He was given two <u>months'</u> salary as severance.
- The four <u>hostesses'</u> coats were missing.
- He will be the Marine <u>Corps's</u> next Commandant.
- The attorney <u>general's</u> appointment was confirmed.
- Who's/<u>Whose</u> file is this?
- The <u>company's</u> annual report disclosed <u>its</u>/it's profits.

Challenge: Punctuation

Correctly punctuate the following:

- Are you familiar with the legal phrase "res ipsa loquitor"?
- The defendant said, "I plead not guilty."
- The plaintiff shouted, "That's the man who robbed me!"

- "I was the court clerk," said Sue, "and everyone knew it."
- She asked him if he would prepare the report.
- The defendant stated, "I did provide an eviction notice; however, it was never received."
- We prepared the following exhibits: the lease, the amendment to the lease, and the eviction notice. (Note that semicolons could be used rather than commas to separate these listed items.)
- The will was witnessed by two witnesses; therefore, it is valid. (Note that these statements could be presented as two separate sentences).
- Lee prepared the complaint; it included three counts. (Note that these statements could be presented as two separate sentences or as *Lee prepared the complaint, which included three counts.*)
- You will need supplies, such as folders, labels, and pens.
- Jake announced the verdict: "The defendant is guilty."
- Kyle excels in research, writing, and interviewing.

Challenge: Parentheses, Hyphens, and Other Marks

Correct the following:

- All co-partners must agree on the admission of a new partner.
- The defendant, Thomas Simmons ("Simmons"), denied the allegations of fraud. (*See* Answer ¶ 5.)
  - Some practitioners would omit the quotation marks around "Simmons."
  - The parenthetical is in *Bluebook* form.
  - *ALWD* would present the parenthetical as follows: *See* Def.'s Ans. ¶ 5 (Exact Date.) Note that *ALWD* Rule 29 permits the reference to the court document to appear in parentheses or brackets, in boldface type, or both bold and parentheses.
- She observed that anti-American sentiment was on the rise.
- William H. Rehnquist served as Chief Justice from 1986–2005.
- He is a well-respected judge who produces opinions that are well reasoned.

Chapter 3

Challenge: Spelling

Select the correct word.

- He has asked for the <u>advice</u>/advise of his attorney.
- Pam will present the <u>argument</u>/arguement to the judge.
- The court calender/<u>calendar</u> is crowded.
- Only <u>relevant</u>/relevent evidence may be admitted.
- She has claimed the attorney-client privelege/<u>privilege</u>.
- He has continued to harrass/<u>harass</u> the employee.
- The evidence is <u>admissible</u>/admissable.

- The <u>maintenance</u>/maintainance of the building is his duty.
- Her <u>counsel</u>/council is representing her in court.

Challenge: Capitalization and Abbreviations

Correct the following:

To get to the <u>offices</u> of Mr. Ian Nelson (or *Ian Nelson, Esq.*), go <u>through</u> <u>South</u> Martin <u>Street</u> and then head <u>northeast</u> on <u>Massachusetts</u> Avenue. <u>One hun-dred</u> yards <u>north</u> of this is the <u>Federal</u> Communications Commission (or *FCC*), which is a <u>department</u> <u>within</u> the <u>federal</u> <u>government</u>. Last <u>spring</u>, the <u>FCC</u> held ten hearings relating to <u>congressional</u> budget shortfalls <u>and</u> issued full decisions in <u>nine</u> of those matters. Most of these <u>hearings</u> relate to <u>U.S.</u> policy as formulated by the <u>President</u>.

Section Two: Features of Effective Legal Writing and Organization

Chapter 4

Challenge: Word Choice

Select the correct word or rewrite to improve meaning.

- Judges and their wives will attend the conference.

  Judges and their spouses will attend the conference.

- He will file a claim for workmen's compensation.

  He will file a claim for workers' compensation.

- An engineer should promptly prepare his reports.

  Engineers should promptly prepare their reports.

  An engineer should promptly prepare his or her reports.

  An engineer should promptly prepare reports.

- We will need to engage with Susan later this week.

  We will need to meet with Susan later this week.

- After the meeting, Ben was asked to own the action.

  After the meeting, Ben was asked to take responsibility for _____.

- Jeff doesn't have enough bandwidth to handle the case.

  Jeff doesn't have enough time to handle the case.

- Let's diary that for next week when we can surface the issue to the board.

  Let's place this on the calendar for next week when we can raise the issue with the board.

- Francie prepared both <u>memoranda</u>/memorandums.
- The court believed/<u>held</u> that the will was invalid.
- The company plans to monetize its assets.

  The company plans to use its assets to raise money.

- The condominium complex is richly amenetized.

  The condominium complex has many amenities.

Challenge: Elegant Variation

Rewrite the following statements.

- The noncompetition agreement was signed on June 10. The executed covenant prohibiting competition was then filed with the court.

  The noncompetition agreement was signed on June 10. The signed agreement was then filed with the court.

- The company has alleged breach of a software license agreement. The plaintiff specifically claimed that the agreement permitting use of the software was invalid.

  The company [or "the plaintiff"] has alleged breach of a software license agreement. The company [or "the plaintiff"] specifically claimed that the software license agreement [or "the agreement"] was invalid.

- The corporation's board of directors called an annual meeting in May. The company managers submitted financial reports at this convention.

  The corporation's board of directors held an annual meeting in May. The directors submitted financial reports at this meeting.

- The applicant must submit an application for employment by July 30. A candidate's failure to submit a résumé is grounds for disqualification.

  The applicant must submit an application for employment by July 30. An applicant's failure to submit an application is grounds for disqualification.

- The purchaser must deposit the purchase price with the seller within thirty days. If the buyer fails to deposit the purchase price within one month the vendor may terminate the contract.

  The purchaser must deposit the purchase price with the seller within thirty days. If the purchaser fails to deposit the purchase price within thirty days, the seller may terminate the contract.

Challenge: Negative Expressions

Rewrite the following negative expressions.

- We are not unfamiliar with the concept of copyright infringement.

  We are familiar with the concept of copyright infringement.

- We are reluctant to say that we do not disagree with you.

  We are reluctant to say that we agree with you.

- Vote for no more than one candidate for the board of directors.

  Vote for one candidate only for the board of directors.

- We do not deny that scandalous trademarks are ineligible for federal registration.

  We acknowledge that scandalous trademarks cannot be federally registered.

- You should not forget to deny the allegations of the complaint.

  Remember to deny the allegations of the complaint.

Challenge: Word Order and Active Voice

Rewrite the following:

- He demanded a jury trial on Monday.

  On Monday, he demanded a jury trial.

  He demanded that a jury trial be held on Monday.

- Preparing the request for the production of documents was a difficult task for Beth.

  It was difficult for Beth to prepare the request for the production of documents.

- It was foggy on the date the accident occurred.

  The accident occurred on a foggy day.

- An extension of time was requested.

  The plaintiff [or _____] requested an extension of time.

- Abandonment of trademarks has been thoroughly discussed by the Second Circuit Court of Appeals.

The Second Circuit Court of Appeals has thoroughly discussed trademark abandonment.

■ An invitation to the defendant to enter into settlement negotiations was issued by the plaintiff.

The plaintiff invited the defendant to enter into settlement discussions.

The plaintiff invited the defendant to discuss settlement.

■ The budget and the compensation report were approved by the board of directors.

The board of directors approved the budget and the compensation report.

Challenge: Parallel Structure

Correct the following:

■ Our litigation plan is to take the expert's deposition, request documents, and interviewing of witnesses.

Our litigation plan is to take the expert's deposition, request documents, and interview witnesses.

■ There are other factors considered by the court: the nature of the display; the source of financial support for the display; and courts may consider the duration of the display.

There are other factors considered by the court: the nature of the display; the source of financial support for the display; and the duration of the display.

■ Her duties are to provide records, attend meetings, and to prepare minutes.

Her duties are to provide records, attend meetings, and prepare minutes.

Her duties are to provide records, to attend meetings, and to prepare minutes.

■ This is a matter not for discussion but action.

This is a matter not for discussion but for action.

■ Either Susan must plead guilty or stand for trial.

Susan must either plead guilty or stand for trial.

■ The most important parts of your project are the beginning and the end.

The most important parts of your project are the beginning and the ending.

Challenge: Legalese

Rewrite the following:

- Pursuant to your request of the seventeenth of July, 2008, enclosed herewith please find the proof of service you requested.

  Pursuant to your request of July 17, 2008, enclosed is the proof of service.

  Enclosed is the proof of service you requested on July 17, 2008.

- In the instant case, plaintiff has alleged and averred that the contractual agreement is void ab initio.

  In this case the plaintiff has alleged that the contract was void from the beginning.

  The plaintiff has claimed that the contract was void from the beginning.

- Concerning the matter of your will, we respectfully request that you forthwith execute said will and deliver it to this office at your earliest convenience.

  Please sign your will and return it to us.

- We are in accord with your previous report albeit we have opined that it includes some inaccurate statements and averments.

  We agree with your report although we believe that it includes some inaccuracies.

- Classroom managers have objected to decreases in budgetary funding as well as negative advancement within their ranks.

  Teachers have objected to budget decreases as well as demotions.

- Many impoverished people experience food insecurity.

  Many poor people are hungry.

- I am returning herewith the settlement agreement, the same having been fully and duly executed by the plaintiff.

  The plaintiff has signed the settlement agreement, which is enclosed.

  I am enclosing the settlement agreement signed by the plaintiff.

Challenge: Keeping Subjects and Verbs Close

Rewrite the following:

- The lease, which included a variety of provisions for early termination as well as covenants relating to habitability, was signed on July 10, 2008.

  The lease included a variety of provisions for early termination as well as covenants relating to habitability. It was signed on July 10, 2008.

■ Mrs. Jacobs, the defendant whose deposition was taken earlier this month and whose testimony was inconsistent with that of her husband, has filed a counterclaim.

Mrs. Jacobs has filed a counterclaim. She is the defendant whose deposition was taken earlier this month and whose testimony was inconsistent with that of her husband.

Challenge: Transition Words

Rewrite the following to make them smoother:

■ The corporation held its annual meeting. First, proxies were tabulated. Then votes were cast. Three directors were elected. They were elected by a plurality of votes. The shareholders then voted to adjourn the meeting. The next meeting will be held in May.

The corporation held its annual meeting. Following the tabulation of proxies, votes were cast, and three directors were elected by a plurality of votes. The shareholders then voted to adjourn the meeting until the next meeting in May.

■ Copyright protects many types of works. Some of these works are literary, musical, and artistic works. For example, poems, songs, and paintings are protected. No copyright notice is needed for protection of a work. The work is protected from the time of its creation. Infringement of a copyrighted work may give rise to damages. An action for infringement may be brought in federal court.

Copyright protects many types of works, including literary, musical, and artistic works, such as poems, songs, and paintings. No copyright notice is needed for protection of a work because the work is protected from the time of its creation. If a work is infringed, an action may be brought in federal court and damages may be awarded.

Challenge: Shifts in Verb Tense

Rewrite the following:

■ In that case, the court upheld the lower court's determination that the scene endorsed a message that is secular.

In that case, the court upheld the lower court's determination that the scene endorsed a message that <u>was</u> secular.

■ Vice-President Diaz mentioned the board's previous decision to award bonuses to employees and comments that any further compensation is unwarranted.

*Vice-President Diaz mentioned the board's previous decision to award bonuses to employees and **commented** that any further compensation **was** [or **would be**] unwarranted.*

- The defendant assaults the victim, who died as a result of the attack.

  *The defendant **assaulted** the victim, who died as a result of the attack.*

- Identifying the documents was straightforward. Most are authored by the employee, leaving only a few that were authored by the employer.

  *Identifying the documents was straightforward. Most **were authored** by the employee, leaving only a few that were authored by the employer.*

Challenge: Conciseness

Select a more concise word or phrase for the following:

- In the above-referenced matter   *In this case*
- Completely unanimous   *Unanimous*
- We are in receipt of   *We have received*
- Situated in the vicinity of   *Near*
- Aware of the fact that   *Know*
- Institute   *Begin*
- In excess of   *More than*
- Advance planning   *Planning*
- Future plans   *Plans*
- Postpone until later   *Postpone*
- For the duration of   *During*
- In the event that   *If*

Rewrite the following:

Minutes of Board of Directors' Meeting

The Board of Directors of ABC Inc. (the "Corporation") held a meeting on July 1, 2008, at twelve noon. The purpose of holding the meeting was to discuss and consider extending the employment contracts and agreements of Thomas Simmons ("Simmons") and Kara Andrews ("Andrews").

The Board is cognizant of the fact that Simmons and Andrews have fulfilled and effectuated all of the terms and conditions of their agreements. In addition to the foregoing, the employees have demonstrated commitment and devotion to the Corporation and its goals, purposes, and vision.

After due discussion and consideration, it was the consensus of opinion of the Board that the employment agreements for Simmons and Andrews should be extended for a duration of two years. Vice-President Beth Harris shall commence preparation of the respective extensions of the employ-ment contracts and give and submit them to the Board upon their final completion for approval by the Board of Directors.

The President of the Corporation then announced that he would summarize briefly the Corporation's financial performance during the course of the past calendar quarter. The President announced that there is no doubt but that the Corporation's performance has met and exceeded all financial and monetary expectations. This success is attributable to the commencement of the Corporation's newly implemented computer accounting systems. Subsequent to the implementation of this system, the Corporation experi-enced demonstrable and significant cost savings. Subsequent to the pres-entation of this report, the President announced an adjournment of the meeting.

Minutes of Board of Directors' Meeting (Revised)

The Board of Directors (the "Board") of ABC Inc. (the "Corporation") met at noon on July 1, 2008, to discuss extending the employment contracts of Thomas Simmons ("Simmons") and Kara Andrews ("Andrews").

The Board is aware that Simmons and Andrews have performed all of the terms of their employment agreements and are committed to the Corporation and its goals.

After discussion, it was the Board's consensus that the employment agree-ments for Simmons and Andrews should be extended for two years. Vice-President Beth Harris will prepare the employment agreement extensions and submit them for the Board's approval.

The President of the Corporation then summarized the Corporation's finan-cial performance during the prior quarter. The President stated that due to implementing a new computer accounting system, the Corporation exceeded all financial expectations and achieved significant cost savings. The President then adjourned the meeting.

Chapter 5

Challenge: Position and Voice

Rewrite the following for the defendant:

- The defendant failed to approve the figures as he was contractually required to do.

  The figures were not approved.

- The defendant attacked the plaintiff.

  The plaintiff was attacked.

- Although corporate profits permit, the defendant corporation has not declared a dividend in two years.

  A dividend has not been paid in two years (or for some period of time).

- In violation of the employment agreement, the defendant employer has failed to pay sales commissions to the plaintiff.

  The plaintiffs have not yet received sales commissions.

- The defendant doctor negligently operated on the plaintiff.

  The plaintiff underwent an operation.

Section Four: Postwriting Steps and Document Design

Chapter 11

Challenge: Proofreading

Correct the errors:

<u>To</u> discourage corporations **from** simply holding onto profits and not distributing them, the Internal Revenue **S**ervice has devised certain **penalties** that **give** corporations a strong incentive to distribute profits to shareholders rather than **hoarding** them. Corporations that **accumulate** earnings beyond the reasonable needs of the **business** to avoid having shareholders pay income **taxes** on earnings that should have been distributed to the **shareholders** are subject to an accumulated income tax **[omit second "tax"]** in the amount of fifteen percent **(15%)** of the accumulated taxable amount in excess of Two Hundred and Fifty Thousand Dollars **($250,000),** **although** certain credits **are** allowed.

Appendix A

Challenge: Citation Form

Using either *The Bluebook* (using the format required for practitioners) or *ALWD*, correct the following citations. You need not include punctuation after the citations. [Note that material shown in italics may be <u>underscored</u>, according to preference.]

- Phillips Company versus Henderson, 102 Federal Supplement, Second Series, page 33, decided by the Southern District of New York in 2006.

  Phillips Co. v. Henderson, 102 F. Supp. 2d 33 (S.D.N.Y. 2006)

- United States of America versus Timothy Taylor, 155 Federal Reporter, Third Series, page 230, decided in 2004 by the Eighth Circuit.

  United States v. Taylor, 155 F.3d 230 (8th Cir. 2004)
  (*ALWD* would present the case name as *U.S. v. Taylor*)

- Harold Anthony vs. Bailey Brothers, a 2005 case decided by the Supreme Court of Minnesota in volume 859 of the relevant reporter, second series, at page 560, with a quotation appearing on pages 565 through 568.

  Anthony v. Bailey Bros., 859 N.W.2d 560, 565-68 (Minn. 2005)
  (*ALWD* would allow the pincites to be presented as either "565-568" or as "565-68.")

- Masterson versus Ellen Caldwell, a United States Supreme Court case decided in 2005, at volume 540, page 118.

  Masterson v. Caldwell, 540 U.S. 118 (2005)
  (*ALWD* would permit parallel citations to S. Ct. and to L. Ed.)

- Section 2244 of Title 18 of the United States Code.

  18 U.S.C. § 2244 (2000)

- California Probate Code Section 1140.

  Bluebook: Cal. Prob. Code § 1140 (Publisher year)
  ALWD: Cal. Prob. Code Ann. § 1140 (Publisher year)

- Section 114 of volume 6 of a book written by Cynthia Dawson, entitled "Calculating Spousal Support," published in its third edition in 2006.

  Bluebook: 6 Cynthia Dawson, *Calculating Spousal Support* § 114 (3d ed. 2006).

  ALWD: Cynthia Dawson, *Calculating Spousal Support* vol. 6, § 114 (3d ed., Publisher 2006)

- A law review article authored by Gregory T. Anderson, entitled "Complying with Sarbanes–Oxley Requirements," and published in 2007 in volume 32 of the South Carolina Law Review, beginning on page 340.

  Gregory T. Anderson, *Complying with Sarbanes–Oxley Requirements*, 32 S.C. L. Rev. 340 (2007)

Appendix B

Challenge

Make corrections to the following passage.

Our client **wishes** to file **a** complaint in federal court. A case may be brought in **[the]** federal court **only** if jurisdiction is based either on a federal question or diversity of the parties. A federal question **exists** if the case involves a federal statute or **a** constitutional provision. For diversity to exist, **both** the plaintiff and the defendant must be from different states and the case **must allege** more than $75,000 in **damages**. Our client **has alleged** that she **has been** subjected to a hostile work environment at **her** job and **therefore** has been sexually harassed. Sexual harassment **is** forbidden **by** federal law. **Therefore,** our client **may** institute a lawsuit in federal **court**.

appendix E

Glossary of Terms

Abbreviation: A shortened form of a word or a symbol used in place of a word, as in the abbreviation *Mr.* for the word *Mister*.

Acronym: An abbreviation that spells out a pronounceable word, such as *AIDS* or *FICA*.

Active voice: A style of writing in which the subject of the sentence performs the action, as in *The corporation held its meeting*.

ALWD: A reference to ALWD & Darby Dickerson, *ALWD Citation Manual* (3d ed., Aspen Publishers 2006), a guide to citation form.

Antecedent: The noun to which a pronoun refers.

Appeal brief: Written document seeking reversal, affirmance, or some modification of a lower court's action.

Appositive: A word or phrase that explains the noun it follows, as in *James, the first witness, was tall*.

Auxiliary verbs: See *Helping verbs*.

Block quotation: A quotation of fifty words or more that is justified and indented from the regular text and set without quotation marks.

Bluebook: A reference to *The Bluebook: A Uniform System of Citation* (Columbia Law Review Ass'n et al. eds., 18th ed. 2005), a guide to legal citation form.

Boilerplate: Standard language in a document, such as a contract.

Brainstorming: A method of outlining in which the writer lists all words related to a project.

Brief: A document submitted to a court that includes legal argument; a summary of a case, namely, a *case brief*.

Certificate of compliance: A document that verifies compliance with court rules.

Certificate of service: A document attached to a court pleading that verifies the pleading has been served on all parties.

Clause: A group of related words containing a subject and a verb.

Clustering: A visual method of outlining that shows relationships among ideas.

Collection letter: A type of letter seeking to collect money for a client from a debtor.

Collective noun: A noun that stands for a group of people or things, such as *jury* or *committee*.

Comma splice: A run-on sentence caused by a comma that joins two main clauses.

Compound predicate: A sentence with one subject and two verbs joined by *or* or *and*, as in *The defendant went home and ate dinner*.

Compound sentence: A sentence with two independent clauses, usually joined by a conjunction such as *but* or *and*, as in *The defendant went home, and the jurors were released for the day*.

Compound subject: A subject made up of more than one word, as in *The jurors and the bailiffs were relaxing in the hallway*.

Compound word: A word comprising two ideas or words, such as *well-intentioned*.

Conjunction: A word that joins together words or groups of words.

Connotation: The suggested meaning of a word.

Coordinating conjunction: The words *and, but, for, nor, or, so,* and *yet* that join together words or groups of words.

CRAC: An acronym for Conclusion, Rule, Application, and Conclusion; a method of analyzing legal authorities.

Dangling modifier: A modifying phrase that does not include a subject and does not modify any word or group of words in a sentence, as in *Driving down the road, the brakes failed*.

Definite article: The word *the*, which identifies a definite, known noun.

Defined term: A label associated with a name or a term in a legal document, which must be used consistently.

Demand letter: A type of letter demanding some form of action, such as the payment of money.

Dependent clause: A clause that cannot stand on its own (also called *subordinate clause*).

Elegant variation: The practice of substituting one term for another in a document to avoid repetition of a term.

Ellipsis: Three periods separated by spaces and set off by a space before the first and after the last period (. . .), used to show omissions from quotations.

ESL: English as a Second Language; a reference to the use of English by nonnative speakers of the English language.

Font: Typeface, such as Times New Roman.

Freewriting: A method of outlining in which the writer writes without stopping for a short period of time.

Full justification: See *Justification.*

Fused sentence: A run-on sentence caused by a lack of punctuation between two main clauses.

Gerund: A verb form that ends in -*ing* and that functions as a noun, as in *pleading* or *drafting.*

Helping verbs: Verbs that accompany main verbs, such as *can, must,* and *will,* as in *You must file the appeal by May 18.*

Idiom: An expression the meaning of which cannot be determined by its actual wording, such as *come up with a remedy.*

Indefinite antecedent: An antecedent that does not refer to any specific person or thing, such as the use of the words *anyone* or *everybody.*

Indefinite article: The articles *a* and *an,* which introduce a noun that has not been introduced previously.

Independent clause: A clause with a subject and a verb that expresses a complete idea and can stand on its own (also called a *main clause*).

Indirect question: A question that indicates what someone asked but not in the exact form of a question, as in *Mother asked me whether I was going* (also called an *indirect quotation*).

Infinitive: The word *to* plus a verb, as in *to argue.*

Inverted sentence: A sentence in which the verb precedes the subject, as in *There is an attorney present in the room.*

IRAC: An acronym for Issue, Rule, Analysis/Application, and Conclusion; a method of analyzing legal authorities.

Jargon: The specialized language of a profession.

Justification: The appearance of margins on a page; full justification refers to a margin in which all words begin and end at the same location in each line.

Legalese: A style of jargon used by legal professionals that uses archaic, stuffy, and unfamiliar terms rather than plain English.

Legend: A notation or warning on a legal document, such as a notation that a letter is subject to the attorney-client privilege.

Linking verb: A verb that links its subject to the material or description following in the sentence; linking verbs include *be, seem, appear*, and other words that refer to a state of being.

Litotes: An expression that makes an assertion by denying its opposite, as in using *not unprepared* to mean *prepared*.

Main clause: See *Independent clause*.

Memorandum: A research document that analyzes a legal problem in an objective manner; usually for interoffice use only.

Memorandum of law: A written argument submitted to a court in support of a certain position; may be called a *brief*.

Misplaced modifier: A modifier that is located in the wrong place in a sentence.

Modifier: A word that limits, qualifies, or describes another word or group of words.

Monospace: Typeface in which every letter takes the same amount of horizontal space.

Motion: A request that a court enter an order in favor of a party.

Nominalization: Conversion of a verb into a noun, which weakens the verb (as in *decide—issued a decision*).

Nonrestrictive clause: A clause that adds information but is not essential to the meaning of a sentence and is set off with commas, as in *The corporation, which had merged, filed its papers with the SEC.*

Notice pleading: The current pleading philosophy that a pleading must be sufficiently clear as to notify another party of the nature of one's claims or defenses.

Open punctuation: A style of punctuation that uses fewer punctuation marks than more traditional approaches to punctuation.

Opinion letter: A type of letter providing a legal opinion; usually provided to clients.

Parallel structure: Correct writing style of using the same pattern of words or phrases in sentences or lists, such as starting all items in a list with a word ending in *-ing*.

Paraphrasing: Using one's own words to summarize or present another's thoughts or writings. Paraphrasing in legal writing must be attributed to the original author.

Phrase: A group of words that lacks a subject, a verb, or both, and cannot stand on its own.

Pinpoint citation: A reference to the specific page on which material, often a quotation, appears; usually required in citation form.

Plagiarism: Taking another's ideas, writings, or expressions and representing them as one's own.

Plain English: A writing movement that calls for straightforward and clear expression rather than legalese.

Pleading: A document, such as a complaint or answer, filed by a party in a pending court action.

Prayer: The ending of a pleading, often a complaint, that requests relief.

Pronoun: A word that takes the place of a noun, such as *he, she,* or *it.*

Proper noun: The name of a particular person, place, or thing, such as *Justice Kennedy, the Washington Monument,* or *Lake Huron.*

Proportional spacing: Use of a typeface in which letters take up different amounts of horizontal space; Times New Roman is a proportionally spaced typeface.

Protection clause: Clause in a letter used when information is incomplete to protect the writer; also called a *savings clause.*

Ragged edge: Reference to a margin, usually the right margin, in which words end at different locations in different lines, producing a ragged-looking edge to the page.

Recitals: Clauses in agreements that identify the nature and purpose of the document.

Redlining: The technique of using a computer's "track changes" feature to show changes in a document, usually one that is prepared collaboratively; changes appear in red on the computer's screen.

Reflexive pronoun: The *-self* pronouns, such as *myself* and *herself,* that are used to refer back to another noun, as in *Mary asked herself that very question.*

Restrictive clause: A clause or phrase that restricts or limits the word it modifies by giving essential information, as in *The case that the defendant cited is on point;* it is not set off by commas.

Reverse outlining: A method of outlining in which the outline is prepared after a document is drafted and then used to analyze the project's structure.

Sans serif: A typeface that does not use decorative strokes at the edge of letters.

Sentence fragment: An incomplete sentence; a sentence lacking a subject and a verb.

Serial comma: The last comma in a series of three or more items, as in *Our flag is red, white, and blue;* required in legal writing.

Serif: A typeface in which small decorative strokes are added to the edges of letters.

Slash: A diagonal line used in punctuation that means *or*; also called a *solidus* or *virgule*.

Solidus: See *slash*.

Split infinitive: An infinitive that is divided by one or more words between the word *to* and the verb, as in *to quickly run*; avoid when possible.

Squinting modifier: A modifier that can refer to the word before it or after it.

Subordinate clause: See *Dependent clause*.

Subordinating conjunction: Words such as *after, although, because, before, if,* and *when* that are used to join dependent clauses to main clauses, as in *Although she testified, she was not an effective witness*.

Tabulation: The listing of items.

Tense: The form of a verb that shows the time of action. For example, *I run* is in the present tense, and *I ran* is in the past tense.

Thesis statement: An assertive introductory statement in a writing project that provides a preview of the analysis to follow; sometimes called an *umbrella statement*.

Topic sentence: The sentence in a paragraph (usually the first sentence) that announces the theme or subject for the information to be presented in the paragraph.

Transactional document: A document, often a contract, that specifies parties' rights, duties, and obligations.

Transitional expressions: Words or phrases that connect parts of sentences, such as *however, for example,* and *therefore,* or sentences that connect paragraphs and sections.

Virgule: See *slash*.

Handle them carefully, for words
have more power than atom bombs.
Pearl Strachan Hurd

appendix F

Glossary of Usage

StyleLinks

http://grammar.about.com/od/words/a/UsageGlossary.htm
About.com provides an excellent glossary of usage with commonly confused words.

http://grammar.ccc.commnet.edu/grammar/faq.htm
Capital Community College provides an excellent list of commonly confused words.

www.bartleby.com
This site offers direct linking to numerous writing resources, including reference materials such as dictionaries and thesauri, which will help in selecting the correct word.

Introduction

Because words change meaning over time and because many words and phrases sound alike, writers can easily become confused when selecting words. This Glossary of Usage identifies troublesome words and phrases that are commonly confused in legal writing.

A, an: The sound of a word, not its spelling, dictates whether the article **a** or **an** will be used before it. Use **a** before all consonant sounds, including a sounded *h*, a long *u*, and the sound of *w*, as in *one*. Thus, say *a brief, a historic event, a one-day event, a union*. Use **an** before any vowel sound (except a long *u*) and words beginning with a silent *h*, as in *an appellant, an hour, an heir, an IRS ruling*.

Accept, except: **Accept** means *to receive something* or *agree to it*. **Except** usually means *other than*. *I will accept all of the contractual revisions except the most recent one*.

Adverse, averse: **Adverse** means hostile or difficult, as in *The adverse party* or *adverse circumstances*. **Averse** means having a strong feeling against or reluctant, as in *We are averse to meeting at the employer's office*.

Advice, advise: **Advice** is a noun meaning *help* and **advise** is a verb meaning *to give help*. *I advise all my clients to take my advice on trial strategy*.

Affect, effect: **Affect** usually means *to influence* and is a verb and **effect**, usually used as a noun, means *result*. *I was affected by John's testimony, which had the effect of changing my opinion*. **Effect** can also mean *to cause*. Tip: If these words cause confusion, do not use either of them. Use their synonyms (*to influence* for **affect** and *to bring about, result*, or *produce* for **effect**).

Also: Many writers object to sentences starting with **also**. Use *additionally, moreover*, and similar words.

Alternate, alternative: An **alternate** is a *substitute*, as in *The court selected an alternate juror* (although it can also mean *one after another*, as in *black alternates with white in this diamond pattern*). Conventional authorities state that **alternative** should be used only when referring to two choices (as in *You have the alternative of making the opening statement or the closing statement*). The more modern approach is that **alternative** means one of several choices or options.

Although: See *While*.

Ambiguous, ambivalent: **Ambiguous** means *having more than one meaning*, as in *the lease is ambiguous as to when rent is due*. **Ambivalent** means *having conflicting feelings*, as in *I was ambivalent toward the third juror*.

Among, between: **Among** is used when referring to three or more items or people. *The damages were divided among all six plaintiffs*. See *Between*.

Amongst: Avoid this British usage for **among**.

Amount, number: Use **amount** for quantities in bulk that cannot be counted. Use **number** for individual items. *The amount of suffering experienced by the plaintiffs cannot be overestimated. We have a large number of pending class actions.*

Ampersand (&) symbol: Do not use the symbol for *and* (called an *ampersand*, a corruption of the phrase *and per se and*) rather than the word *and* in legal writing unless a company or firm name shows this presentation, as in *The law firm of Reed & Smith is located downtown.*

And: **And** is a coordinating conjunction and is generally used to connect words or groups of words. Most legal writers avoid starting sentences with coordinating conjunctions (*and, but, for, nor, or, so, yet*), although such usage is commonly seen in informal writing.

And/or: The use of the expression **and/or** is confusing. It means *one or the other or both*. Write *The employer or the employee, or both, may terminate the contract* rather than *The employer and/or employee may terminate the contract.*

Ante-, anti-: **Ante-** means *before*, as in *antebellum*. **Anti-** means *against*, as in *anti-American*.

Appraise, apprise: **Appraise** means *to estimate value* and **apprise** means *to inform. I will apprise you when I have received the property appraisal.* Avoid possible confusion by using *inform* rather than **apprise**.

Arbitration, mediation: Although both **arbitration** and **mediation** are methods of alternative dispute resolution, in **arbitration**, a binding decision is usually rendered by an impartial third party. In **mediation**, a neutral third party attempts to help the disputing parties resolve their differences and no decision is rendered. *If mediation does not produce a satisfactory resolution, the parties will proceed to binding arbitration.*

As: Do not use **as** in place of **because**. Thus, write *She could not sue because the statute of limitations expired* rather than *She could not sue as the statute of limitations expired.*

As, because, since: Do not use **as** in place of **because** or **since**. *She was expelled from the partnership because she embezzled funds.* Do not write *She was expelled from the partnership since she embezzled funds.*

As follows: Use **as follows** (not *as follow*) to introduce a list. *The directors attending the meeting were as follows: Adams, Baker, and Carey.*

As, like: Use **as** for most comparisons, as in *She looks as if she is angry* rather than *She looks like she is angry.* The word **like** is a preposition. Write, *She argues like an experienced advocate.*

As long as: Use *so long as* not **as long as**.

Assure: See *Ensure, insure, assure.*

As to whether: Substitute the word *whether* in place of this awkward phrase. *The issue is whether the contract was induced by fraud.*

As yet: Substitute the word *yet* in place of this phrase. *The documents have not arrived yet.*

Bad, badly: Write or say *I feel bad the settlement was rejected.* The only way a person feels badly is if his or her hands are damaged. Just as you wouldn't write *I feel sadly*, don't write *I feel badly*.

Being that: Do not use **being that** as a substitute for **because**. *Because I was in Ohio, I could not serve on the jury* (not *Being that I was in Ohio, I could not serve on the jury*).

Beside, besides: **Beside** means *at the side of,* as in *Come sit beside me.* **Besides** means *in addition to,* as in *Besides the directors, the officers also attended the meeting.*

Between: Used when referring to two items or people. *The treaty was entered into between Canada and France. The profits will be divided among the four partners.*

Between you and me: The phrase **between you and me** is correct. Do not write *Between you and I.*

Bi-, semi-: **Bi-** means *two;* **semi-** means *half* or *somewhat.* Thus, a *bimonthly meeting* occurs every two weeks (or, according to some dictionaries, every two months) and a *semi-annual checkup* occurs every half-year or six months. Because of the confusion in using these prefixes, avoid them. Write *The meeting will be held every other month.*

But: The word **but** is redundant with *doubt* and *help.* Thus, write *I have no doubt that he is guilty* (not *I have no doubt but that he is guilty*). Avoid starting sentences with **but** (see *And*).

By contrast, in contrast: When comparing and contrasting cases, use the expression **in contrast** rather than **by contrast**.

Can, may: Use **can** to show *ability* and **may** to show *permission* or *possible action.* *He can introduce the evidence* (meaning he is able to introduce the evidence). *The witness may step down* (meaning that the witness has permission to step down).

Cannot: Spell **cannot** as one word. Do not spell as *can not.*

Capital, capitol: **Capital** means *money* or *the city that is the seat of a government.* **Capitol** (with an *o*) is *the building in which a governmental body meets. The capital of our nation is Washington, D.C. Tours of the capitol building are given daily.*

Case law: Use **case law** rather than *caselaw.*

Cite, citation, sight, site: Use **citation** rather than the less formal **cite** to refer to legal authorities, as in *His brief included four citations to case law.* **Sight** refers to *ability to see* or *the thing seen,* as in *The moon was a beautiful sight.* **Site** refers to a place, as in *the site of the accident.*

Compare to, compare with: **Compare to** is used to show similarities and is used less frequently than **compare with**, which is used to show similarities and differences between like kinds. *The reasoning in* Smith *can be compared to that in* Jones. *Compared with his opening statement, his closing argument lacked force.*

Compose, comprise: **Compose** means *to make up*, as in *The contract is composed of four sections.* **Comprise** means *to include* or *to consist of*, as in *The corporation comprises four separate divisions.* It is correct to say *consists of* or *composed of*, but it is not correct to say *comprised of.*

Continual, continuous: **Continual** means *frequently repeated*. **Continuous** means *without interruption*. *Counsel was continually interrupted by objections. The music from the party next door was continuous.* The distinction between these two words is subtle, and you may wish to use *periodically, routinely,* or *intermittently* in place of **continually**.

Council, counsel: A **council** is a *governing body*. *The city council enacted the ordinance.* **Counsel** means *advice* or *lawyer*. *My counsel gave me good counsel when she suggested that I should draft a new will.*

Criteria, criterion: **Criteria** is the plural of **criterion**. *There are three criteria for proving a breach of contract case.*

Data, datum: **Data** is the plural of **datum**. The singular form **datum** is seldom used and **data** is often used as a singular and a plural word. *The data supports your theory.*

Discreet, discrete: **Discreet** means *careful* and *cautious*, as in *The witness was discreet about his whereabouts on the day of the murder.* **Discrete** means *distinct from others* and *separate*, as in *There were four discrete parts to the pleading.*

Disinterested, uninterested: **Disinterested** means neutral, as in *The arbitrator is a disinterested party.* **Uninterested** means bored, as in *The jurors seemed uninterested in the testimony.*

Due to: Use **due to** only when you mean *caused by*. **Due to** appears only after a linking verb (such as *is, was,* or *seemed*). Thus, it should not be used to begin a sentence. Don't use **due to** as a substitute for *because of*. Thus, the following examples are correct: *The plaintiff's injuries were due to Mr. Lee's negligence. Because of the holiday, the trial was postponed.*

Effect: See *Affect*.

E.g.,: This abbreviation for *exempli gratia* (meaning *for the sake of an example*) is not italicized in legal writing when it is used to introduce an example; however, it is italicized or underscored when it is used as a signal to introduce a supporting legal citation (see Rule 1.2 of *the Bluebook*; Rule 44.3 of *ALWD*). The abbreviation **e.g.,** should always be followed by a comma according to *Bluebook* rules (and the comma is not underscored or italicized), but is not followed by a comma according to *ALWD*. Consider using the phrase *for example* in legal writing rather than **e.g.**, when introducing an example. *He suffered numerous injuries, for example, cuts, bruises, and broken bones.* Do not confuse **e.g.**, with **i.e.**, an abbreviation that means *that is.*

Eminent, imminent: Eminent means *distinguished*, as in *He is an eminent jurist.* **Imminent** means *about to happen* as in *Her appointment to the bench is imminent.*

Ensure, insure, assure: Ensure means *to make definite* or *guarantee* as in *We must ensure that the rent is paid promptly.* **Insure** means *to protect against loss*, as in *You should insure your jewelry for at least $50,000.* **Assure** means *to make a person sure*, as in *I assure you the trial will not be delayed.*

Et al.: This abbreviation for *and others* should be italicized or underscored when used in legal writing to refer to additional people. *The plaintiff sued Anderson, Baker, Levy et al.* Do not use **et al.** in citations of case names (Rule 10.2.1(a) of *The Bluebook*; Rule 12.2(c) of *ALWD*).

Etc.: Do not use this informal abbreviation for *et cetera* (meaning *and other things*). Use the expression *and so forth*, as in *In contracts class, you will learn about offer, acceptance, consideration, and so forth.*

Explicit, implicit: Explicit refers to *something stated expressly.* **Implicit** refers to *something implied. He left explicit instructions in his will. She gave me implicit consent to draft the agreement.*

Fact: A **fact** is *something that has occurred* or *something that can be verified.* Use the word **fact** only when describing an event or something proved. *It is a fact that the plaintiff has blue eyes. It is not a fact that a defendant is guilty until a court or jury says so.* **Fact** is often used in long-winded phrases such as *Due to the fact that.* Substitute *Because* for such phrases.

Farther, further: Farther refers to *physical distance*, as in *I can throw the ball farther than I thought.* **Further** refers to *time, quality, or additions*, as in *I will discuss this matter further tomorrow.*

Feel: Feel refers to *emotion* or *touching.* Courts do not feel. Courts reason, state, rule, or hold. Avoid the use of the wishy-washy expressions *I feel* or *the court felt* in legal writing.

Fewer, less: Fewer refers to *objects or people that can be counted* as in *The plaintiff took fewer depositions than planned.* **Less** refers to *general amounts and things that cannot be counted*, as in *Ellen has less compassion than Bill does.*

Finding, holding: In the strictest sense, a court makes **findings** on questions of fact and issues **holdings** on questions of law.

First, firstly: Use **first, second, third** rather than the archaic *firstly, secondly, thirdly.*

Forgo, foregoing: Forgo means *to give up*, as in *She was forced to forgo her third cause of action.* **Foregoing** is an adjective meaning *preceding*, as in *As provided in the foregoing paragraph, the goods shall be delivered on June 1, 2008.*

Former, latter: **Former** refers to *a first item or person* and **latter** refers to *a second item or person*. Consider using labels such as *The Seller sold the property to the Buyer* rather than *The former party sold the property to the latter party*.

Good, well: **Good** is used as an adjective, as in *She is a good judge*. Well is used as an adverb or to refer to health, as in *He performed well today* or *I feel well*.

Guilty, liable: Use **guilty** to refer to *criminal wrongdoing*. Liable refers to *responsibility for a civil wrong*. *Defendant Smith is guilty of robbery while Defendant Jones is liable for damages for breach of contract*.

Hanged, hung: **Hanged** is the past tense of *hang* only for an execution. *He was hanged at dawn*. **Hung** is used for all other meanings and usually means *suspended*. *We framed and hung the photos in the gallery*. Informally, you may refer to a *hung jury*.

Have to: Do not use this informal phrase. Use **must**. *We must file the complaint by Monday*.

Holding: See *Finding*.

Hopefully: Use **hopefully** to mean *in a hopeful manner: The victim awaited hopefully for the verdict*. Although **hopefully** is often used to mean *I hope* or *it is hoped that*, most experts object to such usage. Thus, avoid writing *Hopefully, the jury will render its verdict soon*. Write instead, *I hope the jury will render its verdict soon*.

However: Many experts object to using **however** to begin a sentence when it is used to mean *nevertheless*. Better placement is in the middle of a sentence, as in the following two examples: *The jury that was selected, however, was diverse. Donna was anxious about testifying; however, she was an effective witness*.

i.e.,: This abbreviation for *id est* (Latin for *that is*) is used to introduce further explanation, as in *The defendant was a partnership, i.e., an association of two persons*. The abbreviation **i.e.,** is always followed by a comma and appears in Roman type, not in italics or underscoring. Do not confuse **i.e.,** with **e.g.,** which introduces an example.

Illegible, unreadable: **Illegible** means *handwriting that cannot be read or deciphered*, as in *The testator's handwritten will was illegible*. **Unreadable** refers to *content that is unclear*, as in *The judge stated the brief was so poorly written it was unreadable*.

Impact: Many experts recommend using this word only as a verb to mean *a collision*, as in *His car impacted mine*. Avoid using **impact** as a noun in place of *affect*. Thus, write *My actions affected your decision* (not *My actions impacted your decision*).

Implicit: See *Explicit*.

In contrast: See *By contrast*.

Innocent, guilty: A defendant pleads or is found *guilty* or *not guilty*. A defendant does not plead *innocent* and is not found *innocent*; however, a defendant is presumed *innocent* until proven *guilty*.

In regards to: Avoid this nonstandard phrase. Use *regarding* or *in regard to* (or possibly *as regards*, although that phrase is somewhat stuffy). *I am writing you regarding your lease.*

Irregardless: **Irregardless** is a glaring nonstandard form of *regardless*. It may be a combination of *regardless* and *irrespective*. Always use *regardless*, as in *Regardless of her alibi, she was found guilty.*

Is when, is where: Do not use these terms in giving a definition. Thus, write *A guaranty is a promise to perform another's obligation* (not *A guaranty is when a person promises to perform another's obligation*).

Its, it's: **Its** is the possessive form of the word it and means *belonging to it*. The only meaning of the contraction **it's** is *it is* (or possibly *it has*). *The corporation held its meeting last week. It's a Fortune 500 corporation listed on the New York Stock Exchange.* Contractions (such as **it's** for *it is*) are seldom used in legal or formal writing. There is no such word as *its'*.

-ize: Words ending in **-ize** (*monetize, colorize, strategize*) are often "made up" words borrowed from modern business settings and are usually too informal for legal writing. Avoid such words unless they appear in a standard dictionary.

Judicial, judicious: **Judicial** refers to courts, as in *A review showed no abuse of judicial discretion.* **Judicious** means *using good judgment*, as in *A judicious use of graphs makes a document visually appealing.*

Kind of, sort of: Use *somewhat* or *rather* in place of these informal terms, as in *She was somewhat reluctant to testify.*

Lay, lie: **Lay** means *to put* or *place something* and its forms are *lay, laid, laying,* and *lays*. **Lie** means *to recline* and its forms are *lie, lay, lain, lying,* and *lies*.

> **Correct:** *I lay the document in the folder. I laid it there last Monday.*

> **Correct:** *I will lie down and nap when I have a moment. I lay down yesterday for a brief rest.*

Lead, led: **Led** is the past tense for **lead**. Write *I usually lead the list of defense counsel but yesterday Ann led the list.*

Lend, loan: **Lend** is a verb and **loan** is a noun. *I will lend you money because you need a loan.*

Less: See *Fewer*.

Lessor, lessee: Do not spell as *leasor* or *leasee*.

Liable, libel, slander: **Liable** means *responsible for some civil wrong*, as in *She is liable for damages caused by her negligence.* **Libel** is written defamation, as in *His* *newspaper article libeled the plaintiff by calling her a crook.* **Slander** is oral defamation, as in *She slandered me in her speech yesterday.*

Like, as: **Like** is a preposition. Use as follows: *We need another expert like Dr. Harris.* **As** is usually a conjunction and introduces a clause. Use as follows: *She acted as if she didn't know me.*

Literal, literally: The word **literal** (meaning *in fact* or *actually*) is often used incorrectly to show exaggeration. It would be incorrect to write *When the client received the bill, he literally exploded.* Use *almost* or *nearly* in such cases.

Loose, lose: **Loose** means *not tight,* as in *Her clothing was loose.* **Lose** means *to misplace* or *not win,* as in *Did you lose the document?* or *Never tell clients they cannot lose a case.*

Lots, a lot of: Avoid using these informal expressions. Use *many* or *significant,* as in *The defendant had significant resources.*

Manner: Avoid writing *in a ___ manner.* Thus, write *She walks awkwardly* rather than *She walks in an awkward manner.*

May: See *Can.*

Maybe, may be: **Maybe** means *possibly,* as in *Maybe the defendant will not appear at the hearing.* **May be** is a verb. Use as follows: *She may be the court clerk, but I am not sure.*

Media, medium: **Media** is the plural of **medium** and should be used with a plural verb, as in *The media have distorted my client's record.* **Media** and other similar words (such as *agenda, criteria, data*) are often used in common parlance as singular words. See *Data.*

Mediation: See *Arbitration.*

Memoranda, memorandum: The word **memoranda** is plural and refers to *several documents.* **Memorandum** is a *single document.* Use as follows: *He prepared all six memoranda. The first memorandum was the most persuasive.*

Might of: This is the incorrect and nonstandard use of *might have.*

More important, more importantly: **More important** is often used at the beginning of a sentence to mean *what is more important,* as in *More important, the statute of limitations had expired.* **More importantly** means *in a more important manner,* as in *The scheduling of the deposition was treated more importantly than it deserved.* Consider avoiding these expressions as they are often overused to signal a reader, "What I'm about to tell you is important. Pay attention." Use strong writing to convince a reader, not gratuitous instructions.

Must: See *Shall, must, will.*

Myriad: **Myriad** means *many* and should not be followed by *of.* Thus, write *There were myriad contracts to be reviewed* (not *There were a myriad of contracts to be reviewed*).

Not guilty: See *Innocent.*

Number: See *Amount.*

Of, have: It is incorrect to use the preposition **of** in expressions such as *could of* or *might of.* The correct uses are *could have* and *might have,* as in *I could have attended the conference.*

On, upon: Use **on** rather than the stuffier **upon,** as in *On discovering the defect, the tenant sued the landlord.*

Oral, verbal, written: **Oral** means *something spoken,* as in *Her oral testimony at trial confirmed her earlier deposition testimony.* **Verbal** means *a communication in words* and can refer to either *written* or *spoken communication.* Thus, the statement *We had a verbal agreement* is confusing because it could refer either to a written agreement or to a nonwritten agreement. To avoid confusion, use **oral** or **written** and avoid the use of **verbal.**

Overrule, reverse: A court **overrules** earlier decisions in its jurisdiction. *In 1954, the Supreme Court case* Brown v. Board of Education *overruled the 1896 case* Plessy v. Ferguson. A court **reverses** the very case before it on appeal and changes its result, as in *The defendant in* State v. Thomas *was found guilty. He appealed his conviction, and the appellate court agreed and reversed the trial court's decision.*

Passed, past: **Passed** is used as the past tense of the verb *to pass,* as in *The defendant passed the truck in the right-hand lane.* **Past** usually refers to a *former time* or *age,* as in *My past caught up with me.*

People, persons, parties: Use **people** to refer to a group of individuals collectively, as in *The people summoned for jury duty have arrived.* Use **persons** to refer to small numbers of specifically identified individuals, as in *The persons responsible for the negligence have been sued.* Generally, however, the word **people** sounds more natural in most contexts. Use your ear. The word **parties** is used to refer to the individuals or entities involved in litigation, as in *The parties have settled the case.*

Per: Generally, use *a* or *an* rather than the Latin **per,** as in *The firm bills $200 an hour* (not *The firm bills $200 per hour*).

Percent, percentage: Spell **percent** as one word and use only after a specific number, as in *Interest was assessed at five percent.* **Percentage** is used when no fixed number is given, as in *A significant percentage of new businesses fail.*

Plead, pleaded, pled: The correct past participle of the verb **plead** is **pleaded,** as in *The defendant pleaded guilty.* Avoid the less preferred **pled.**

Plus: Do not use the informal word **plus** when you mean *moreover* or *additionally. The defendant was old; moreover, he was sickly.*

Practicable, practical: **Practicable** usually means *feasible,* as in *It is not practicable to learn the meaning of every Latin phrase.* **Practical** means *useful* or *sensible,* as in *It is not practical to structure the business as a partnership.*

Precede, proceed: **Precede** means *to come or go before,* as in *The clerk will precede the judge into the courtroom.* **Proceed** means *to go ahead,* as in *You may proceed with the cross-examination.*

Precedent, precedence: A **precedent** is a previous judicial decision, as in *The court followed its earlier precedent in reaching its decision.* **Precedence** means *priority* or *the act of coming or going before,* as in *Working on the brief takes precedence over all other matters.*

Prescribe, proscribe: **Prescribe** means *to order,* as in *The doctor prescribed complete bed rest.* **Proscribe** means *to forbid* or *to prohibit* as in *Iowa laws proscribe littering.*

Principal, principle: **Principal** means *a supervisor at a school, a dominant item,* or *a sum of money.* **Principle** means a *fundamental rule.* Match the *le* in *principle* with the *le* in *rule.*

> Correct: *The principal rang the opening bell of school.*
> *The principal office of the corporation is in Los Angeles.*
> *You must repay the principal amount of the debt.*

> Correct: *The principles of physics are complex.*

Procedural, substantive: **Procedural** refers to legal procedures, such as the rules for pleading and other similar practical matters. **Substantive** refers to the law itself. For example, a law requiring a complaint for medical malpractice to be filed within one year of the wrongful act is a matter of substantive law. A court rule requiring the pleading to be filed on white, opaque paper is a matter of procedural law.

Protection clause: A clause in a letter or document that protects the writer (often from a claim of legal malpractice); also called a *savings clause.*

Proved, proven: Use **proved** as a past participle of **prove**, as in *The attorney proved his case.* **Proven** is an adjective, as in *The proven facts were clear.*

Quotation, quote: Use **quote** only as a verb, as in *Don't quote me on this.* Use **quotation** as a noun, as in *The decision included several quotations from the U.S. Supreme Court.*

Raise, rise: **Raise** means *to lift or bring up* and requires a direct object, as in *The plaintiff raised a serious objection* or *The foundation will raise the funds for diabetes research.* **Rise** means *get up* or *move upward* and is not used with an object: *They will rise at 6:00 a.m.* or *You must rise to the occasion.*

Reason is because, reason why: Avoid the redundant expressions **reason is because** and **reason why**. Write *The reason the partnership dissolved was that the general partner died* (not *The reason why the partnership dissolved was that the general partner died*).

Rebut, refute: **Rebut** means *speaking or writing against something,* as in *The defendant's opening statement rebuts the plaintiff's opening statement.* **Refute** means *to disprove something,* as in *How will you refute the claim that you breached the contract?*

Recur, reoccur: **Recur** means *to happen repeatedly,* as in *Her recurring dream was to win the lottery.* **Reoccur** refers to *something happening a second time,* as in *If the leaks reoccur, contact the landlord.*

Regardless: Use this word to mean *notwithstanding*, as in *Regardless of his protestations of innocence, he was found guilty.* Never use *irregardless*, which is not a word. See *Irregardless*.

Respectfully, respectively: **Respectfully** means *with respect* and is a commonly used closing in a document, as in *Respectfully submitted, Mary Harris.* **Respectively** means *in a certain order*, as in *The three landlords were Smith, Allen, and Madison, respectively.*

Sanction: This word has two meanings. When used as a noun, **sanction** means *a penalty*, as in *The judge imposed sanctions against the plaintiff for failing to appear in court.* When used as a verb, **sanction** means *approved*, as in *The fundraiser was sanctioned by the governing board.*

Savings clause: See *Protection clause*.

Seem: Avoid this weak word whenever possible. For example, avoid the following: *Your letter did not seem to include the invoice.* Write instead, *Your letter did not include the invoice.*

Shall, must, will: **Shall** is generally used only in legal documents or in statutes and refers to *mandatory action*, as in *The tenant shall pay rent on the first of every month.* **Will** refers to *future action*, as in *Ted will attend the shareholders' meeting next month.* **Must** is becoming more commonly accepted as a replacement for **shall** in legal writing, as in *The seller must convey the property to the buyer.* Because **shall** is somewhat archaic, consider using **must** in place of **shall.**

Sight, site: See *Cite*.

Since, because: Avoid using **since** as a substitute for **because**; otherwise, ambiguity results, as in the sentence *Since the tariffs were lifted, trade has increased.* It is not clear in this sentence whether **since** means *after a period of time* or whether it means *because*. To avoid confusion, use **since** to refer to the *passage of time*, as in *It has been four weeks since we filed the appeal* and use **because** to show *causation*, as in *Because the jury was improperly charged, the judgment was reversed.*

Sometime, some time: **Sometime** means *at some time in the future*, as in *The trial will be scheduled sometime soon.* **Some time** means *a period of time*, as in *It has been some time since the defendant was arraigned.*

Supposed to, used to: Avoid these informal expressions and if you use them, always include a *d* in the verb. Consider using *should* or *accustomed to*, as in *You should have attended the deposition* (rather than *You were supposed to attend the deposition*) and *He has become accustomed to his client's tardiness* (rather than *He is used to his client's tardiness*).

Sure and, sure to: Use **sure to**, not *sure and*, as in *Be sure to argue forcefully*.

Than, then: Overenunciate these words to select the correct one. **Than** is used to refer to *comparisons*, as in *I have been practicing law longer than Sue has.* **Then** refers to *time*, as in *The plaintiff argued and then the defendant responded.*

That, which: Use **that** to introduce essential material, as in *The brief that I filed last week was missing an exhibit.* **That** is not set off by commas. Use **which** to introduce nonessential material, as in *The will, which he signed, was entered into evidence.* A clause beginning with **which** is usually set off by commas.

That, who: Use **that** when referring to *animals and things*, as in *The dog that barked was vicious* or *The corporation that held the meeting is bankrupt.* Use **who** or **that** for *people or for animals with names*, as in *Maria is the woman who called*, or *Daisy is a dog who is clever*, or *Phil is the attorney that was hired today.*

Therefor, therefore: **Therefor** means *for that*, as in *He pledged to donate funds to build the school and the land therefor.* **Therefore** is used *to show causation*, as in *The defendant infringed the plaintiff's trademark. Therefore, damages were awarded to the plaintiff.*

Thus, thusly: Use **thus** instead of the more archaic word **thusly**.

Till, until: Both **till** and **until** are correct, although **until** is preferred in legal writing. Do not use the informal *'til*.

Tortious, tortuous, torturous: **Tortious** refers to *acts that give rise to civil actions*, as in *She sued for tortious interference with contract.* **Tortuous** means *full of twists and turns*, as in *We climbed the tortuous path.* **Torturous** refers to *torture or pain*, as in *I have a torturous toothache.*

Toward, towards: Americans use **toward**. The British use **towards**.

Treble, triple: These words mean the same but **treble** is often used in statutes to refer to *the tripling of damages*, as in *The court awarded treble damages because of the willfulness of the defendant's conduct.*

Try to, try and: Use **try to**, not **try and**, as in *Try to keep your argument brief.*

Ultimate, penultimate: **Ultimate** means *the last* and **penultimate** means *next-to-last.*

Unique: This word means *one of a kind* and should not be modified. Thus, write *The defendant's claim was unique* (not *rather unique, somewhat unique*, or *very unique*).

Unreadable: See *Illegible*.

Usage: **Usage** refers to *a customary practice* or often *a customary way of using words*, as in *The correct usage of "whom" is confusing to most people.*

Use, utilize: Prefer **use** to **utilize** in most instances. **Use** means *to put into action, make use of*, or *to employ*, as in *Use your main argument first.* **Utilize** often suggests *a practical purpose* or *making use of a utensil*, as in *Utilize a black marker to make the exhibits more noticeable.*

v., vs.: In case citations, use a lower case *v* followed by a period, as in *Smith v. Jones*. In other instances, including court pleadings, **vs.** is sometimes used.

Verbal: See *Oral*.

Verbiage: The word **verbiage** generally means *wordiness* and is usually used in a critical manner, as in *The document's verbiage made it impossible to read.*

Via: **Via** means *by way of*, as in *We flew to New York via Boston.* **Via** does not mean *by means of* and thus should not be used as follows: *We flew to New York via plane.*

Void, voidable: A contract or act that is **void** has *no effect*. A contract that is **voidable** *is effective until a party (with cause) declares it void*, as in *The agreement will be voidable at the option of either party after sixty days.*

Where: **Where** refers to a *location* or *place*. It is not a substitute for *when* or *in which.* Use as follows: *Oregon is where the defendant was convicted* (not State v. Jackson *is a case where the defendant was convicted*).

Whether, whether or not: Generally, the phrase *or not* is redundant and can be omitted, as in *The issue is whether the defendant acted recklessly.*

Which: See *That, which.*

While: Traditionally, **while** has meant *during the time that*, as in *While the defendant was in jail, he confessed.* In more modern usage, **while** has come to be an accepted substitute for *although*, as in *While the contract was long, it was readable.* To avoid ambiguity, consider using *although* at the beginning of a sentence to show contrast and using **while** when you mean *concurrently or during the time that.*

Who's, whose: **Who's** is a contraction meaning *who is*, as in *Who's the witness?* **Whose** is the possessive form of *who*, as in *Whose client pleaded guilty?*

Will: See *Shall, must, will.*

Willful, wilful: Prefer the first spelling, which is the American spelling, to the second spelling, which is the British spelling.

appendix G

Sample Case Brief

StyleLinks

www.4lawschool.com/conlaw/conlaw.htm
This site offers a number of sample case briefs posted by law students.

www.lib.jjay.cuny.edu/research/brief.html
This site provides instructions on preparing case briefs.

Introduction

Formats for case briefs vary from person to person. Following is a suggested format for a typical case brief.

Cobaugh v. Klick-Lewis, Inc., 561 A.2d 1248 (Pa. Super. 1989)

Procedural History

Plaintiff Cobaugh sued an automobile dealer to compel delivery of a car offered as a prize. The trial court entered summary judgment for the plaintiff and the defendant appealed. The Pennsylvania Superior Court affirmed.

Statement of Facts

Amos Cobaugh, a golfer playing at a golf tournament, observed a car and a sign at the ninth tee stating that a hole-in-one would allow a golfer to receive a car as a prize. Cobaugh made a hole-in-one and attempted to claim his prize. The car dealership refused to deliver the prize, stating that the car had been offered as a prize for an earlier golf tournament and that it had neglected to remove the car and the posted sign prior to Cobaugh's hole-in-one.

Issue

Does an offer to award a prize in a contest constitute an enforceable contract?

Answer

Yes. An offer to award a prize in a contest will result in an enforceable contract if the offer is properly accepted by appropriate performance prior to revocation of the offer.

Reasoning

When a promoter of a contest makes an offer and another party acts on the offer before it is withdrawn, the promoter must perform his promise. A person reading the sign at the golf course would reasonably understand that he or she could accept the offer and win the car by performing the feat of shooting a hole-in-one. There was thus an offer that was accepted when Cobaugh shot a hole-in-one. The court held that consideration existed in a bargained for exchange in which the car was to be given in return for the feat of making a hole-in-one. Moreover, the defendant benefited from the publicity generated by the contest. This was adequate consideration. Additionally, there was no mutual mistake such as to make the contract voidable. When a mistake is not mutual but is due to the negligence of one party (in this case, the defendant's failure to remove the sign), rescission of the contract will not be granted. Finally, a contest to award a prize to a golfer for a hole-in-one is not illegal gambling because some skill is involved.

index

A

Abbreviations, 65-69
  acronyms, 66
  addresses, 66
  ampersand, use of, 67-68
  blunders and, 214
  capitalization and, 68
  citations, 242
  company names, 65, 66, 69
  dates, 66
  general rules, 65-68
  legal abbreviations, 68
  money, 67
  numbers, 67
  paragraph symbol, use of, 68
  percentages, 67
  period use, 31, 65
  section symbol, use of, 68
  spelling, 65-69
  tips for use, 69
  titles, 65-66
  United States, 66
Accuracy, 75-84
  intentional vagueness, 79
  made-up words and phrases, 80-81
  offensive language, 82-83
  overused words, 80-81
  slang and colloquial expressions, 81-82
  vague words, 78-79
  word choice, 76-77, 84
  word connotation, 79-80
Acronyms, 66
Active voice
  conciseness and, 114
  dangling modifiers, correcting, 12-13
  readability and, 91-92
  word order, 89
Acts, capitalization rules for, 63
Addresses
  abbreviations, 66

comma use in, 33, 38
legal correspondence
  inside, 130-131, 134
  letterhead, 130, 134
Adjectives
  comma use with parallel structure, 34, 38
  English as second language, 250
Adverbs
  English as second language, 251
Advice, giving of, 257-258
Affirmative and positive terms, use of, 88
Agreements. *See* Contracts; Transactional
    documents
ALWD. See Citations
Ambiguous reference and pronouns, 18
Amendment of pleadings, 189
American Jurisprudence Legal Forms 2d, 197
*American Jurisprudence Pleading and Practice
    Forms, Annotated,* 189
Among, word choice of, 77
Amounts, final check of, 225
Ampersand, use of, 67-68
Analysis, legal, 156-160
  English as second language, 258
Ancient proper names, 41
and/or, use of, 51, 76
Antecedents, pronoun agreement with,
    17-18. *See also* Pronouns
Apostrophes, 39-44
  contractions, 39, 43
  numbers and letters, 43
  possessives, 40-42
Appellate briefs, 174-178. *See also* Briefs
  appendix, 177-178
  argument, 177
  certificate of compliance, 177
  certificate of service, 177
  conclusion, 177
  constitutional and statutory provisions,
    176

Appellate briefs (*continued*)
  cover sheet, 175
  elements, 175-178
    trial court brief compared, 178
  headings, 175, 176, 177
  identification of parties, 175
  jurisdictional statements, 176
  question(s) presented, 176
  sample brief, 259-278
  signature, 177
  statement of case, 176-177
  statutory provisions, 176
  summary of argument, 177
  table of authorities, 175-176
  table of contents, 175
  thesis statements, 177
Appositives, 35, 38
Archaic words, 98-99, 102
Argue, word choice of, 76
Arguments
  appellate briefs, 177
  trial court briefs, 173
Articles "a," "an," "the"
  English as second language, 253, 254
"As" or "than," use of, 25
At, symbol for, 68
Attachments
  legal correspondence, 133
  transactional documents, 196
Authorities. *See* Legal Authorities

B
Bad news in legal correspondence, 144
Bender's Federal Practice Forms, 189
Between, word choice of, 77
BlackBerrys, 152
Blind carbon copy, 133
Block quotes, 48. *See also* Quotations
The Bluebook. See Citations
Blunders in legal writing, 208-214
  abbreviations, 214
  addressing readers, 211
  authors of court opinions, 212
  citations, 212
  collective nouns, 214
  complete discussion, 210-211
  complete information, failure to
    provide, 211
  conclusory language, 210
  concurring opinions, overreliance on, 211
  court rules, violation of, 214
  cross-references, 214
  defined terms, 208
  dissenting opinions, overreliance on, 211

facts from cases, failure to include, 210
first person, use of, 213
headings, 213
headnotes, use of, 211
including facts, 210
incomplete discussion, 210-211
labels and numbering, 208
mini-conclusions, failure to use, 212
new topics, 212
numbering, 208
other legal authorities, failure to use, 210
over-quoting, 212
party designation, use of, 213
party names, use of, 213
plagiarism, 209
supporting authorities, 209
tense, 213
third person, failure to use, 213
"this case," confusion from overuse of, 214
title headings in statutes, 210
tone in court documents, 210
writing "this case," 214
Brainstorming and freewriting, 116-117.
    See also Outlines
Brief answer in memoranda, 156, 160
Briefs, 169-186
  appellate, 174-178. *See also* Appellate
    briefs
  case briefs, defined, 170
  closing, 174
  conclusions, 121
  covers for, 119
  defined, 170
  footnotes, 179-180. *See also* Footnotes
  honesty in, 171
  introductory statement, 172
  party designation in, 170
  personal pronouns in, 178
  persuasive writing, 170-171
  position and voice in, 121-122, 123
  quotations, 178
  rules of court, 119, 171-172, 178
  sample, 180-186, 259-278
  sarcasm, humor, or irony in, 178
  tips for writing, 170-172, 178-179
  trial court, 172-174. *See also* Trial court
    briefs
Burying negative information. *See* Negative
    information

C
Capitalization, 60-64
  abbreviations and, 68
  colons, use of, 61

Commonwealth or State, 64
Constitution, 63
Court, 63
defined terms, 61
general rules, 61-63
initial phrases, 207
judge or justice, 64
legal documents, 63-64
party designation, 64
proper names, 61
State or Commonwealth, 64
tips on, 63
titles, 61, 62, 64
Captions
  briefs, 172
  pleadings, 188
Carbon copies, 133
Case analysis, 156-160
  authors of court opinions, citing, 212
  concurring opinions, overreliance on,
    211
  dissenting opinions, overreliance on, 211
Case briefs, 170
  instructions on preparation, link to site
    with, 319
  samples, link to site with, 319
Cell phones, 152
Certificate of compliance, 174, 177, 178
Certificate of service
  appellate briefs, 177
  pleadings, 189
  trial court briefs, 174
Citations. *See also* Legal authorities;
    Quotations
  abbreviations, 242
  Bluebook and *ALWD* differences, 246-247
  blunders and, 209, 212
  font, 242
  form, 235-247
  guides, 236
  new topics, 212
  over-quoting, 212
  pinpoints, 243-244
  plagiarism, 209
  in pleadings, 188
  punctuation, 243
  quick reference to, 237-241
  quotations, 244
  short forms, 245-246
  spacing, 242-243
  special issues, 242-246
  typeface, 242
Clarity, 84-90
  elegant variation and, 86-87

idioms in legal writing, 84-85
  negative expressions, 87-89
  word order and, 89-90
Closing, 132-133, 134
  comma use, 32, 38
  merged closing, in legal correspondence,
    133
  prayer for relief, 189, 192
Clustering, 117
Collective nouns, 214
  blunders and, 214
  pronouns, 18
  subject-verb agreement, 8-9
Colloquial expressions, 81-82
Colons, 44-45
  capitalization rules, 61
  incomplete sentences, 45
  lists, 44
  minutes and hours, separating, 44
  quotation marks, 48
Commas, 32-39
  addresses, 33, 38
  adjectives, parallel, 34, 38
  appositives, 35, 38
  closings in letters, 32, 38
  dates, 32, 38
  digits, 33, 38
  independent clauses, 35, 38
  interruptive or transitional expressions,
    33-34, 38
  introductory elements, 33, 38
  law firm names, 208
  lists, 46
  misuse of, 37
  nonrestrictive phrases, 36, 37, 38, 39
  numbers, 33, 68
  quick reference chart, 38
  quotations, 36, 38
  rules for use, 32-39
  salutations in letters, 32, 38
  semicolons, use with lists, 46
  separating contrasting elements,
    34, 38
  series, 34, 38
  splices, 5
  "that" and "which," use of, 20-22
Common blunders. *See* Blunders in legal
    writing
Common idioms in legal writing, 82,
    84-85
Commonwealth, capitalization of, 64
Company names
  abbreviations, 65, 66, 69
  subject-verb agreement, 8-9

Comparisons
  parallel structure, 95
  "than" or "as," use of, 25
Complaints. *See also* Pleadings
  responding to, 189
  sample, 190-192
Compliance, certificate of, 174, 177, 178
Complimentary closing, 132-133, 134
Compose, word choice of, 76
Compound words
  hyphens, use of, 50, 58-59
  possessives, 42
  spelling, 58-59
  subject-verb agreement, 7
Comprise, word choice of, 76
Conciseness, 109-114
  active voice, use of, 114
  English as second language, 257
  needless words, omitting, 110-111
  redundancy, avoiding, 112
  repetition, avoiding, 114
  "throat-clearing" introductions,
      avoiding, 111
  tips to achieve, 114
  wordy phrases, 110
Conclusions
  appellate briefs, 177
  briefs, 174
  formal, 121
  in letters, 32, 38, 121
  memoranda, 160
  mini-conclusions, use of, 212
  in writing projects, 121
Concurring and dissenting opinions,
    overreliance on, 211
Confidentiality, 130
  cell or car phones, 151
  email and, 149, 150
  facsimile, 150-151
  voice mail, 151
Confirming letters, 138. *See also* Legal
    correspondence
Confusing words and phrases
  glossary, 306-318
Conjunctions, 27-28
  coordinating, 5, 27, 35, 37, 95
  correlative, 27-28, 95
  "old" rules of writing and, 15
  subordinating, 28
Consideration, 195
Constitution
  capitalization rules for, 63
  provisions in appellate briefs, 176
Consumer protection, 140

Contention, word choice of, 77
Contractions, 39, 43
  letters, use in, 137
Contracts. *See also* Transactional
      documents
  complaint for breach, 190-192
  sample partnership agreement, 197-203
Contradictions, phrases that show, 34
Conventions, legal, 206-208. *See also* Legal
      conventions
Coordinating conjunctions, 5, 27, 35, 37, 95
Copies of legal correspondence, 133
Correlative conjunctions, 27-28, 95
Correspondence. *See* Legal correspondence
Court
  capitalization rules for, 63
  citing authors of court opinions, 212
  word choice and, 76
Court rules
  following, 119, 171-172, 178
  violation of, as biggest writing blunder,
      214
Cover letters, 137. *See also* Legal
      correspondence
Cover sheets for appellate briefs, 175
CRAC or IRAC approach, 156-157, 158,
    173
Criminal prosecution, threatening, 140
Cross-references, blunders and, 214
Current Legal Forms with Tax Analysis, 197

D
Dangling modifiers, 12-13. *See also*
    Modifiers
Dashes, 49-50
Dates
  abbreviations, 66
  comma use in, 32, 38
  final check of, 225
  legal correspondence, 130, 134
  slashes in, 51
d/b/a (doing business as) references, 51,
    207-208
Debt collection, 140
Defined terms
  capitalization rules, 61
  common blunders and, 208
  legal conventions and, 206
Demand letters, 138-142. *See also* Legal
      correspondence
  arguing the case, 140
  common pitfalls in, 139-140
  content, inappropriate, 140
  elements, 139

ethical issues, 140
factual pitfalls, 139
failure to follow through, 140
inappropriate tone and content, 140
legal pitfalls, 140
sample, 141-142
tone, inappropriate, 140
Dependent clauses
comma use, 37
subordinating conjunctions and, 28
Design of documents. *See* Document
design
Diagrams
tree diagrams, 117
Dicta, word choice of, 76
Dictating as writing method, 124
Dictionary
use of, for spelling, 54
Digits, comma use in, 33, 38. *See also*
Numbers
Dissenting and concurring opinions,
overreliance on, 211
Document design, 228-234
formatting and layout, 230-234
headings, 232-233. *See also* Headings
justification, 230
length of document, 231-232
paper, 228
principles of, 228-230
spacing, 231
typeface, 228-230. *See also* Typeface or
font
visuals, 234
white space and margins, 230
Doing business as (d/b/a) clauses, 51,
207-208
Double quotation marks, 46

E

Effectiveness of legal writing. *See* Features
of effective legal writing
Electronic communication, 149-152.
See also Technology, use of
BlackBerrys, 152
email, 149-150
facsimile, 150-151
personal digital assistants, 152
telephone, 151
text messaging, 152
voice mail, 151
Elegant variation, 86-87
Ellipsis, use of, 48
Email, 149-150
Em dash, 50

Emphasis, 233
Enclosures in legal correspondence, 133
En dash, 50
Endnotes, avoidance of, 180
English as second language, 249-258
adjectives, 250
adverbs, 251
advice, giving of, 257-258
analysis, inclusion of, 258
articles "a," "an," and "the," 253, 254
conciseness, 257
cultural comments, 256-258
demonstrative pronouns, 255
directness, 257
grammar, 250-255
help, asking for, 258
noncount nouns, plurals of, 254
nouns, 253-255
prepositions, 251
pronouns, 251, 255
spelling, 255-256
tense, 251-253
vocabulary, 255-256
word order, standard, 250
Essential and nonessential phrases. *See*
Nonrestrictive phrases; Restrictive
phrases
Ethical issues
consumer protection, 140
corresponding with person represented
by counsel, 140
threatening criminal prosecution, 140
Exclamation points, 30, 32
Expressions in legal writing, 84-85

F

Facsimile (fax) communication, 150-151
Facts
blunders and, 210
in briefs, 173
from cases, inclusion of, 210
in memoranda, 156, 162
in opinion letters, 143
word choice of fact, 77
Features of effective legal writing, 73-114
accuracy, 75-84. *See also* Accuracy
clarity, 84-90. *See also* Clarity
conciseness, 109-114. *See also*
Conciseness
plain English movement, 74-75
readability, 90-109. *See also* Readability
Federal Practice and Procedure (Wright and
Miller), 189
Findings, word choice of, 77

Flesch Reading Ease Formula, 90
Font. *See* Typeface or font
Footnotes, 179-180
  cons, 179
  numbering of, final check of, 225
  pros, 179
  rules for, 179-180
Forceful words, 103-104
Form books
  pleadings, 189
  transactional documents, 195-197
Forms and templates, use of, 222
Fragments of sentences, 4
Freewriting and brainstorming, 116-117.
      See also Outlines
Full justification, 135
Fused sentences, 5

G
Gender-neutral language, 23-24
  letters, 24-25
  pronouns, 23-24
  techniques for, 23-24
General correspondence, 137-138. *See also*
      Legal correspondence
Generic nouns, 18
Gerunds, 26
Glossary
  of terms, 297-302
  of troublesome/confusing words and
      phrases, 304-316
  of usage, 304-316
Grammar, 3-28. *See also* Punctuation
  conjunctions, 27-28
  English as second language, 250-255
  modifiers, 10-14
  pronouns. *See* Pronouns
  sentences, 4-5. *See also* Sentences
  split infinitives, 14-15
  subject-verb agreement, 6-10
  "that" and "which," use of, 20-22
  "who" and "whom," use of, 19-20
Guilty, word choice of, 77

H
Headings
  blunders and, 213
  briefs, 170-171
    appellate, 175, 176, 177
    trial court, 171, 173
  emphasis, 233
  formatting and layout, 230-234
  legal correspondence, 132, 137
  lists, 233

memoranda, 155, 160, 163
  neutral, 171
  numbering of, final check of, 225
  parallel structure, 95, 96
  persuasive, 170-171
  phrasing, 233
  placement, 233
  in statutes, 210
  title headings in statutes, 210
  transactional documents, 194
Headnotes, use of, 211
He/she, use of, 24, 51
His/her, use of, 24, 51
Holdings, word choice of, 77
Humor
  use of, in briefs, 178
Hyphens, 50-51, 58-59

I
Idioms, 82, 84-85
Implied reference and pronouns, 19.
      See also Pronouns
"Including but not limited to" phrases, 207
Incomplete sentences, 4
  colon use and, 45
Incorporation by reference, 189
Indentation, and legal correspondence
  formatting, 135
Independent clauses
  commas, 35, 38
  semicolon use, 45-46
  subordinating conjunctions and, 28
Indirect writing, 100
Infinitives, split, 14-15
Informative letters, 137. *See also* Legal
      correspondence
Intentional vagueness, 79
Interruptive expressions, comma use and,
      33-34, 38
Intervening words and subject-verb
      agreement, 9
Introductory material
  overuse of words in, 111
  in sentences, 33, 38
Introductory sections
  of briefs, 172
  of pleadings, 188
  of transactional documents, 194
  of writing projects, 119-120
Inverted subjects, 9-10
IRAC or CRAC approach, 156-157, 158,
      173
Irony
  use of, in briefs, 178

Issues, 120. *See also* Question(s) presented
It, indefinite use of, 19
"It is," use of, 78, 114
"Its" and "it's," use of, 43

J
Jargon. *See* Legalese
Judge or Justice, capitalization of, 64
Judgment, spelling of, 77
Jurisdictional statements, appellate briefs, 176
Justification and margins, 230-231
    letters, 135
    white space and margins, 230

L
Labels, 206
    numbering and, 208
Law firm names
    presentation of, 208
    punctuation of, 208
Layout of document, 230-234
Legal analysis, methods of, 156-160
Legal authorities. *See also* Citations; Quotations
    authors of court opinions, citing, 212
    blunders and, 209, 210
    concurring opinions, overreliance on, 211
    dissenting opinions, overreliance on, 211
    headnotes, use of, 211
    supporting, 209, 210
    table of authorities in appellate briefs, 175-176
    using, 119
Legal briefs. *See* Briefs
Legal conventions, 206-208
    capitalization of initial phrases, 207
    d/b/a references, 207-208
    defined terms, 206
    "including but not limited to" phrases, 207
    initial phrases, capitalization of, 207
    labels, 206
    law firm names, 208
    money amounts, 207
    numbers, 207
    ordinals, 208
    pagination, 208
    repetitive terms, 206
    "whether" clause, 207
Legal correspondence, 129-152
    audience and tone, 136-137
    bad news, 144

conclusions in, 121
contractions, use of, 137
electronic communication, 149-152.
        See also Electronic communication
elements of letter, 130-135
    body, 132, 134
    closing, 132-133, 134
    complimentary closing, 132-133, 134
    copies, 133
    date, 130, 134
    enclosures, 133
    final notations, 134
    headers, 132
    headings, 132, 137
    inside address, 130-131, 134
    letterhead, 130, 134
    merged closing, 133
    Re:, 131, 134
    reference initials, enclosures, and copies, 133
    reference or subject notation, 131, 134
    salutations, 32, 38, 44, 131-132, 134
    signature block, 132-133, 134
    special mailing notations, 130, 134
    subject notation, 131, 134
enclosures, 133
format considerations, 134-135
    arrangement and indenting, 135
    attachments, 133
    blind carbon copy, 133
    carbon copy, 133
    font and typeface, 135
    headers, 132
    indentation, 135
    justification, 135
    margins, 135
    orphans and widows, 135
    paper size and spacing, 134
    spacing, 134
    typeface, 135
    widows and orphans, 135
gender-neutral language, 24-25. *See also* Gender-neutral language; Offensive language
headings, use of, 137
legalese in. *See* Legalese
to opposing parties/counsel, 137
personal pronouns, use of, 136, 138
protection clauses, 145-146
purpose, 137
text messaging, communicating by, 152.
        See also Electronic communication
tips for, 148

Legal correspondence (*continued*)
  tone, 136-137
  typeface, 135
  types of letters, 137-152
    confirming, 138
    cover letters, 137
    demand, 138-142. *See also* Demand
        letters
    general correspondence, 137-138
    opinion, 142-148, 150. *See also*
        Opinion letters
    status report, 150
  we or I, use of, 138
Legalese, 98-102
  archaic words, 98-99, 102
  curing, 101
  form books, 196
  indirect writing, 100
  jargon, 98-99
  pleadings, 192
  pretentious writing, 100
  redundancies, 98
  terms of art, 98
  transactional documents, 196
Legal memoranda. *See* Memoranda
Legal writing, effectiveness of. *See* Features
    of effective legal writing
Letterhead, 130, 134
  law firm names, punctuation and
      presentation of, 208
Letters. *See* Legal correspondence; specific
    type of letter
Letters and numbers
  apostrophe use with, 43
  typeface or font, 135
Liability, word choice of, 77
Limiting modifiers, 12. *See also* Modifiers
Lists
  colon use and, 44
  formatting and layout of, 233
  parallel structure. *See* Parallel structure
  semicolons, use with, 46
  use of, 92-93

M
Made-up words and phrases, 80-81
Margins and justification. *See* Justification
    and margins
Measurement, units of
  possessives, 42
Memoranda, 153-167
  format, 154-167
    analysis or discussion, 156-160, 162
    brief answer, 156, 162

conclusion, 160, 162
    example of elements, 162
    heading of document, 155
    headings, 155, 160, 163
    IRAC or CRAC, 156, 158-159
    paragraphs in, 163
    question(s) presented, 155, 162
    quotations and paraphrasing, tips for,
        161
    recommendations section, 160
    "Re:" line, 155
    sample, 163-167
    statement of facts, 156, 162
    thesis statement, 157-158
  guidelines for, 154
  neutrality, importance of, 154
  objectivity, importance of, 154
  parties, identification of, 163
  personal pronouns in, 77, 163
  position and voice, using for emphasis,
      121-122, 123
  specificity, importance of, 154
  third person, use of in, 160
  thoroughness, importance of, 154
  tips to prepare, 163
  word choice of, 77
Merged closing, in legal correspondence, 133
Metadata, 196
Micro-editing, 123
Middle section and paragraphs, 120-121
Minutes and hours, colon use in, 44
Mnemonic devices, 55
Modifiers, 10-14
  dangling, 12-13
  limiting, 12
  misplaced modifier phrases, 11
  misplaced prepositional phrases, 11
  squinting, 13
Money
  abbreviations for, 67
  amounts, 207
  verb use, 9
Motion
  defined, 77
  word choice of, 77
Multiple word subjects and verb
    agreement, 6-7

N
Names, final check of, 225
Needless words, 110-111
Negative expressions, 87-89
Negative information
  burying, 89, 122

forceful language and, 122
  passive voice, use of, 122
  strong start and finish needed, 122
Neutral language, use of, 83
Nominalizations, 97-98, 114
Nonrestrictive clauses, 20-22, 37, 38, 39
Nouns. *See also* Pronouns
  appositives, 35, 38
  collective, 8-9, 18
  company, 8-9
  gerunds, 26
  "one," use of, 24
  plural, 6, 7, 10, 23
  singular, 6, 7, 9, 10, 23
Numbering, final check of
  footnotes, numbering of, 225
  headings, numbering of, 225
  pages, numbering of, 225
Numbers
  abbreviations, 67
  apostrophe, use with, 43
  comma use in, 33, 68
  hyphen, use of, 51
  indefinite expressions, 69
  legal abbreviations, 68
  legal conventions for use of, 207
  money amounts, 207
  ordinals, 208
  plural, 69
  spelling, 69
  statutes, 69
  tips on use, 69

O
Offensive language, 82-83
"One," use of, 24
Opinion letters, 138, 142-148. *See also*
      Legal Correspondence
  bad news, 144
  date, 143
  explanation of opinion, 145
  instructions, 145
  introductory language, 143
  introductory section, 120
  opinion, 144
  protection clauses, 145-146
  recommendations, 145
  review of facts, 143
  sample, 146-148
Opinions, legal
  authors of court opinions, citing, 212
  concurring opinions, overreliance on,
      211
  dissenting opinions, overreliance on, 211

Oral, word choice of, 77
Orders, proposed, 174
Ordinals, 208
Organization and writing process, 115-126
  avoid micro-editing during drafting
      stage, 123
  conclusions, 121
  internal organization, 116-123
  introductory section, 119-120
  legal authorities, use of, 119
  methods of writing, 123-124
  middle section and paragraphs, 120-121
  order and internal organization, 116-123
  outlines, 116-118
  overview of writing projects, 119-121
  position and voice, use for emphasis,
      121-122, 123
Organization names. *See* Company names
Orphans and widows, 135
  final check of, 225
Outlines, 116-118
  reverse outlining, 118
Overrule, word choice of, 77

P
Page numbering
  final check of, 225
Pagination
  legal conventions, 208
Paper
  document design, 228
  letters, 134
Paragraphs, 120-121
  legal correspondence, 132, 134, 135
  length, 120
  memoranda, 163
  orphans and widows, 135, 225
  pleadings, 188
  transitional words and phrases, 121
  use of word "paragraph" or paragraph
      symbol, 68
  widows and orphans, 135, 225
Parallel structure, 94-97
  check for, 96
  comparisons, 95
  coordinating conjunctions, 95
  correlative conjunctions, 95
  headings, 95, 96
  lists, 95, 96
  series, 96
  tips on use, 96
Paraphrasing, tips for, 161
Parentheses, 47, 49
Partnership agreement, sample, 197-203

Party designation
  briefs, 170
  capitalization, 64
  legal convention of, 206
  memoranda, 163
  use of, 213
Passive voice
  dangling modifiers and, 13
  negative information and, 122
  readability, 91-92
  word order, 90
Past tense, use of, 107-108
Percentages, 67
Percolating, 117-118
Periods
  abbreviations, 31, 65
  quotation marks, 48
  titles, 65-66
  using, 31
Personal digital assistants, 152
Personal pronouns, 15-16
  briefs, 178
  first person, use of, 213
  legal correspondence, 136
  legal documents, 77
  memoranda, 160, 163
  third person, failure to use, 213
Pinpoints, citation form, 243-244
Plagiarism, 209
Plain English movement, 74-75
Pleadings, 188-192
  in alternative, 188
  amendment of, 189
  caption, 188
  certificate of service, 189
  citations, 188
  defined, 170
  endings, 189
  format, 188-189
  from form books, 189
  incorporation by reference, 189
  introductory matter, 188
  legalese in, 192
  numbering of paragraphs, 188
  paragraph content, 188
  prayer for relief, 189, 192
  responding to, 189
  sample, 190-192
Plural nouns, 6, 7, 10, 23
  forming, 43, 57
  possessives, 40, 41
  spelling, 57
Positive and affirmative terms, use of, 88

Possessives, 40-42
  abstract words, 42
  ancient proper names, 41
  apostrophe use, 40-42
  compound words, 42
  general rules, 40
  individual, 41
  joint, 41
  measurement, units of, 42
  plural nouns, 40
  proper names, 40-41
  quick reference chart, 42
  silent letters, 42
  singular nouns, 40
  "s," words ending in, 40, 41
  time, units of, 42
Postwriting steps, 217-226
  cite checking, 225
  content and meaning review, 219
  final run-through, 225
  proofreading and proofreader's marks, 223-224, 226. *See also* Proofreading
  spell checkers, 220
  style sheet, use of, 220
  technical errors, review for, 220-223
  technology, use of, as aid, 222
  templates and forms, use of, 222
  tips for successful reviews, 218, 225
Prayer for relief, 189, 192
Prepositions
  colons, use after, 45
  English as second language, 251
  misplaced prepositional phrases, 11
  "old" rules of writing and, 15
Prescribe, word choice of, 77
Present tense, 108
Pretentious writing, 100
"Privileged and Confidential," 130
Project checklist, 221
Pronouns, 15-26
  agreement, 17-18
  alternating he and she, 24
  ambiguous reference, 18
  collective nouns, 18
  consistency in, 26
  demonstrative, 255
  English as second language, 251, 255
  gender-linked, 23-25
  generic nouns, 18
  gerunds, 26
  he/she, use of, 24
  "he," use in transactional documents, 24
  implied references, 19

indefinite
  agreement with antecedent, 17
  plural, 7
  singular, 7
  subject-verb agreement, 7-8
indefinite use of "it" and "they," 19
"one," use of, 25
personal, 15-16, 77, 136
reference, 18-19
reflexive, 22
shifts in, 26
"than" or "as," use of, 25
"that" and "which," use of, 20-22
tips for use, 16
vague reference, 19
"we" and "us" use of, 25, 138
"who" and "whom," use of, 19-20
"you," use of, 24
Proofreading
  help from others, 222
  marks, 223-224
  for others, 223
  slowing down, techniques for, 220
  spelling, 55
  technology, use of, as aid, 222
Proper names
  ancient, 41
  capitalization rules, 61
  law firm names, 208
  possessives, 40-41
  titles before, 62, 65-66
Proscribe, word choice of, 77
Punctuation, 29-52. See also Grammar
  apostrophes, 39-44
  citations, 243
  colons, 44-45
  commas, 32-39
  dashes, 49-50
  end, 30-32
  exclamation marks, 32
  hyphens, 50-51, 58-59
  law firm names, 208
  parentheses, 47, 49
  periods, 31
  question marks, 31
  quotation marks, 46-47, 48
  semicolons, 45-46
  slashes, 51

Q
Question marks, 31
Question(s) presented
  appellate briefs, 176
  memoranda, 155, 162

Quotation marks, 46-47, 48
  double, 46
  other punctuation with, 48
  single, 46
Quotations. See also Citations; Legal
      authorities
  block quotes, 48
  briefs, 178
  citation form, 244
  colon use and, 44, 48
  commas, 36, 38
  ellipsis, 48
  explanatory words in, 48
  number of words, 48
  omissions in, 48
  over-quoting, 212
  plagiarism, 209
  signal phrases and, 48
  tips for, 161

R
Racial designations, 83
Readability, 90-108
  active voice, 91-92
  conciseness, 109-114. See also
      Conciseness
  effective transitions, 105, 106
  forceful words, use of, 103-104
  keeping subjects and verbs close
      together, 102-103
  legalese, 98-102
  lists, use of, 92-93
  nominalizations, 97-98, 114
  parallel structure, 94-97
  passive voice and, 91-92
  repeating strong words and phrases, 104
  sentence length, 104-105, 111
  tense shifts, 106-108
  tests for, 90
Recitals, 194
Redundancy, 98, 104, 112
Reference and pronouns, 18-19. See also
      Pronouns
Reflexive pronouns, 22
Repetition
  avoiding, 114
  repetitive terms, 206
  strong words and phrases, 104
Report letters, 150
Restrictive phrases, 20-22, 37, 39
Reverse outlining, 118
Reverse, word choice of, 77
Review of writing projects. See Postwriting
      steps

Right justification, 135
Rules of court
  briefs, 119, 171-172, 178
  U.S. Supreme Court, 119, 171-172
  violation of, as biggest writing blunder,
    214
Run-on sentences, 4-5

S

Salutations, 131-132, 134. *See also* Legal
    correspondence
  colon use and, 44, 132
  comma use and, 32, 38, 132
  formality of, 131-132
  informal letters, 32, 38
  striking through, 132
  unknown recipients, 132
Samples
  appellate court brief, 259-278
  briefs, 180-186, 259-278
  case briefs, link to site with, 317
  complaint, 190-192
  demand letters, 141-142
  memoranda, 163-167
  opinion letters, 146-148
  partnership agreement, 197-203
  pleadings, 190-192
  trial court brief, 180-186
Sarcasm
  use of, in briefs, 178
Semicolons, 45-46, 48
Sentences
  colon use and, 44
  fragments, 4
  fused, 5
  incomplete, 4, 45
  introductory material in, 33, 38
  keeping subjects and verbs close
    together, 102-103
  length, 104-105, 111
  run-on, 4-5
  starting with abbreviation, numerals, or
    symbols, 69
  word order, 89-90
Series
  comma use in, 34-35, 38
  numbers in, 69
  parallel structure, 96, 97
Service, certificate of
  appellate briefs, 177
  pleadings, 189
  trial court briefs, 174
Sexist language. *See* Gender-neutral
    language; *see also* Offensive language

S/he, use of, 24, 51
Short forms of citations, 245-246
Signal phrases and quotation marks, 48
Signature block, 133
  appellate briefs, 177
  trial court briefs, 174
Silent letters, 42
Single quotation marks, 46
Singular nouns, 6, 7, 9, 10, 23
Slang and colloquial expressions, 81-82
Slashes, 51
Slender Yellow Fruit Syndrome, 86-87
Snail mail, 150
Solidus, 51
Spacing, 132, 134, 231
  citations, 242-243
Spell checkers, 55, 150, 220
  limitations of, 220
Spelling, 53-69. *See also* Grammar; Spell
    checkers
  abbreviations, 65-69
  capitalization, 60-64
  compound words, 58-60
  double consonants, 57
  English as second language, 255-256
  plurals, forming, 57
  rules, 55-57
  strategies to improve, 54-57
Split infinitives, 14-15
Squinting modifiers, 13. *See also* Modifiers
State, capitalization of, 64
Statement of case in appellate briefs,
    176-177
Statement of facts. *See* Facts
Status letters, 150. *See also* Legal
    correspondence
Statutes
  authority in appellate briefs, 176
  numbers, use of, 69
  title headings, 210
Story telling, 117. *See also* Outlines
Strong words and phrases, 104
Style sheet, 220
Subject-verb agreement, 6-10
  collective nouns, 8-9
  company names, 8-9
  compound subject preceded by "each"
    or "every," 7
  indefinite pronouns, 7-8
  intervening words, 9
  inverted sentence order, 9-10
  multiple-word subjects, 6-7
  plural nouns, 6, 7, 10
  singular nouns, 6, 7, 9, 10

Subordinating conjunctions, 28
Symbols
    at, 68
    paragraph signs, 68
    starting sentences with, 69

T
Table of authorities in appellate briefs, 175-176
Table of contents in appellate briefs, 175
Tabulation. *See* Lists
Technical errors, review for, 220-223
Technology, use of
    electronic communication. *See* Electronic communication
    proofreading, help with, 222
Telephone, communicating by, 151
Templates and forms, 222
Tense
    blunders and, 213
Tense shifts, 106-108
Terms of art, 98
Text messaging, 152
    texting, 152
    text speak, 152
"Than" or "as," use of, 25
"That" and "which," use of, 20-22
"That," when necessary, 20
"There is," use of, 78, 114
Thesis statements, 156-157
    appellate briefs, 177
    trial court briefs, 173
They, indefinite use of, 19
"Throat-clearing" introductions, 111
Time
    abbreviation, 66-67
    colon use and, 44
    minutes and hours, separating, 44
    possessives, 42
    verb use and, 9, 106
Title headings in statutes, 210
Titles
    capitalization rules, 61, 62, 64
    proper names and, 65
Tone
    in court documents, 210
    in legal correspondence, 136-137
Transactional documents, 193-203
    attachments, 196
    confidentiality of documents, 196
    defined, 193
    drafting considerations, 193-194
    elements, 194-195
        consideration, 195

    introductory matter, 194
    operative terms, 195
    recitals, 194
    signatures, 195
    standard provisions, 195
    ethics concerns, 196
    form books, 195-197
    gender-neutral language, 24
    headings, 194
    legalese in, 196. *See also* Legalese
    metadata mining, 196
    sample partnership agreement, 197-203
    statutes and, 193-194
Transitional words and phrases
    comma use, 33-34, 38
    effective use of, 105
    paragraphs and, 121
    semicolon use and, 45
    word patterns and, 121
Tree diagrams, 117
Trial court briefs, 172-174. *See also* Briefs
    argument, 173
    caption, 172
    certificate of compliance, 174
    certificate of service, 174
    conclusion, 174
    elements, 172-174, 178
        appellate brief compared, 178
    exhibits, 174
    headings, 171, 173
    introductory statements, 172
    IRAC or CRAC, 173
    orders, proposed, 174
    sample, 180-186
    signature and date, 174
    statement of facts, 173
    thesis statements, 173
Troublesome words and phrases
    glossary, 304-316
Typeface or font, 228-230
    citations, 242
    letters, 135
    mixing, 229
    monospace, 229
    proportional or monospace, 229
    Roman, 229
    size of, 229-230
    style of, 228-229

U
United States, abbreviation of, 66
U.S. Supreme Court rules for briefs, 119, 171-172
"Us" and "we," use of, 25

V

Vagueness, 78-79
   intentional vagueness, 79
   pronouns and, 19
Verbal, word choice of, 77
Verbs
   colon use after, 45
   nominalizations, 114
   past tense, 107-108
   present tense, 108
   subject agreement. *See* Subject-verb
      agreement
   tense shifts, 106-108
Virgule, 51
Visuals, formatting and layout, 234
Vocabulary
   English as second language, 255-256
Voice mail, use of, 151

W

Weak positions, burying, 89, 122. *See also*
   Negative information
"We" and "us," use of, 25
West's Legal Forms 2d, 197
"Whether" clause, 207
"Which" and "that," use of, 20-22, 36-37

White space and margins, 230. *See also*
   Justification and margins
"Who" and "whom," use of, 19-20
Widows and orphans, 135
   final check of, 225
Word choice, 76-77, 84
Word connotation, 79-80
Word order, 89-90
   English as second language,
      250
Word patterns, 121
Word processors, 123, 124
Wordy phrases, 110
Wright and Miller *(Federal Practice and
   Procedure),* 189
Writing
   dictating, 124
   by hand, 123
   methods of, 123-124
   organization. *See* Organization and
      writing process
   tips for getting started, 125-126
   word processor use, 123, 124

Y

"You," use in gender-neutral language, 24